PATH TO THE LIGHT

Kabbalah Centre Publishing is a registered DBA of
Kabbalah Centre International, Inc.

For further information:

The Kabbalah Centre
155 E. 48th St., New York, NY 10017
1062 S. Robertson Blvd., Los Angeles, CA 90035

1.800.Kabbalah www.kabbalah.com

ISBN: 978-1-952895-32-6
Path to the Light Volume 9

eBook ISBN: 978-1-952895-40-1

Design: HL Design (Hyun Min Lee) www.hldesignco.com

PATH TO THE LIGHT

DECODING THE BIBLE WITH KABBALAH

KABBALAH CENTRE PUBLISHING

An Anthology
of Commentary
from Kabbalist
Rav Berg

BOOK OF
BAMIDBAR
Volume 9

Chukat
Balak
Pinchas
Matot
Masei

TABLE OF CONTENTS

Portion of Chukat 1

Portion of Balak 57

Portion of Pinchas 123

Portion of Matot 205

Portion of Masei 261

BOOK OF BAMIDBAR:

PORTION OF CHUKAT

PORTION OF CHUKAT

Bamidbar 19:1 And the Lord spoke to Moses and to Aaron, saying: 2 "This is the statute of the law which the Lord has commanded, saying: 'Speak to the children of Israel, that they bring you a red heifer, faultless, with no blemish, upon which no yoke has been laid.

Purification and Cleansing

To religious scholars, the word *chukat* derives from the word *chok*, meaning "law or statute." According to this interpretation, the Red Heifer is considered a statute without the rationale to support it. The Zohar, however, states that there is a clear explanation: The Red Heifer represents absolute judgment. It is red, female, never yoked, and its ashes are used for purification after it has been burned. The High Priest who performs the act of purification becomes ritually impure through this process. This is to teach us the nature of true giving. The High Priest was prepared to reach the level where he could feel the pain of another person to help them. Because of this intense giving consciousness, the disease would leave the afflicted person.

The portion of Chukat pertains to purification and cleansing. Achieving quantum consciousness means that the future is here and now—the right thoughts come at the right time and we can know a person at a glance. It is written in the Zohar that no matter how many good deeds, or how much charity a person gives, nothing will help them gain control over their life unless they connect to the inner power of the weekly portion and the reading of the Torah

Scroll (Bible). The Torah gives us strength to control our lives and prevent disaster.

The portion of Chukat always comes in the month of Cancer (Tammuz). The month of Cancer is said to be one of the three most negative months of the year. According to Abraham the Patriarch, the disease of cancer begins in this month. Nonetheless the Hebrew name for this month is Tammuz and it has the same numerical value as the word *shalem*, which means "complete."

By listening to the reading of the Torah and connecting to the Hebrew letters of the portion of Chukat we receive the power of cleansing, as well as prevention of the disease of cancer. Cancer can begin in our bodies twenty years or more before it becomes symptomatic. By means of this portion, we draw both the physical and the metaphysical power of cleansing. After experiencing a difficulty, or a falling of consciousness under an illusion, things can be restored to their natural state.

This portion also provides an immunity to judgment. The month of Cancer is a time of judgment; there is an enormous amount of Light available. However in this cosmic timeframe the source of Light comes only from the moon, therefore there is a need for immunization. There are no really negative months, there is only a time of a great deal of Light without balance.

The Red Heifer is the quintessence of the *klipot*, the negative shells. It purifies the negative energy of the sin of the Golden Calf, which brought death to the world—as it is written, "This is the law: when a man dies in a tent...." (Bamidbar 19:14)

How can a weekly Bible portion affect a cure? Why is the choice of animal specifically a heifer—a young cow? Korach was to blame for this trap of consciousness because he thought being a priest was simply a job, and so he disconnected himself from the quantum.

The ashes of the Red Heifer cause the ritually pure to become ritually impure, and the ritually impure to become pure. The power of the ashes created from the burnt heifer would forge a connection to the individual's inner consciousness, whether it was positive or negative. The Red Heifer relates to *Klipat Noga* and the Tree of Knowledge of Good and Evil, which we want to transcend. The portion of Chukat remedies the actions of Korach.

Rav Shimon Bar Yochai said: "I could write better stories if they were only to be interpreted literally." We would be foolish to believe only the literal meanings of stories in the Bible.

"And from the desert, a gift," explains that a gift is from the Light. When a person behaves according to the Bible—even if everyone else is wild, as was the case in the wilderness—and receives it, he or she can then receive the Light as a gift.

Those who would rather golf than hear a Torah reading on Shabbat should go golfing. I, personally, would not miss even one Shabbat because I know the truth about how Shabbat provides protection from negativity.

Improving our Immune System; Overcoming the War of Consciousness

To combat the metaphysical causes of illness and death, chaos and negativity, it is of the utmost importance to drastically improve our immune system.

If we want to eliminate the disease of cancer, the month of Cancer is the most appropriate time to do so. The power of the Red Heifer can remove all the pollution in the world. The world is now experiencing the effects of the highest degree of pollution ever generated by humans. Why wait decades for cancer to manifest on a physical level, when instead we can take proactive steps, at the seed level, to combat the disease of cancer from within our consciousness where it lives now. The spiritual technology of the Creator is the only way we can accomplish this.

According to kabbalists, the Third Meal of Shabbat is the way we can completely prevent the War of Armageddon, known as the War of Consciousness, from entering our lives. We are mired in the War of Armageddon at this moment and the Central Column energy of this meal protects our lives and the lives of our families from chaos.

The study of the wisdom of Kabbalah provides the needed tools for removing all chaos in our lives. Chaos is everywhere. Economists today are discussing how chaos operates in modern economies. It exists everywhere; even leading scientists refer to the Heisenberg Uncertainty Principle. Yet we are not obliged to accept chaos in our lives.

The Bible has survived for thousands of years and provides direction and guidance. Interpreted correctly, with an elevated consciousness, one becomes capable of comprehending the hidden meanings contained within the literal text. What else in this world has such a life of its own?

The portion of Chukat is for immortality. It is very important because it relates to the concept of *mati velo mati*. This is a profound secret in Kabbalah which requires much explanation but for our purposes in this discussion it is a connection to immortality.

According to Gematria—the study of kabbalistic numerology that assign numerical value to each of the 22 Hebrew letters, allowing us to uncover coded meaning in the Torah—the number 86 is Pei-Vav, which are the two Hebrew letters related to the month of Iyar (Taurus), which according to Kabbalah is the month of healing. The portion of Chukat contains 87 verses, and number 87 corresponds to the words *Parah Adumah* (Red Heifer). The purpose of the Red Heifer is to cleanse—on a very deep level—those individuals who have become contaminated.

It is now understood that cancer does not begin when the tumor appears, it starts decades earlier. Cancer originates in a very concealed place, which contaminates us at the root. We are so involved in physicality that it is difficult for us to understand this. Of course I am not advocating doing away with physicality; the problem arises when we consider physicality to be the most important aspect of life. The Talmud says that the greatest form of contamination comes from being in a room with a dead person, or in touching a dead person, because this negativity spreads. The purpose of the Red Heifer is not only to remove severe forms of contamination, but also even the small contaminations which are equally serious and infectious. *Lashon Hara* (Evil Speech) was the cause for the Destruction of the Holy Temple. The Red Heifer was used in the Temple, yet modern technology today tells us it is invalid.

How are we meant to rid ourselves of such contamination today if we do not have a Temple or a red heifer? The Torah is our opportunity to experience the cleansing, restorative power of the Red Heifer. When a person leaves this world, they are to be buried immediately because the body is contaminated and negativity can be spread around. The Zohar says every death is truly brought about by the Angel of Death (*Malach haMavet*) no matter what the cause of death. The importance of the portion of Chukat is that we

7

can receive the cleansing and restoration of the Red Heifer when listening to this Torah reading on Shabbat—but this is too abstract for most to understand.

Inner Essence of the Red Heifer

The Bible, in Bamidbar 19:1, says: *Zot chukat haTorah asher tziva haShem le'emor.* (This is the statute of the Lord which the Lord had commanded.) Once the word *chukat* has been associated and brought into focus on any particular subject, the general translation of that word is "statute," and this is something we cannot understand. Rav Shimon bar Yochai disagrees and says this is a corruption that displays total ignorance of what is taking place here. Everything that concerns this aspect of the Red Heifer relates to an understanding of what its inner essence is all about.

What was the Red Heifer? The Bible says very clearly that it must be red (*adumah*), it must be a young female cow that has not borne a calf (*parah*), it must be faultless/complete (*temimah*), in which there is no blemish. It seems that the phrase "in which there is no blemish" is redundant because the Bible has already stated she should be faultless/complete (*temimah*). If the heifer is *temimah* then obviously she is without blemish. Why do we need to know that the cow is without defect as well? The Bible then says that it must be an animal that has never been yoked.

The purpose of the Red Heifer was to cleanse *tumah* (impurity). The word *tumah* is often translated to mean "unclean." This is a corruption of the word. The word for "unclean" is *lo naki*. The purpose of the Red Heifer, according to the Bible, was to remove uncleanliness. Why do we need to remove uncleanliness? And furthermore, what about those of us who are here today, when there is no Red Heifer available, why do we need this portion?

From the explanation in the Zohar we come to understand that *adumah* means Left Column, and the word *temimah*, meaning "faultless/complete" has nothing to do with being free of blemishes. What is completeness? It is when opposites exist and yet they are part of one unified whole.

What the Bible is describing here is a channel of energy, which is the Heifer, the Left Column, the negative energy. Why was the Heifer chosen to be a channel of the Left Column, negative energy? What is being implied when people are described as either negative or positive? From a kabbalistic perspective, a negative person channels negative vibrations, negative fields of energy, whereas a positive person transmits or emits positive fields of energy. These opposites also both exist within each individual. It is within a person's free will to choose to act as a channel for positivity or negativity. The animal kingdom has no free will; animals have been designated as either positive channels or negative channels.

The Hebrew word *tamei* does not mean "uncleanliness," it means "to become short circuited." The circuit is closed. They have now become closed-minded—generating an aspect of darkness, opaqueness though which they cannot see—to their own detriment. Those who are open-minded can see things on many levels; they take it all in and form a realistic conclusion. When an individual is closed-minded, this is a liability. When someone is close-minded, meaning he or she is not taking all of the facts presented in daily life into account, not taking them all together to try to understand all of these factors, then such a person fails in their endeavors. What does an accountant tell a proprietor whose business has failed? "You forgot to take into account this, that or the other thing." When people in hindsight say, "Had I known this or that," these people did not know because they were closed off to a certain extent or in a certain area.

The Red Heifer was meant to restore a circuit of energy; to open individuals up, to remove that opaqueness, to remove that closed-mindedness, so they could see the whole picture, almost from beginning to end.

The Red Heifer was an animal designated at the time of Creation, in Beresheet (Genesis), for the sole purpose of channeling the most intensified negative form of energy. It is only when you have the most intensified form of energy that you can have the most intensified flow of energy. For example, the difference between a generator and a five watt bulb is that the generator produces a greater intensity of energy, and the five watt bulb very little intensity. In the five watt bulb there is very little negative charge for drawing that electrical current into the bulb.

The animal had to be red, a heifer, and with no blemishes because anything that could disrupt the flow of cleansing, restorative energy would not produce the desired result of restoring a complete circuit of energy.

The reason we come to the War Room on Shabbat to listen to the Torah reading of this portion concerning the Red Heifer is because the Torah permits us to go back to the time, when there was the Red Heifer, when there was this form of restoration. It is for those who, for whatever reason, have created negative flows of energy, resulting in short circuits in their lives. When we connect via the Torah reading we go back in time to when this was established, drawing to ourselves, not to the physical extent of what took place there, but the equivalent of that kind of energy. So, the reading of this section is not to review another part of the Bible that seems to be meaningless for most of us today, but actually to connect to that very procedure, the most powerful restoration of energy, different than what the High Priest could establish. On Yom Kippur, the High Priest did not restore energy. Instead he was a channel for bringing down that kind of immense energy. But the channel for the restoration of individual energy for each person was the Red Heifer. This was and is the significance of this portion.

3 And you shall give her to Elazar, the priest, and she shall be brought forth outside the camp, and she shall be slain before his face. 4 And Elazar, the priest, shall take of her blood with his finger, and sprinkle of her blood toward the front of the Tent of Meeting seven times. 5 And the heifer shall be burnt in his sight; her skin, and her flesh, and her blood, with her dung, shall be burnt. 6 And the priest shall take cedar-wood, and hyssop, and scarlet, and cast it into the midst of the burning of the heifer. 7 Then the priest shall wash his clothes, and he shall bathe his flesh in water, and afterward he may come into the camp, and the priest shall be unclean until the evening. 8 And he that burned her shall wash his clothes in water, and bathe his flesh in water, and shall be unclean until the evening. 9 And a man that is clean shall gather up the ashes of the heifer, and store them up outside the camp in a clean place, and it shall be kept for the congregation of the children of Israel for the purification water of sprinkling; from sin. 10 And he that gathered the ashes of the heifer shall wash his clothes, and be unclean until the evening; and it shall be to the children of Israel, and to the stranger that dwells among them, as a statute forever. 11 He that touches the dead, even any man's dead body, shall be unclean seven days; 12 the same shall purify himself therewith on the third day and on the seventh day, and he shall be clean; but if he does not purify himself on the third day and the seventh day, he shall not be

clean. 13 Whoever touches the dead, even the body of any man that is dead, and does not purify himself, has defiled the Tabernacle of the Lord, and that soul shall be cut off from Israel; because the water of sprinkling was not dashed against him, he shall be unclean; his uncleanness is yet upon him. 14 This is the law: when a man dies in a tent, every one that comes into the tent, and everything that is in the tent, shall be unclean seven days. 15 And every open vessel, which has no covering close-bound upon it, is unclean. 16 And whoever in the open field touches one that is slain with a sword, or one that dies of himself, or a bone of a man, or a grave, shall be unclean seven days. 17 And for the unclean they shall take of the ashes of the burning of the purification from sin, and put it together with running water in a vessel. 18 And a clean person shall take hyssop, and dip it in the water, and sprinkle it upon the tent, and upon all the vessels, and upon the persons that were there, and upon him that touched the bone, or the slain, or the dead, or the grave. 19 And the clean person shall sprinkle upon the unclean on the third day, and on the seventh day; and on the seventh day he shall purify him; and he shall wash his clothes, and bathe himself in water, and shall be clean in the evening. 20 But the man that shall be unclean, and shall not purify himself, that soul shall be cut off from the midst of the assembly, because he has defiled the Sanctuary of the Lord; the water of sprinkling has not

been dashed against him: he is unclean. 21 And it shall be a perpetual statute to them; and he that sprinkles the water of sprinkling shall wash his clothes; and he that touches the water of sprinkling shall be unclean until the evening. 22 And whatever the unclean person touches shall be unclean; and the soul that touches him shall be unclean until the evening.'"

A Crazy Change?

Was it crazy, 80 years ago, to think of changing what is normal, to seize this great opportunity for change? Rav Ashlag decided to be considered crazy and remove what was thought to be normal, and thereby eliminate any seed of cancer. I suppose we kabbalists must be crazy, since we connect to the portion of Chukat in order to receive cleansing and affect change. In essence, we are still faced with a fairly primitive form of medicine today. We have no reasons to consider the medical community ill-intentioned, yet physicians are, to date, not very successful in removing cancer, disease, at its root. Kabbalah is here, however, to assist us to do just that.

The rules and regulations for the Red Heifer are enumerated in this section. Only the Red Heifer and the way it was being prepared here, with herbs and so forth, could purify a person who came into contact with a corpse. Once the person is cleansed, the priest who performed this ritual service became, himself, unclean. Why? Biblical commentators often say there is no sense to this, no rationale to the idea that one who purifies becomes unclean because of the act of purifying what is unclean.

The Bible prescribes that a corpse should be buried immediately. Why? I will come back to answer this in a moment. When any physical disease emerges, its origins may well lie 30 or 40 years in the past. Science cannot deal with these root causes because at the root level disease is immaterial, cancer is immaterial. Science does not know how to deal with the immaterial. A tumor is physical so it can be addressed. Science is grounded in the physical, and disease is not; only symptoms are physical.

The Bible describes illnesses as "clean" and "unclean." However, these translations are corruptions of the original words used by the Bible. Although this is how these terms have long been translated, a more proper interpretation is "circuitry" and "short-circuit." The Bible is constantly addressing the issue of clean and unclean, which is the superficial level. The root of all illness is being without the Lightforce (*tamei*).

Therefore the reason the Bible says that a corpse should be buried immediately is because one who touches a corpse, which is totally devoid of all Light, assumes and permits the beginning and origin of a most severe form of short-circuitry that can exist in the human body, thus creating an opening for disease to manifest at some point. A diseased body is different, meaning it may be experiencing an interruption in the flow of the Lightforce, but the Light is nonetheless still present.

We read this portion every year to eliminate our confusion. The portion of Chukat will always be read during the month of Cancer, the month of confusion. And so it is that with Shabbat Chukat we have an opportunity to eliminate confusion. Cancer is accepted as a label for confusion, whether we call it cancer of the body, or cancer in a society, and so forth. Cancer cells are literally confused. This is an opportunity to remove all forms of confusion.

The Red Heifer, with all the requirements and prescriptions, was chosen to remove confusion. This instrument is not aimed at clearing the branches of confusion's tree because it is not about the effects or symptoms, instead the Red Heifer strikes at the roots, the very core of negativity itself. There are many reasons for which this is used to cleanse, one is, coming in contact with a corpse and not knowing how to purify oneself. The Mikveh does not remove this type of uncleanliness. We come to this particular Shabbat for such an opportunity—and we dare to challenge normalcy with our radical methods for healing.

The priests who handled the procedure of administering the ashes of the Red Heifer were contaminated, taking the whole disease on themselves. Why? The Bible tells us, if you come in contact with a sick person, only if you feel their pain can the illness be cured, can the impurity be truly removed. This is also true for standard medicine, law, and other professions. Wherever services are rendered, if the individual providing the service does not come in contact with the pain or grave concerns of his client, he or she will not be able to remove that pain or assuage those concerns. If a doctor, lawyer, or accountant cannot feel the problem personally, they should be released from that duty. Only the person able to connect to the pain of another can truly help remove that pain. The Zohar says that every time we visit the sick we can remove 1/60th of their illness, but only if we are properly prepared and genuinely able to feel the pain of the ailing person.

Preparing our Consciousness

The Temple was destroyed because the Kohanim, the Priests, became corrupt—they sold their right to perform Temple services to the highest bidder. They did not appreciate their lofty position but were willing to let it go for financial gain.

We have to remember that we must prepare our consciousness. If we do not understand, and if we go about all of this without knowledge of what it can do for us, we do not make the connection and we do not receive anything from the reading. This reading of the Torah is the way to remove the layers of confusion enveloping us.

The reason we kiss the Torah is worth mentioning here. Is it done because of awe, reverence or respect? No, we kiss the Torah to create a connection with the Lightforce of God. Only through such a connection can we alter that which is normal and mundane.

Mind over Matter

On Shabbat Chukat, we can collect and draw to ourselves something of an extremely unusual nature. A vague notion of this unusual nature has recently begun to penetrate medicine: mind over matter has influence over our physical bodies. We do not participate in a Shabbat at the Kabbalah Centres to pay homage and take part in a very nice service. There is much more to it than that, which we have come to understand as it relates to the portion of Chukat and the Red Heifer. The Bible tells us that this Heifer was completely red; she did not have even a single hair of any other color. Accompanied by certain rituals, she first had to be slaughtered, and only then would her ashes remove uncleanliness. What does this mean? Does this mean there were people who did not bathe, who were literally unclean? The answer is no.

The Red Heifer had a short-lived existence, indeed she only lived at the time of the Holy Temple. What then is the purpose of reading or listening to this story now? It seems so outdated and serves no apparent purpose. The Zohar tells us the Red Heifer concerned a special kind of purification, which had to do with the removal of negativity.

Kabbalah teaches us that the Bible was given because God needed to give us an instrument to use for our correction. The Zohar states categorically that the Ten Utterances are not Ten Commandments or principles to live by. These Torah verses and the Hebrew letters comprising them, are coded forms of a universal language designed to bring about immortality and the end of chaos in this world. There is no dispute about this, either in the Zohar or in the Talmud. Where, then, did this confusion, this chaos, come from? It comes from the Satan. The event of the Giving of the Bible at Mount Sinai is generally seen as one of the main elements in monotheistic religion—but it was not intended as such.

The same is true for the Red Heifer; such accounts possess a much deeper significance than they at first seem to have. Upon this reading of the Red Heifer's story, we are presented with the opportunity to receive an incredible 25th century medical procedure. If we imagine ourselves living for centuries henceforth, it becomes easy to see that 21st century medicine will appear to have been very primitive. We may even wonder, as we look back to today, why it was that we would cut into people to remove cancers. A hundred years is a long time in medicine. But it may come as a surprise to learn that today we have the good fortune to perform 25th century surgery on any medical condition because this biblical portion is an instrument to tap into the awesome power of removing uncleanliness, which is the metaphysical root of all disease.

It is a very simple concept: you flip on a light switch and the darkness disappears. Darkness expresses every form of chaos. In the darkness, we are unable to see the way forward. Darkness and chaos are the very same thing. But with this portion we can tap into the awesome power of the Light, using it to remove chaos at the root level. As stated previously, Cancer's origins are 30-40 years before the tumor appears, and no physical, material tool or device can detect that which is immaterial—the root cause of cancer. This portion reaches into the inner recesses of the body and performs spiritual-immaterial surgery, and we have to perform this spiritual surgery now to avoid physical surgery later.

Should one accept these claims? Should one accept whatever is written or said? Rav Shimon bar Yochai told his pupils not to accept anything he said—the proof of a pudding is in the eating of that pudding. If a person, God forbid, ends up in the hospital and does not require surgery, the point is proven. We at the Kabbalah Centres, come to hear the Torah reading, for the spiritual-immaterial surgery that will remove a condition within our bodies, which we may or may not be aware exists. I shall leave the issue here, since it would require another book to fully explain so deep an idea.

Benefits of the Red Heifer

In Chukat there is a very powerful and very negatively enlightened section. The reading begins with the Red Heifer, an instrument of cleansing, at the time of the Holy Temple in Jerusalem. There is so much commentary about the Red Heifer; those of us who have the merit to have the Zohar in our midst, and can refer to the Zohar as a body of information, can walk away with something so incredible. The Red Heifer was present while there was a Holy Temple. It was used for spiritual cleansing, which also means the cleansing of our soul that is necessary as long as we are in this world of Malchut. For those of us whose effort in this world is toward elevated awareness, the cleansing of the soul means that to whatever extent we can, we place our consciousness to emulate the Creator. Now the Creator does not need cleansing, nonetheless by desiring to emulate the Creator, we can cleanse the body and the soul. The energy of the Red Heifer was such that any impairments of the body seen or unseen could and can be cleansed. A malady like cancer can go undetected for 30 or 40 years. There are many aspects of negativity that are unseen; yet we become so concerned with the necessities of life that we forget that there are negative activities going on in our body and our soul. With this reading, we have the opportunity to cleanse everything in our frame. We are all here to share in this energy, which the Creator with so much compassion for humanity, has provided us this instrument.

According to the Zohar, in its interpretation of the Red Heifer, we become cleansed of any negativity—just as we were when the Temple existed. Yet being cleansed of every aliment in our physical body is a difficult concept to accept and, in fact, there are those of us who would more readily to accept bad news. It ought to be the reverse. We ought to ask ourselves the question: Why do I not want to accept such a truth? Why do we prefer to believe that we, ourselves, are not that gullible, which is a common first reaction to something so extraordinary? Why is it so hard to accept that the Bible takes us to this next state where we can connect to those disciplines, those methodologies, that energy that served all people at the time of the Temple? Today, we are going to make a resolution that we are going to know that we are being cured of everything. Why does it not happen? Because although there are miracles that are incredible we think they are not for everybody. Today, we will know that we have had the full procedure as it was done in the Temple.

The Power of the High Priest

The High Priest who administered this potion to cure anyone from the ultimate scourges of disease, contracted the disease himself. The Zohar explains that for the Priest or any healer to administer cleansing, they had to be prepared to remove that illness by taking it into themselves. The Priests (Kohanim) have extraordinary powers; they can channel healing, and literally snatch from the sick the very aspect of death itself. We cannot simply cut out an illness but we can convert it. There are trillions of cells, and even if 99.9% of a disease has been removed, there are still a couple of billion diseased cells left, which is why surgery is not the answer. What we learn from the Zohar is that disease must be converted, restored back to a healthy cell. This is 50th century physics, medicine. This is the power of the Kohen and the power of the Red Heifer.

Bamidbar 20:1 And the children of Israel, the whole congregation, came into the wilderness of Zin in the first month; and the people stayed in Kadesh; and Miriam died there, and was buried there. 2 And there was no water for the congregation; and they assembled themselves together against Moses and against Aaron. 3 And the people contended with Moses, and spoke, saying: "Would that we had perished when our brethren perished before the Lord! 4 And why have you brought the assembly of the Lord into this wilderness, to die there, we and our cattle? 5 And why have you made us to come up out of Egypt, to bring us in to this evil place? It is no place of grain, or of figs, or of vines, or of pomegranates; neither is there any water to drink." 6 And Moses and Aaron went from the presence of the assembly to the door of the Tent of Meeting, and fell upon their faces; and the glory of the Lord appeared to them. 7 And the Lord spoke to Moses, saying: 8 "Take the rod and assemble the congregation, you and Aaron, your brother, and speak to the rock before their eyes, that it give forth its water; and you shall bring forth to them water out of the rock; so you shall give the congregation and their cattle to drink." 9 And Moses took the rod from before the Lord, as He commanded him. 10 And Moses and Aaron gathered the assembly together before the rock, and he said to them: "Hear now, you rebels; are we to bring you forth water out of this rock?" 11 And Moses lifted up his hand

and smote the rock with his rod twice; and water came forth abundantly, and the congregation and their cattle drank. 12 And the Lord said to Moses and Aaron: "Because you did not believe in Me, to sanctify Me in the eyes of the children of Israel, therefore you shall not bring this assembly into the land which I have given them." 13 These are the waters of Meribah, where the children of Israel contended with the Lord, and He was sanctified in them.

Transcending Time, Space, and Motion

Why do we read about the Red Heifer when we no longer have the Temple or the Tabernacle? Why is the portion of Chukat always read in the month of Tammuz (the month of Cancer)? Why is it important to read and hear the Torah? Because it is the instrument that can bring us back in time and not because it is commanded for us to do so. With the help of the readings we can transcend time, space, and motion, which are an illusion. There is no other technology that offers us the ability to transcend time, space, and motion.

With this reading we can receive a cleansing more powerful than any Mikveh (spiritual immersion), even if we were to immerse ourselves over and over again. Although we do not have a Red Heifer, the power of this Torah reading can remove and cleanse us of the negativity of a short-circuit. When a person dies, the soul, which is part of the Light, leaves and only the body, the dark part, remains behind. Even if one is only in the same room, this negativity becomes attached. And we cannot rid ourselves of it.

There is a debate in Israel today whether one should be able to go to the Temple Mount. The reason for the debate is not the idea of to go or not to go. Rather, a person might carry the negativity of a dead person, which most of us carry, especially in the land of Israel, with all the wars throughout history. The Zohar says every powerful nation that has existed has tried to conquer Israel. If we go to the Temple Mount and we are not totally pure, we can experience a considerable short-circuit. We read the portion of Chukat to receive the most powerful form of cleansing from death.

Cancer, Confusion, and Consciousness

Abraham the Patriarch named this month *Sartan* (Cancer). The word *tan*, which is the second syllable of the word, means "confusion." The negative force of confusion begins in this month. Even though scientists do not know what causes cancer, they recognize that the cancer cell acts in confusion and abnormally. When the cancer cell attacks a healthy cell, the cell dies and eventually the whole organism dies and the cancer dies with it. The cancer cell acts with total Desire for One Self Alone.

In the month of Cancer all manner confusion occurs. This is the true cause of problems and diseases. The reason that there are Holidays at particular times or specific Torah readings at particular times is because the Creator gave us these connections as a protection. It is when the confusion sets in that we have the opportunity to remove the source and thereby the problem.

In nature, wherever the disease is found, the cure is also found. This is a big secret. That is why, within the month of Cancer there is already a cure to remove the confusion. Even the doctors agree, cancer can begin in a person years before it manifests. Kabbalah wants to eliminate the source of the tumor from the root, to remove the confusion. Everything is consciousness. We receive the technology to eliminate the confusion with this portion of Chukat.

Tamei, which is referred to as uncleanliness is not discussing something physical; *tamei* is metaphysical. How can we remove something metaphysical? There is no medicine in the world that can remove that which is not physical. There is no cure for mental disease even though we have medications to control the physical symptoms. This confusion starts in either this life or the last life.

We have the Red Heifer to cleanse us of this metaphysical short-circuit. If all the world would hear this Torah reading, all the confusion in the world will disappear and there would be no need to hide our negativity. God willing, with this portion of Chukat, and with the consciousness of cleansing, we will have wonders and miracles soon.

Striking the Rock

The passing of Miriam is also found in this portion. When a righteous person passes away they remove judgment, darkness. In Bamidbar 20 it says "...And the Israelites ....came and Miriam died... There was no water for the people..." The people began complaining. God told Moses, "... speak to the rock." Yet instead Moses hits the rock twice and God tells Moses that because he hit the rock he will not bring the people to Israel.

The Zohar compares this with the Golden Calf incident, when the two sons of Bilaam—Yunus and Yumbrus—who made the Golden Calf, covered up the process of how to make it, so the Israelites would not be able to see. Why would they cover it up? And why would the Zohar compare the two?

I like to compare it to a magician who first covers the hat and then reveals the bird. Why is this part of the show? We know that what we are seeing is a trick on the five senses and we know that it is not real, nonetheless we pay good money to be fooled. For 2,000 years (according to the order that was prepared by the Great Assembly) the people prayed to cover the real truth from the eyes. The sons of Bilaam knew this and so they covered the process with the gold. If there is no trickery, we complain. Yet if we see the truth, meaning that the bird does not come out of the hat, we ask for our money back.

Moses knew—after what happened with the spies and with Korach—that the consciousness of the people was so low that they would not believe in a reality where water could come out of a stone. Even though they had already seen it before, they would have forgotten. They preferred to be fooled.

The commentators say that there was no water because Miriam died. However there were rocks around. Moses had already taken water out of the rock and he knew that the people wanted a trick; by hitting the rock, they could believe that water came out the stone—like we do when we see a magic show. This is what the Torah wants to show us about human nature. That is why it is so hard to bring Kabbalah to the world. People want to see a magic trick and if there is not one, there is the complaint that Kabbalah is not real and they want their money back. People want to be conned and are willing to pay the price for someone to do so.

When we look at the verse from the Torah, the Creator is saying, "...because you did not believe in Me." We have to ask, what did Moses not believe in? If the water had come out only by speaking, there would be no trick. This is the problem with spreading the wisdom of Kabbalah: when something is false it is easy to convey and when it is truth it is much harder because people are very connected to the lie.

My teacher, Rav Brandwein, told me once that Rav Ashlag had a chance to tell a small lie; however, he decided not to do so even though in telling the lie a person would have been saved from being hurt. He did not want to say even the smallest lie in order not to put this energy into the cosmos.

Any person who lies connects to the false. Moses knew this; especially after the spies and Korach lied. This is why Moses hit the stone: the people were connected to the lie because the truth is not obvious.

There is so much opposition to teaching Kabbalah to the public. Today, it is not as much of a problem as it was 30 years ago when we were the only people teaching it. Nonetheless, the Kabbalah Centres may not be popular but to study Kabbalah is popular.

What can we learn from what God said? God said, "You did not believe in Me," meaning in the power of the Light. We can see today all the problems of the world. At the Centre we work to elevate the consciousness of the world. This is the power of the Light, the minute you turn on a small light, the darkness disappears. I do not know how but it disappears. This is the miracle.

Water does not normally come out of a rock, yet in this case there is an opportunity. The minute we place the Light into a situation no one can say what is going to be. We see that the Kabbalah Centre has an influence and that we are changing the consciousness of the world. Any sparks of Light that we put into the world with prayer, the Zohar, and positive actions, replace the negative actions that would have taken place because people are learning Kabbalah. *Bila hamavet lanetzach*, which means "death can be swallowed up forever," can come in an instant. In a split second there is more Light in the world. Yet most would not know the cause. For 2,000 years only a few righteous people brought a little Light to the world, but today the masses are doing it. This is what God told Moses. God told him that these people do not believe. They will not believe it even if they see the trick.

Go with the Light

Moses struck the rock instead of speaking with the rock—as God had commanded. According to the simple meaning of this text, this is the reason Moses was not permitted to enter Israel. Why was this sin so great that it warranted such a "punishment"? Instead of speaking to the rock, Moses smote the rock. Why did Moses not do exactly as the Creator told him?

The Zohar tells us that whoever seeks to understands the meaning of the Bible in the most simple, literal manner is a fool. Even inert entities, like rocks, have an inner intelligence, and the Creator told Moses to speak with the inner intelligence of the rock. Moses struck the rock because he saw that the people's consciousness was limited. They were incapable of connecting to the inner aspect of the rock. They needed the physical contact. Therefore he struck the rock, which is a lower level of consciousness, instead of acting in accordance with the highest consciousness of the Light. By striking the rock, the people would either accept it or not; they would believe it or not.

The lesson for us here is to go with the Light, and reveal the Light without fear or concern whether or not it will be accepted. When Karen and I began distributing the truth of Kabbalah, especially in the beginning, everyone was against it, we persevered fearlessly, all the same—and then a door opened. A true teacher, a good teacher, transmits the information of the Light whether it is accepted or not. He or she cannot be influenced.

Striking the Rock of Consciousness

Why did Moses strike the rock? Moses did not succeed in raising the people's consciousness to the level of speech, which is why he did not enter Israel. Had he entered, it would have manifested more Light than the Israelites could handle at that time. This is why he smote the rock—so that he would not be able to enter Israel. Smiting is a physical action. Speaking is less involved with matter and more involved in thought, and thus it is more metaphysical. Moses wanted to effect a unification by striking—that is establishing the Returning Light. He thought this action would awaken the people.

The Magic of Moses

If I were a magician, you would all pay $100 to see my performance. First, I would show you an empty hat, then I would put my *Talit* (Prayer Shawl) across it—and next thing you know a pigeon would fly out. This would probably be worth $100 to you. If no pigeon came out, you would be running to the box-office cash register for a refund. We all pay good money to be fooled.

Rav Ashlag explained that the sons of Bilaam hid the process of how the Golden Calf was fashioned and because of this, Moses then understood the real nature of Israelites' consciousness. Moreover, after the death of Miriam, as soon as the miracle of the traveling well was gone from their memory, they immediately forgot about these gifts, and they started to complain.

Moses hit the rock because there is no performance in merely speaking to a stone. Their consciousness was not prepared for the acceptance of a miracle; their consciousness could only accept a magic trick. A complete metaphysical immaterial communication was something they would not understand or believe at this stage.

God's response to Moses was, to paraphrase: "When I asked you to speak to the stone, I too knew that their consciousness was low, but it was up to you to make an attempt to elevate them. This is what was called for in order to take their consciousness out of the realm of "magic" into the realm of the metaphysical. However, because you thought changing the mindset of the Israelites was impossible, you are no longer able to connect to them, and you cannot lead them into the Promised Land."

Avoiding Corruption

Here we learn about the trait of the evil people (*erev rav*), which was one of complaining, even after witnessing all the miracles brought about through Moses. The children of Israel came to a place where there was no water. What did they do—they complained! The point that the Bible wants to make clear is that corruption will emerge, and we must strive to avoid it. They had no water to drink. Previously, they had a well that travelled with them wherever they went; and it was known as the Well of Miriam. But now there was no well, so they complained and wanted to go back to Egypt.

You might think they would be happy to leave slavery behind, instead they cried, "Why did you take us out of Egypt?"

It is considered that during Passover those of Jewish persuasion celebrate the liberation from Egyptian bondage. However, if you read the words of the Bible, the people actually did not want to leave Egypt; they constantly asked to return. Often conditions in Egypt are compared to those in Auschwitz. Yet this is illogical as the Bible repeats that the desire of the Israelites was to remain in Egypt. It is therefore illogical to assume that things were so bad in Egypt.

Now there was no water, God told Moses, "Speak to the stone and tell the stone to give you water." Is there water in stone? Yes, there is; all things consist of water. We consist of approximately 80% water, and scientists are now telling us that even inanimate objects, such as stone, consist mostly of molecular water.

What did Moses do? He struck the stone with his staff. This appears to be confusing. God told Moses: "Take the staff; assemble the Israelites; and speak to the stone"—speak, not strike. In an earlier portion, Moses was told to strike the stone to obtain water, yet now he is told not to strike but to speak to the stone, and to draw water from it for the children of Israel. What did Moses do? He took the staff and struck the stone, disobeying God. Because he struck the stone and did not speak to the stone as instructed, Moses was not allowed to enter the land of Israel.

Restoring Mind over Matter; Tikkun haNefesh

This sounds a little excessively cruel, and we may ask what this incident has to do with the portion. The answer to this question is that what we are reading here is the very thing the Kabbalah Centres have been trying to achieve for the past 80 years. The Centre wants to achieve one objective: to restore within human consciousness the knowledge of mind over matter, to restore the birthright that has never fully disappeared. In our dealings with time, space, and motion, more specifically our ability to move through space, man is useless if he cannot achieve mind over matter. The physical world places limitations upon us. We are limited through space, time, and motion. It takes time to move from one country to another, but if I could rise above space it would be much quicker.

To return to our thoughts about spiritual/immaterial surgery— this too is mind over matter. We have tools we can use to realize this state of consciousness. With the *Tikkun haNefesh*, we can create a condition of Light in our physical system, in the body – and, as we know, Light makes darkness disappear. But this creates a problem. How many of us believe we can remove chaos from our bodies? Science is now proving mind over matter on a theoretical level. Empirical proofs will follow.

God was telling Moses: "Just speak to the stone, do not use any physical medium (the staff) on the stone, because this could be seen as the result of some form of trickery, like that which is performed by a magician. The staff could have had some hidden water in it that gushed out when the stone was struck. Can a magician speak to a hat and make a rabbit emerge from it? No, he has to tap the hat to facilitate the trick.

Humanity must try progressing to the point where we accept mind over matter. Science confirms that mind over matter exists as a principle. The wisdom of Kabbalah has expressed this truth for centuries: mind over matter exists as a natural and universal law. The Centre advances the understanding of mind over matter. A few years ago, we raised the idea of Immortality, and the media put us down for it at every opportunity. Nonetheless science then found "the immortality gene." Now the Centre is furthering the idea of spiritual, as opposed to physical, surgery—science will, no doubt, uncover this soon too!

The Importance of Water

What came first, the water or the stone? According to Rav Shimon bar Yochai, the water came first. Our bodies are made up of 70–80% water. At a fundamental level, everything is water. The Zohar says that the water is Yesod (cause) and the rock is Malchut (effect) and that a cause always presides over the effect, the effect never rules over the cause; whatever comes first always has dominion over what comes second.

Moses knew the internal energy of the stone; he understood the stone is physicality but physicality disappears; energy, on the other hand, does not disappear. It can only transform, just as water, when heated, becomes steam. Moses knew the immaterial nature of the stone, for the stone is 99% water. Moses was at a level of mind over matter—this is a simple truth conferred on us. Why, then, do we not exercise mind over matter? Because we are searching for truth in all the wrong places.

So what did God really want of Moses in this situation? If Moses simply spoke to the stone, it would be clear to all that it was only the mind without the physicality, which would corrupt the consciousness of the people. A magician always uses a physical element to create the illusion. This is what God wanted. He wanted Moses to make the connection without using physicality, to make the connection with universal consciousness.

This story teaches us the Israelites were not ready to do this yet; they had not achieved the consciousness of mind over matter. Thus when God told Moses he could not go into Israel, He was really saying the people were not ready yet. However, using the technology of the Bible, we today, can overcome chaos in our lives.

The Merit of Miriam

As we mentioned previously, when Miriam passed away, the well that had traveled with the Israelites disappeared. The miracle of the well was because of the merit of Miriam and, when she passed on, immediately there was no water for the congregation. This is how the Zohar connects Miriam to water. The people complained to Moses. It does not make sense, because an hour earlier they had water. They were of a totally unappreciative consciousness, failing even to appreciate the ability to create a masterpiece such as a well in the desert that went with them wherever they travelled. This generation had the ability to comprehend the secrets of the universe and yet they complained to Moses and wanted to go back to Egypt!

This is a problem we face today. Those Israelites are us, and, knowing this, perhaps we can understand a little about our nature. Everyone here has experienced some kind of miracle, yet we still question what the Light is doing for us now. How far does this misunderstanding really go? Once we have made a connection to this reading, we may say, "God, I just got finished with this reading, why did nothing happen?"

Do we consider that perhaps there is something we have not yet fulfilled ourselves in the requirements to alleviate disease? After making our connection today, do we stop and give the time to the person who asks it of us or do we say, "Please ask someone else, I'm in a rush." When we walk out of the Centre, our spiritual work is not over; there are still requirements to be fulfilled.

The reason the Israelites were able to forget all the miracles they had experienced and continued complaining to Moses that he had brought them to the wilderness to die, is because they did not appreciate what was being given to them. We, today, have the Zohar and the wisdom of Kabbalah, and yet can also not appreciate all that we are being given—to the extent that we can ignore a person asking for help.

God said, "Speak to the stone," and instead Moses brought all the Israelites together and beat the stone twice. Water came out, and the congregation drank. Perhaps he was distressed?

Even though God told Moses to speak to the stone, Moses realized that the Israelites were not going to believe a miracle had occurred, and this is why he struck the stone. God then condemned Moses to never lead the Israelites into Israel.

A consciousness of mind over matter is what we must achieve to receive what we are here to receive.

A Travelling Well

In the desert there was one miracle after another. The Israelites had a well that traveled with them, supplying all the water needed for 600,000 men, women, and children, and millions of cattle. We have all seen a travelling well of such magnitude, have we not? When Miriam passed from this physical realm, the well stopped and in a reaction typical of the people, they started to complain about where their water would come from now. This is abnormal. It is like Israelis in Gaza beating up other Israeli's because they are spreading the Zohar. How do we explain such aberrations?

There have always been people like this; they are part of the Creation. While we cannot understand how people could react in such ways, God can. When they said they were scared they would all die because there was no water, God spoke to Moses and told him to speak to the rock to obtain water. And there is another miracle.

Next, the Israelites complained because there was always food in Egypt and now they have nothing to eat. Imagine, they say this when they have the manna. Whatever flavor they wanted manna to be would become the taste of that food. If anyone decided they wanted a medium steak, they got a medium steak. If, the next day they desired a steak prepared well-done, the manna now tasted like well-done steak. And still they complained. What could they complain about, that it was prepared differently in Egypt? Nothing in the wilderness had the same physicality they were used to.

It seems that God began to get tired of these people and many of them died as a result. What is the limit to griping? Is it remotely reasonable to complain because someone, somewhere in the world has something that we do not?

With this reading we are given the opportunity to restore the consciousness of mind over matter. This was lost because of the complaining and the shortsighted type of consciousness in the Israelites. The only free will we truly have is to act like the Creator. Now we have the cleansing needed to help us get back that right.

14 And Moses sent messengers from Kadesh to the king of Edom: "So says your brother Israel: You know all the hardship that has befallen us; 15 how our fathers went down into Egypt, and we dwelt in Egypt a long time; and the Egyptians dealt ill with us, and our fathers; 16 and when we cried to the Lord, He heard our voice, and sent an angel, and brought us forth out of Egypt; and, behold, we are in Kadesh, a city in the uttermost of your border. 17 Let us pass, I pray you, through your land; we will not pass through field or through vineyard, neither will we drink of the water of the wells; we will go along the king's highway, we will not turn aside to the right hand nor to the left, until we have passed your border." 18 And Edom said to him: "You shall not pass through me, lest I come out with the sword against you." 19 And the children of Israel said to him: "We will go up by the highway; and if we drink of your water, I and my cattle, then will I give the price thereof; let me only pass through on my feet; there is no hurt." 20 And he said: "You shall not pass through." And Edom came out against him with many people, and with a strong hand. 21 Edom refused to give Israel passage through his border; so Israel turned away from him. 22 And they journeyed from Kadesh; and the children of Israel, the whole congregation, came to mount Hor. 23 And the Lord spoke to Moses and Aaron in Mount Hor, by the border of the land of Edom, saying: 24 "Aaron shall be gathered to his people; for he shall

not enter into the land which I have given to the children of Israel, because you rebelled against My word at the waters of Meribah. 25 Take Aaron and Elazar his son, and bring them up to Mount Hor. 26 And strip Aaron of his garments, and put them on Elazar his son; and Aaron shall be gathered to his people, and shall die there." 27 And Moses did as the Lord commanded; and they went up into Mount Hor, in the sight of all the congregation. 28 And Moses stripped Aaron of his garments, and put them upon Elazar, his son; and Aaron died there in the top of the mount; and Moses and Elazar came down from the mount. 29 And when all the congregation saw that Aaron was dead, they wept for Aaron thirty days, all the house of Israel.

The Death of the Righteous is an Atonement

Miriam and Aaron died, and the Zohar says that the death of the righteous is an atonement. It also concerns clearing up cancer, the death of Aaron and Miriam, connecting us with the power of cleansing.

Bamidbar 21:1 And the Canaanite, the king of Arad, who dwelt in the South, heard that Israel came by the way of Atharim; and he fought against Israel, and took some of them captive. 2 And Israel vowed a vow to the Lord, and said: "If You will indeed deliver this people into my hand, then I will utterly destroy their cities." 3 And the Lord hearkened to the voice of Israel, and delivered up the Canaanites; and they utterly destroyed them and their cities; and the name of the place was called Hormah. 4 And they journeyed from Mount Hor by the way to the Red Sea, to compass the land of Edom; and the soul of the people became impatient because of the way. 5 And the people spoke against God, and against Moses: "Why have you brought us up out of Egypt to die in the wilderness? For there is no bread, and there is no water; and our soul loathes this light bread." 6 And the Lord sent fiery serpents among the people, and they bit the people; and many people of Israel died. 7 And the people came to Moses, and said: "We have sinned, because we have spoken against the Lord, and against you; pray to the Lord, that He take away the serpents from us." And Moses prayed for the people. 8 And the Lord said to Moses: "Make a fiery serpent, and set it upon a pole; and it shall come to pass, that every one that is bitten, when he sees it, shall live." 9 And Moses made a serpent of brass, and set it upon the pole; and it came to pass, that if a serpent

had bitten any man, when he looked at the serpent of brass, he lived.

The Caduceus

What is the sign of the physician? It is entwined snakes on a pole. How strange it is to find that such a symbol comes from this portion.

10 And the children of Israel journeyed, and pitched in Oboth. 11 And they journeyed from Oboth, and pitched at Ije-Habarim, in the wilderness which is in front of Moab, toward the sunrise. 12 From there they journeyed, and pitched in the valley of Zered. 13 From there they journeyed, and pitched on the other side of the Arnon, which is in the wilderness, that comes out of the border of the Amorites. Arnon is the border of Moab, between Moab and the Amorites; 14 where it is said in the book of the Wars of the Lord: Vaheb in Suphah, and the valleys of Arnon, 15 And the slope of the valleys that inclined toward the seat of Ar, and leans upon the border of Moab. 16 And from there to Be'er; that is the well where the Lord said to Moses: "Gather the people together, and I will give them water." 17 Then sang Israel this song: "Spring up, well, all of you sing to it."

A Song in the Wilderness

The Song of the Well here, unlike the Song of the Sea, is understood as totally encoded and completely in accordance with the mystical. As we know, that which is hidden is always more exalted. The Song of the Sea—the 72 Names—is about when Nachshon jumped into the sea and the visible miracle of the parting of the Red Sea occurred. In this portion, they did not know there was danger, and yet a miracle also occurred. A hidden miracle is greater. We have a special prayer of thanksgiving that we recite daily (Psalms 100) for the miracles we do not see.

18 The well, which the princes sank, which the nobles of the people had dug, with the sceptre, and with their staves. And from the wilderness to Mattanah; 19 and from Mattanah to Nahaliel; and from Nahaliel to Bamoth; 20 and from Bamoth to the valley that is in the field of Moab, by the top of Pisgah, which looks down upon the desert. 21 And Israel sent messengers to Sihon, king of the Amorites, saying: 22 "Let me pass through your land; we will not turn aside into field, or into vineyard; we will not drink of the water of the wells; we will go by the king's highway, until we have passed your border." 23 And Sihon would not allow Israel to pass through his border; but Sihon gathered all his people together, and went out against Israel into the wilderness, and came to Jahaz; and he fought against Israel. 24 And Israel smote him with the edge of the sword, and possessed his land from the Arnon to the Jabbok, to the children of Ammon; for the border of the children of Ammon was strong. 25 And Israel took all these cities; and Israel dwelt in all the cities of the Amorites, in Heshbon, and in all its towns. 26 For Heshbon was the city of Sihon, the king of the Amorites, who had fought against the former king of Moab, and had taken all his land out of his hand, to the Arnon. 27 Therefore those that speak in parables say: "Come you to Heshbon! Let the city of Sihon be built and established! 28 For a fire has gone out of Heshbon, a flame from the city of Sihon; it has devoured Ar of

Moab, the lords of the high places of Arnon. 29 Woe to you, Moab! You are undone, people of Chemosh; he has given his sons as fugitives, and his daughters into captivity, to Sihon, king of the Amorites. 30 We have shot at them—Heshbon has perished—to Dibon, and we have laid waste to Nophah, which reaches to Medeba." 31 So Israel dwelt in the land of the Amorites. 32 And Moses sent to spy out Jazer, and they took those towns and drove out the Amorites that were there. 33 And they turned and went up by the way of Bashan; and Og, the king of Bashan, went out against them, he and all his people, to battle at Edrei. 34 And the Lord said to Moses: "Do not fear him; for I have delivered him into your hand, and all his people, and his land; and you shall do to him as you did to Sihon, king of the Amorites, who dwelt at Heshbon." 35 So they smote him, and his sons, and all his people, until there was no survivor remaining; and they possessed his land.

Bamidbar 22:1 And the children of Israel journeyed, and pitched in the plains of Moab beyond the Jordan at Jericho.

A Deep and More Profound Understanding of the Red Heifer

The Red Heifer was like the Golden Calf—a calf, a heifer, an ox, it is all the same, it is all one family of beasts. Its power is from the side of Gevurah (Left Column), and this power draws down the Light of Chochmah (Light of Wisdom).

43

For example, if someone has cancer, it is this Heifer, the Left Column, that attracts the Light of Chochmah, especially during the month of Cancer and the weekly portion of Chukat. The primary goal of everything we learn in Kabbalah is to create a connection between us and the Light of Chochmah. The Left Column is the connection, the conductor, the transmitter of the Light of Chochmah, which actually fixes everything and eliminates all the problems to the extent that it can create new things.

A phantom limb is an experience where a limb that has been removed or amputated is still present in the body. Amputees can experience sensations including pain in the phantom limb. At the time of the Resurrection of the Dead, for someone whose limb had been removed, it will again be revealed. And the tooth that had been removed will be revealed. What does this mean?

Based on a comment by the Ra'avad (Rabbi Avraham ben David of Posquieres or Provence, 1125-1198), that a blind person can give birth to healthy children who can see, if someone does not have a limb or teeth, the problem is not that the tooth or hand or leg is really lost, the problem is that thought is reality. If I have a desire to go for a stroll on the beach tomorrow, the physicists say that when I go there tomorrow, I will be walking in my own footprints, which were imprinted by me a day earlier when I thought about walking in the sand.

We live in a world of physical things that limit us; but things that limit also reveal. As we say, how does a person become revealed on the street? Only when he covers himself, when he gets dressed, can he go out to the street. This is the paradox of our lives: to reveal we must first conceal.

A blind person can give birth to a person that sees because he or she has eyes and the power of sight. He has teeth. He has hands and feet. What happens is that he is lacking the power of concealment, which enables things to be revealed. Therefore, the Light of Chochmah that is revealed is only revealed when a connection is made with the Light of Chochmah. The Light of Chochmah can create physical power. What is going on here?

In *Sefer haLikutim* ("Book of Compilations"), Rav Isaac Luria (the Ari) writes that the five final letters of the Hebrew alphabet form a word *MaNTZePaCH* ((ך"מנצפ, and are the Five Gevurot (letters of Judgment) and have the same numerical value as the word *parah* (heifer).

There are five levels that are called Gevurah in every vessel, which comprise the Gevurah of the vessel. What happened here with the Heifer? We are hoping to actualize the Resurrection of the Dead. What does this mean? The Red Heifer is the vessel, the channel that contains the Light of Chochmah. When we deal with physical objects, it is the material that reveals the content. Even though it conceals, it reveals. For instance, there are already teeth but there are no teeth, because I do not have any. It is as when a person is born, the real teeth are born, together with the force that reveals them, but then we lose this.

When the Israelites made the Golden Calf, they lost their jewelry. What does this mean? It is written in the Zohar that this refers to *MaNTzePaCh*, which is something we can take advantage of as well. *MaNTzePaCh* is the same force of energy that recreates the ability to reveal the teeth, to reveal the leg. And it is the same force that conceals the leg so that it becomes possible to reveal the leg on the material plane.

I want to explain what *MaNTzePaCh* can do for us. We want to begin using the ability of control over physicality, that is, the power to create physical objects. People have teeth even if they cannot be seen. So is a tooth missing? Is a leg missing? No, Rav Ashlag gives the example that when a person wants to go outside, he must get dressed, and by covering himself, he may be revealed. This is the paradox of the physical world; a person cannot go outside naked— to reveal himself out there, he must cover himself.

What do I cover? I cover the body that I already have There is a prohibition against going naked in the street because it is against spirituality and morality. It is forbidden that things be revealed in their crude form. For a soul to be revealed it needs a body. A person is a basic entity, like an atom. As for atoms, my hand can pass through billions of atoms which cannot stop the hand. But the second there is a table in the way, what happens? It reveals the power that was there but could not be seen. How do I feel it? With the table, for example, the power of the physical reveals the atoms, billions of which are in every square inch. Why do we not feel them in the air? Because there is nothing physical to reveal them, and there has to be something that reveals what exists.

MaNTzePaCh is the power of what we once had. This is why the Israelites were able to make a Golden Calf. What did they do? They took the atoms and they took a Golden Calf that was actually alive. Why is gold the most precious? Because the special quality of gold is that it is a channel for the Light of Chochmah, just as it is a good conductor of electricity. The Golden Calf contained the Light of Chochmah in a passive manner. By the power of *MaNTzePaCh*, the letters were able to reveal the Light of Chochmah, which is concealed. We do not see the Light of Chochmah; the Light of Chochmah is a Light that radiates from God and it can only be revealed by *MaNTzePaCh*.

Regarding the portion of Chukat, we come to realize that the letters *MaNTzePaCh* were used to activate the Red Heifer, which had the Five Gevurot. Just like the gold, the five letters were already combined. What is lacking is the knowledge of how to use *MaNTzePaCh* to reveal the Light of Chochmah.

What was the power of the Red Heifer? It was to cleanse someone who had become ritually impure due to contact with a dead body. If someone touches a dead body, the power of death is transmitted. The person who becomes impure does not die, yet sometimes there is a sense that the person is dead. The person is connected to the ritual impurity brought on by contact with dead bodies. What does the impurity as a result of contact with death mean? It means that the energy a person reveals to be alive, the power of the body, is not working.

The soul is not dead. The active power of *MaNTzePaCh* acts so that the body will awaken and then the body is covered. Only an active body can be revealed, like the table with the atoms. If the table is dead, if it has been burnt, for example, the power returns to the atoms, and the power that vitalizes the physical, the *MaNTzePaCh* is taken away.

This is why the Red Heifer is associated with a ritual impurity caused by contact with death. Before the Israelites made the Golden Calf, during the giving of the Bible at Mount Sinai, "death had been swallowed up for all time." When a person is born, he or she already has a natural *MaNTzePaCh* of the teeth, so the teeth can exist even when they do not yet exist. It is *MaNTzePaCh* that revives the dead. It is through *MaNTzePaCh* that death is swallowed up forever.

What is death? It is the power that can destroy the animating force. When a tooth is taken out, though it was already manifested there is no life on the physical plane, so there is no life in the tooth, therefore the physical tooth cannot be revealed.

The Red Heifer can help us reveal the power of *MaNTzePaCh*, even though we do not have that knowledge today. But the Israelites had such knowledge when they made the Golden Calf. Therefore, when a person touches a dead body he has lost the *MaNTzePaCh*. What does this mean? It means his whole body could rot away. To this day, we do not have the power of the Red Heifer.

What goes missing is *MaNTzePaCh*. When someone touches a dead body, that person loses the *MaNTzePaCh*. What constitutes contact with a dead body? According to the rules of Halacha even if a person is only in the same house as a dead body, the person becomes ritually impure thereby without its *MaNTzePaCh* an entire body can lose its power, God forbid, and die without its *MaNTzePaCh*.

The Creator has compassion. He gave us this Torah reading of Chukat on Shabbat so that if we have been exposed to death in any way, intentionally or unintentionally, we may, by the reading of the Torah, regain our *MaNTzePaCh*.

At the time of the Resurrection of the Dead, everyone will be able to use the power of the letters, *MaNTzePaCh*, and revive the dead. Today, we do not know how to do it but when the time comes we will. On Shabbat we can listen to the reading of Chukat and awaken the *MaNTzePaCh* within us.

The seed of the disease of cancer takes its place in a person in the month of Cancer, so when we read the portion of Chukat and connect with *MaNTzePaCh*, we can destroy the seed of all negativity, not only the cancer, anything connected with death. With the cleansing available to us this month through these readings, we can revive the physical force for everything lacking in our body, so Satan cannot enter and cause us to lose the body's strength. What we are lacking is the power to vitalize the body.

If Satan has no more power, then the seed that began to grow has been cut off. This pertains to what had already begun. So why are we not capable of growing back a tooth or leg and why can we not revive the dead? The Zohar says that the time of the Resurrection of the Dead has not yet come.

Why did Moses strike the rock twice? One function of MaNTzePaCh is to eliminate the power of Satan that was in the object, to remove the power of death, and then, when the force of Satan is no longer present, we may, with the help of *MaNTzePaCh*, infuse life—if we know how.

Moses needed to accomplish two things: one was to show that the rock could be like the Golden Calf, and the other to revitalize. Therefore two actions were needed, one to remove the power of Satan, the power of impurity, the power of death and one to revitalize. To revitalize an additional action is necessary. When the Creator told Moses to speak with the rock, speaking is the additional action needed to revitalize, and this was the mistake Moses made.

What is the power of Chukat? It is to cleanse, to do the one action, to extricate the power of death from the inert or inactive. For example, in the case of teeth, the power of death must first of all be removed from the mouth, while the matter of revitalizing is the additional power of *MaNTzePaCh*. We are on the level that requires two actions. Therefore, when the Creator told Moses to only speak, he did not understand because speaking is only one action. The Revival of the Dead, by means of only our speech, our thoughts is something we, as yet, do not know how. We have the letters *MaNTzePaCh* in the Musaf Prayer (Additional Prayer) we pray on Shabbat. We connect with *MaNTzePaCh*, and this is the intention. However, we have not yet reached the level of knowing how to activate the second force.

The Creator therefore said, "Moses, you do know how to perform the two acts." Moses followed his own common sense. He said, "I know the rules and the laws. I know *MaNTzePaCh* works for the Israelites through two actions." That is why it is written that Moses hit the rock twice. He knew two actions were needed. What he did not know was that if the ultimate goal was the Resurrection of the Dead, how would these conditions enable this Resurrection? It would be by means of thought—which was his mistake. Moses thought it was not possible by means of thought and this is why he smote the rock.

The Endless Blessings of Every Second

One of the daily problems we encounter is that we completely forget the endless blessings of every second. Some people can only see the faults or the lacks they have. We forget to see the blessings we have. Think of what it means: if there is something within our physical body that may go wrong in 20 years from today, in 30 years from today, we can have it cleansed when we connect to the reading of Chukat. We cannot take this for granted. The blessing does not come like that. Let us take advantage of Chukat.

Nonetheless, if our consciousness still remains in the garbage of what we do not have, the reading itself is pointless. We are never going to find happiness and peace of mind. It does not work that way. We need to focus on how to appreciate what we have, and not complain about what we do not have.

The Armageddon War

The War of Armageddon, the War of Consciousness, is happening right now. Chaos and negativity are manifesting in everyone's life at an alarmingly increased rate, and they will not go away on their own. Chaos is part of this reality, and it always has been. The War of Armageddon is a metaphysical war which manifests in airborne disease, cancer, pollution, contaminated water, and so forth. This metaphysical war can only be won if we all become conscious of how we are being attacked by chaos, and use the metaphysical technology provided by the Creator to Moses on Mount Sinai for the overcoming of negativity.

The story of the Red Heifer in the portion of Chukat is only one of the 52 specific sections into which the sages divided the Torah Scroll. Each specific section corresponds to one of the 52 weeks of the year. Millennia ago, the sages saw and knew that the computer system they were using—the Bible—was so advanced they determined that Chukat would always coincide with the month of Cancer in the Hebrew calendar.

The Priest mentioned in this biblical story had been experiencing the ultimate chaos by administering the total remedy to cleanse a sick person, also known as *tumah*, the highest form of chaos. This is what the Red Heifer is really about—a remedy. The Priest absorbed the chaos of the sick person into himself, and then he had to be cleansed in order to remove the absorbed negativity. You may ask, "Why could he not protect himself? Why did he have to suffer and contract that horrible disease?" What do we see in this and what does it teach us?

Not all antibiotic treatments work; we should know that bacteria have become so smart they now quickly develop immunity to existing antibiotics. With antibiotics being no foolproof solution, science has now turned to gene therapy as the answer to emerging super bacterial strains of the present and future. This is all well and good, except gene therapy, is not the "total solution" it is being promoted as. Currently, the most advanced applications of gene therapy research have involved developing ways to shut off the genes that allow cancer cells to multiply. The first trial of the leading treatment resulted in a virtually unprecedented 90% success rate. However, the second trial did not work at all. Why? The cancer cell changed its own genes to resist the treatment and render it ineffective by the second trial.

The Third Meal of Shabbat

What we have discovered from Kabbalah is that science is employing an ineffective approach by searching for the "magic bullet" to cure cancer and other illnesses. We are here now to tap into and make use of a relatively new concept to overcome cancer and negativity in our lives—the Third Meal of Shabbat.

The Third Meal of Shabbat provides healing and protection for the human immune system. Unless the human immune system functions at 100% efficiency, disease has an opening to overcome the body. If the human immune system is operating at less than 100% we are vulnerable to all diseases, such as airborne disease. Airborne disease postings are common in hospitals, and for a good reason. Hospitals know of the risks of airborne disease contamination and want to mitigate liability risks.

The solution, as promoted by Kabbalah, is to turn on the Light in midst of the darkness. The moment the full immune system is activated and switched on, its full potential protects us from cancer and illness. Unfortunately, the Kiddush of the Third Meal of Shabbat is not more widely understood and used because it seems too simple and we have been conditioned to believe medicine provides the only answer to illness. Are we to believe that the Kiddush will work? Yes. There is not, and never has been, a medical system that can improve our immune system. Science is looking for a magic bullet that will not be found.

We must be able to overcome the hostile environment existing in these days—the War of Armageddon. I cannot condemn governments for not revealing the truth about the metaphysical War of Armageddon because they have no options when it comes to avoiding the widespread panic that would follow; therefore they are not totally wrong in the approach of trying to contain panic and maintain order, but as kabbalists we must take action.

Kabbalah is not just a tradition. In fact, because the knowledge of Kabbalah has been kept secret and suppressed for so long a vast majority of people do not even know about the Third Meal of Shabbat. At this moment in time, we can cancel the negative effects of the War of Armageddon by using the technology of the kabbalists from the past 4,000 years.

How can this be the War of Armageddon? Is the world not expecting hail, fire and brimstone? The truth is Kabbalah provides technology from the 25th Century today to battle this war. Kabbalah has taught us about hostile environments and also how to overcome them.

By using the 25th Century technology of the Third Meal of Shabbat we will overcome the War of Armageddon. I hope the whole world learns this, and very quickly too.

Removing Chaos

We have all been using the kabbalistic tools for the removal of chaos, but somehow chaos still stays with us. What is the reason we have not done the job yet? Is it that we do not have the critical mass necessary? The spiritual fact is that we do not yet have the Vessel to capture all of this profound and enormous energy of the Lightforce that is available with the tools of Kabbalah.

In this portion, we read about the Red Heifer that has the power to cleanse all impurities, all forms of negativity, every conceivable act and entity of darkness. We have this benefit because this reading of the Bible on Shabbat connects us to the power of the Red Heifer, even though it does not now physically exist just as it was at the time of the Temple. Nonetheless, this can be achieved on Shabbat because Shabbat is the one day of the week when there is no interference between us and the Lightforce of God, which wants nothing more than to come to us. The only problem is that our vessels are not capable of containing all the energy we draw through the tools we are given from the study of Kabbalah and the Zohar.

We learn something strange in this portion: the priest who administered the Red Heifer remedy to the people who had suffered extreme negativity, such as touching the corpse of a dead person (the highest form of negativity), became impure himself. The priest became infected with everything with which the person he helped to purify was afflicted. All the commentators ask why this is. Why, in the cleansing process, does the priest become infected with that same malady? The answer, according to the Zohar, is that in order to cleanse, one must personally feel the pain he wants to assist to heal. Without empathy, it can be an exercise in futility.

This is very profound for something that was written thousands of years ago. The doctor, while he is treating his patient, cannot be interested in the stock-market; he must be present and feel the patient's pain. Modern day science has not come to this understanding yet. Maybe it will in 50 years?

This is what the Zohar tells us: If we want to help others, yet if we do not feel their pain, if we do not feel what is afflicting them, if we cannot comprehend it, the chances of our success are very slim.

Human Dignity

We are learning that it is important to have sympathy, to have empathy for our neighbor, for our family, to feel what they feel. The spiritual has been lost to the materialism we all strive for—the human dignity of things has been lost.

Anytime we enter into an argument or a discussion, and certainly a war, we need to understand that what brought about chaos in the first place is the lack of human dignity toward others.

What we are asking for when we read and connect to the portion of Chukat is to achieve a total cleansing. When I say total cleansing I mean of all those impurities which lurk in our bodies, and have been there for 20, 30, 60, 80 or 100 years. We must rid ourselves of all these different forms of infections.

But if we do not know about it, if we have no consciousness of it, if we are not aware of it, it is a wasted opportunity. For us at the Kabbalah Centres, there is more to it, something deeper. It is to help and support each and every individual in their own pursuit of happiness, which means being free of chaos. Happiness cannot coexist with chaos.

Does the fact that I am experiencing happiness and the world is experiencing chaos mean the world is no longer in chaos, because I do not experience it? To think this would be like the ostrich, putting its head in the ground and not seeing around. At the Kabbalah Centres, we do not look at reality this way. We are looking for the ultimate—that everyone will be relieved of chaos. Not only me, not only you, but everyone in this universe, and this is the possibility of the energy of this portion. With right consciousness and right thought throughout the reading, this should be uppermost in our minds, not the stock-market, not the individual chaos that we might have but a certainty that we collectively remove all forms of chaos in all the infinite ways it appears. It is indescribable, the pain that chaos inflicts on humanity each and every minute of the day. It is time we brought it to an end.

And bringing chaos to an end is what Kabbalah and the Zohar are all about.

BOOK OF BAMIDBAR:
PORTION OF BALAK

PORTION OF BALAK

The Nature of Balak

We are next going to discuss the portion of Balak. Included within this discussion is what I personally consider to be one of my most controversial commentaries. The content will probably come as a shock to many, and will certainly bring little comfort to most. Nevertheless, the time has come for us to face the reality rather than the illusion. We are connected with the Age of Aquarius, a time when everything will become revealed in one way or another.

Balak was one of the most formidable enemies of the nation of Israel. According to the Zohar he was a very powerful mystic, but from the dark side. All the commentaries on the Torah say Balak's power was so profound that the world feared him.

Through this portion, we come to realize that Balak's intention was to destroy the Israelites, not on a physical level, but on a metaphysical level. The Zohar describes much of the battle between Balak (and Bilaam) against the Israelites. The two worked together in an attempt to bring about the end of the nation of Israel— God forbid.

The Month of Cancer

Why did Abraham the Patriarch designate this month as Cancer? Everything he wrote in the Book of Formation was to provide us with the necessary information whereby we can take control our lives. Humanity has experienced cancer in one way or another for so long. It seems clear that Abraham foresaw this.

Sometimes we indulge in the luxury of melancholia or depression, since it is easier to be negative than it is to be positive. We can become so habituated with depression that we are reluctant to part with it.

The Zohar tells us that the commentaries in the Book of Formation state that during this month we can literally tear out the roots of all forms of illness, and acquire something valuable: the ability to give up depression. It takes more effort to frown than to smile, and yet there are people who never smile.

This is Bilaam. We are so enthralled by him that we do not want to give him up and would rather frown. If we are in a state of Bilaam, then we have not only failed to uproot the seed of all illness but are the principle agents in the cause of our own malady. Satan has perfected this technology. If we frown now in this month, God forbid, we can ignite the force of cancer and forty years later the cancer can appear. We have the merit of this wisdom: to know that in this month we cannot afford the luxury of being unhappy. I know it is difficult to maintain even one month of happiness but we do it to protect ourselves for the rest of the year and years to come. This is the message Abraham was sending us about this month in naming it Cancer.

Bamidbar 22:2 And Balak, the son of Tzipor saw all that Israel had done to the Amorites. 3 And Moab was exceedingly afraid of the people, because they were many; and Moab was overcome with dread because of the children of Israel. 4 And Moab said to the elders of Midian: "Now this multitude will lick up all that is round about us, as the ox licks up the grass of the field." And Balak, the son of Tzipor, was king of Moab at that time. 5 And he sent messengers to Bilaam, the son of Beor, to Pethor, which is by the River, to the land of the children of his people, to call him, saying: "Behold, there is a people come out from Egypt; behold, they cover the face of the earth, and they are settling next to me. 6 Come now, I pray you, curse this people for me; for they are too mighty for me; perhaps I shall prevail, that we may smite them, and that I may drive them out of the land; for I know that he whom you bless is blessed, and he whom thou curse is cursed." 7 And the elders of Moab and the elders of Midian departed with the diviner's fee in their hand; and they came to Bilaam, and spoke the words of Balak to him.

Bilaam, Balak, and the Bible

The portion of Balak is named after our greatest enemy. We find that the Bible often names a portion for a person, such as Noah, Sarah, Jethro, and even Korach. Then along comes Balak, who, because he wanted to uproot everything, is worse than Korach. Balak thought that, together with Bilaam, he would be able to uproot the future of the Israelite nation. Why then is this portion named after Balak? Why are some weekly portions named after people?

What has been the problem of the Israelites for 2,000 years? It can be said that it was the problem of uncertainty, the power of darkness that causes an individual not to believe in the power of the Light. Certainty comes from the Light; an absence of problems comes from the Light; health comes from the Light. Such is the power of the Light. The secret therefore is that the cause of all our problems is a lack of certainty. This includes every problem we face, from health to relationships to financial worries.

What does this mean? How does uncertainty include illness? How does uncertainty include failure in business? How does uncertainty cause family problems? How does this one aspect of consciousness, uncertainty, bring about all of these problems? The answer is this: in the Light there is no doubt, everything is known. This does not refer to any framework we are accustomed to in the Realm of the Tree of Knowledge of Good and Evil, but in the Realm of the Tree of Life, where the Light exists, everything is known and there are no doubts.

Both of the names Balak (בלק) and Bilaam (בלעם) begin with the letters Bet (ב) followed by Lamed (ל). Bet and Lamed together add up to the number 32. The entire world is based on the thirty-two paths of *Elohim* (God). What do the thirty-two paths signify? The Name *Elohim* appears thirty-two times in the story of Creation, and *Elohim* refers to the attribute of Judgment and is a force connected to our world. In the beginning, in Beresheet, a positive force was infused but the moment Adam sinned, things reverted to how they had been. God made the components of the world in such a way that they contrast with each other. With their power, Balak and Bilaam wanted to usher in the power of the thirty-two paths of Judgment among the Israelites.

The emphasis here is that reading the Bible is a shield of protection. Throughout the course of our lives, we interact with this force that is Balak and Bilaam continually, although we are not necessarily aware of it. Obviously, someone who enjoys good health, a good income, and lives a good life, is less aware that this is happening. Regardless, this is a force that exists in the world, and Balak and Bilaam are people who were able to realize this force to influence people. They wanted to uproot the Israelites with this power, because they were in control of the thirty-two paths of Satan.

Again, we must ask ourselves why the portion is named Balak. What we know is that the power of Balak was to actualize, manifest in action what Bilaam realized through thought and speech. Balak actualized, which is much worse than the mere contemplation of them. As long as something is not realized it is possible to correct. Once things are manifested it is much more difficult.

Why did Balak need Bilaam if he was capable of making things happen himself? He could take action as an implementation of a plan. However, as long as the people were not receptive to anything bad, no evil plan could happen to them. When a person does not create an opening, no evil can happen to them. Even if someone takes an action against them, nothing untoward will manifest.

Balak asked Bilaam to use the evil eye, to create an opening that would allow entry for something bad to happen. God forbid. Such an occurrence only happens if a person has first received the evil eye, God forbid. Through evil eye, a person's whole system of defense is then cracked, and uncertainty is activated, which includes all problems, maladies and so on. It is then that Balak's work can begin. Balak needed Bilaam because without his evil eye there was no difficulty that would create an opening for Balak to enter.

8 And he said to them: "Lodge here this night, and I will bring you back word, as the Lord may speak to me." And the princes of Moab stayed with Bilaam. 9 And God came to Bilaam, and said: "What men are these with you?" 10 And Bilaam said to God: "Balak, the son of Tzipor, king of Moab, has sent them to me, saying: 11 'Behold the people that have come out of Egypt, cover the face of the earth; now, come curse them for me; perhaps I shall be able to fight against them, and shall drive them out.'" 12 And God said to Bilaam: "You shall not go with them; you shall not curse the people; for they are blessed." 13 And Bilaam rose up in the morning, and said to the princes of Balak: "Go back to your land; for the Lord refuses to give me leave to go with you." 14 And the princes of Moab rose up, and they went to Balak, and said: "Bilaam refuses to come with us." 15 And Balak sent yet again more princes, and more honorable than they. 16 And they came to Bilaam, and said to him: "So says Balak, the son of Tzipor: 'Let nothing, I pray you, hinder you from coming to me; 17 for I will promote you to very great honor, and whatever you say to me I will do; come therefore, I pray you, curse this people for me.'" 18 And Bilaam answered and said to the servants of Balak: "Even if Balak would give me his house full of silver and gold, I cannot go beyond the word of the Lord, my God, to do anything, small or great. 19 Now therefore, I pray you, also stay here this night that I may

know what the Lord will speak to me more." 20 And God came to Bilaam at night, and said to him: "If the men come to call you, rise up, go with them; but only the word which I speak to you, that shall you do." 21 And Bilaam rose up in the morning, and saddled his donkey, and went with the princes of Moab. 22 And God's anger was kindled because he went; and the angel of the Lord placed himself in the way for an adversary against him. Now he was riding upon his donkey, and his two servants were with him. 23 And the donkey saw the angel of the Lord standing in the way, with his sword drawn in his hand; and the donkey turned aside out of the way, and went into the field; and Bilaam smote the ass, to turn her into the way. 24 Then the angel of the Lord stood in a hollow way between the vineyards, a fence being on this side, and a fence on that side. 25 And the donkey saw the angel of the Lord, and she thrust herself to the wall, and crushed Bilaam's foot against the wall; and he smote her again. 26 And the angel of the Lord went further, and stood in a narrow place, where was no way to turn either to the right hand or to the left. 27 And the donkey saw the angel of the Lord, and she lay down under Bilaam; and Bilaam's anger was kindled, and he smote the donkey with his staff. 28 And the Lord opened the mouth of the donkey, and she said to Bilaam: "What have I done to you, that you have smitten me these three times?" 29 And Bilaam said to the ass: "You have mocked me; I wish there were a sword in my hand, for I would have killed you." 30 And the donkey said to Bilaam: "Am I not your donkey, upon which you have ridden all your life long to this day? Was I ever disposed to do so to you?" And he said: "No." 31 Then the Lord opened the eyes of Bilaam, and he saw the angel of the Lord standing in the way, with his sword drawn in his hand; and he bowed his head, and fell on his face. 32 And the angel of the Lord said to him: "Why have you smitten your donkey these three times? Behold, I have come forth as an adversary, because your way is contrary to me; 33 and the donkey saw me, and turned aside before me these three times; unless she had turned aside from me, surely now I would have slain you, and saved her alive." 34 And Bilaam said to the angel of the Lord: "I have sinned; for I did not know that you stood in the way against me; now therefore, if it displeases you, I will turn back." 35 And the angel of the Lord said to Bilaam: "Go with the men; but only the word that I shall speak to you, shall you speak." So Bilaam went with the princes of Balak.

Bilaam and the Tree of Life

Did Bilaam speak to God? Bilaam knew that the Tetragrammaton—*Yud*, *Hei*, *Vav*, and *Hei* (ה.ו.ה.י), God, is concerned with certainty whether to act or not act and that within his own framework there was no Tetragrammaton. The framework of *Elohim* is in the framework of good and evil, and there the Tetragrammaton cannot speak and cannot approach. Certainty about whether to act or not to act comes from the Tetragrammaton—the Tree of Life Reality. When the connection to the Tree of Life (Tetragrammaton) is removed then the certainty that enters people, like Bilaam, is covered. It is no longer clean, as when a person receives it directly from the Light—pure, without any admixture from the realm of this world of good and evil. Therefore, when this knowledge reached Bilaam, it says *Elohim* and not *Yud*, *Hei*, *Vav*, and *Hei* (the Tetragrammaton) because Bilaam was in a framework of filth.

It is written in the Zohar that if a person is sullied, even if they use a pure clean channel like the Sefirot or the Alef-Bet to connect to the Light, the Light will be transmitted by means of *Elohim* and the person will thus not receive the clean power of *Yud*, *Hei*, *Vav*, and *Hei*. Bilaam also knew this.

The teaching is that when we are in a negative framework, we are in a framework of uncertainty. Even when an individual makes all his or her connections, according to the method of Rav Isaac Luria (the Ari) including the Ana Beko'ach, and it does not help, it is because all is dependent on where a person's consciousness is. Communication is all fine and good but if a person is in the muck then the power emerges through *Elohim*.

Although he understood the power of *Yud*, *Hei*, *Vav*, and *Hei*, Bilaam realized that his connection with God came through *Elohim*. When *Elohim* came to Bilaam, Bilaam told *Elohim* everything—all that Balak wanted from him. *Elohim* responded to Bilaam, "Do not go with them, do not curse the people, for they are blessed."

The next morning Bilaam told this to the messengers, he said "God refuses to allow me to go with you." Bilaam understood that his words came through *Elohim*, though he knew that there was a level of *Yud*, *Hei*, *Vav*, and *Hei*. The messengers returned to Balak and

informed him that Bilaam would not come, so Balak tried again—
"Please do not refuse to come to me."

In Bamidbar 22:18, Bilaam said to Balak, "Even if you give me
your entire house full of silver and gold, I would not be able to
defy the word of the Lord, to do good and not evil." Bilaam told
the ministers of Balak to remain for the night so they could listen
to the word of God. What does this mean? Did he think he could
convince the Creator to give him a different answer?

Bamidbar 22:20 says: "*Elohim* (God) came to Bilaam at night and
said to him, "If these men come to call you, rise up, go with them,
but only the word I speak to you, shall you do." The Creator is
now saying "You can go?" Why should Bilaam go? What is written
following this exchange? Bilaam rose up in the morning, saddled
his donkey, and went with the princes of Moab. And God's was
kindled because he went…." Was it not the Creator who told him
he could go?

What is the answer? Sometimes people come to ask me a question,
even though the individual has already decided what they want to
do. When they ask, I tell them what I really think; let us say I say
"No." They then ask again, "What about if we do it this way?" I
will then answer, "Yes, it is possible." Why? Because the person has
already decided what they want to do; they did not ask to receive
guidance, they came for validation.

This is like the story of a man who left his spiritual path. When his
friends asked him, "Why did you leave?" "I had a lot of questions,"
he replied, "and I didn't receive any answers, so I left." They then
asked him, "Did you start questioning, before or after you decided
to leave?" Once a person has decided to leave, they then find all the
reasons to justify why they should leave.

Elohim (God) told Bilaam to go, but also told him not to do anything. The reason God's anger was sparked is that Bilaam's desire to go was already established—and this is the problem with us as well. When we ask questions, many times the question itself is already the answer. We make decisions without looking deeply into things. Who decides? Satan decides. Like Bilaam, he decides. Bilaam is Satan. He decided, and then he asked the Creator should he go or not; yet in his mind, he had already decided.

The mistake in our lives is that, when we decide to leave a place, we ask the Light if it is right or wrong, yet we have actually already decided on the answer – and we just want to rationalize our actions, our good or bad deeds. This is the influence of Satan. God's anger was kindled, not because Bilaam was going but because he had already decided to go. Even the level of Elohim told him not to go, but it is obvious that he went the second time because he had already wanted to go the first time. What came first was the decision to go. The questions and answers should be to the Light, and then the answers will come from the Light—and Bilaam was well aware of this, but he had already decided.

Next, the Bible tells us that an angel of the Lord stood in the way of Bilaam, obstructing his path as he was riding on his mule. What we want to know is why it is mentioned repeatedly that Bilaam strikes the donkey three times? Rashi (Rav Shlomo Yitzchaki, 1040–1105) comments that it is as if the donkey told Bilaam, "You would like to uproot the people who celebrate the three Festivals (Pesach, Shavuot, and Sukkot), but you cannot." What does this have to do with Bilaam hitting her three times? The answer is that Bilaam knew that even if he could uproot them, as Rashi says, once they realize that they have the protection of the three Festivals (even if Bilaam's blows are actualized) he cannot uproot anything.

Bilaam did not want to see the angel. The donkey told him: "You don't understand. You cannot uproot anything as long as the Israelites are connected." Bilaam became angry, and then suddenly he realized what was happening. God opened his eyes, and he saw the Angel of the Lord standing in his way.

The truth is that, when someone wants to accomplish something, the Light is with them at that moment—so they will not err. However, if a person has already made a decision and does not want to see what is really happening, then they are not permitted to see. This is why we often ask ourselves, after we do stupid things, how it was we missed what was so obvious? It was right there. It was so simple that even the donkey could see it! However, if a person makes a decision without the Light, then they will not see the Light—even if it is right in front of them.

Bilaam's Connection and His Death

Bilaam had a direct connection with the Lord, as we see throughout Bamidbar 22. The Bible in Bamidbar 22:20 says, "And God came to Bilaam at night, and said to him: 'If the men come to call you, rise up and go with them but only the word which I speak to you shall you do.'" And again in verse 31, "Then the Lord opened the eyes of Bilaam, and he saw the angel of the Lord standing in the way, with his sword drawn in his hand; and he bowed his head; and fell on his face." We have discussed previously that the Tetragrammaton—the *Yud, Hei, Vav,* and *Hei* and Elohim, which also means the Lord, are different expressions of revelations of Light. The Tetragrammaton is on a higher level than that of *Elohim*. Here, in this section, we see that the Tetragrammaton is expressed to Bilaam. Both the Talmud and the Midrash tell us that in the nation of Israel there shall never arise a prophet as great as Moses. However, the Midrash, states that only in the nation of Israel shall there never arise a prophet greater than Moses, nonetheless among the other nations of the world there will arise a prophet on the level of Moses—and this is Bilaam because it says, he is "amongst the nations of the world."

Just to confuse matters a little more, Rav Isaac Luria (the Ari) tells us that after the disaster of Bilaam, where his curses were twisted, and he did not succeed in damaging the Israelites, and he was about to be punished, he pleaded with the Lord not to be punished nor die an unnatural death. He said: *Tamot nafshi mot yesharim*; in other words, he prayed to the Lord that he would die a death of natural causes. Even though he felt that his conduct was deserving of an unnatural death, he prayed that it should not happen. The Ari and the Zohar both say that Bilaam was struck down by a sword—and thus he did not die a natural death, which seems to be contrary to the verse.

In *Sefer haLikutim* ("Book of Compilations"), Volume 17 of Kitvei Ha'Ari ("Writings of the Ari"), the Ari helps us to understand this by saying: "But know the secret of this matter is that Bilaam, who was of the other nations and not an Israelite, was incarnated in Naval, who was an Israelite, and Bilaam was also Laban, the father-in-law of Jacob." The Ari explains that the letters that spell the name of Laban in Hebrew—*Lamed, Bet, Nun* (לבן)—are the same letters of Naval—*Nun, Bet, Lamed* (נבל). The Ari says Bilaam's wish was granted, but it was granted only when he was incarnated as an Israelite. All of the commentators express the view that he was speared, and that this is the way he died, even though he had asked God for a natural death. Since he asked this in the form of a question, the Ari says, Bilaam's words were not decisive—thus he did not die a natural death. The Midrash tells us Pinchas did not want to kill Bilaam because he did not want Bilaam to draw this kind of energy from him, since in death the victim is, in a way, drawing energy from the one who kills them. In this case, it would mean that Bilaam would be drawing energy from Pinchas. The Ari

explains that the act of murdering someone means that the act is
a transfer of the energy into the victim and Pinchas did not want
that. If Pinchas had speared Bilaam, then he would have died what
would have been considered a natural death as Bilaam would have
been the recipient of the enormous power that was within Pinchas,
and that, in and of itself, would have been considered a justifiable
and righteous kind of death.

Why was Bilaam's request even mentioned in the portion if he was
not going to die a natural death? The Bible ought not to mention
it at all. However, the Ari concludes that Bilaam *did* die a righteous
death but not at the hands of Pinchas, and not with a natural
death, as it is stated. Rather in his incarnation as Naval, who was
an Israelite, who suffered a death by spear, and then was again
incarnated, was the death a natural one. So, the verse is not without
reason. Bilaam died a natural death and he died an unnatural death,
and both are correct.

What is a Jew?

What seems to emerge from Rav Isaac Luria (the Ari's) commentary
is that non-Jews reincarnate as Jews, and vice versa. This leads to
another question: What is a Jew? It may be said that a Jew is an
individual born of a Jewish mother, and conversely, if one is not
born of a Jewish mother, one is not Jewish. This, however, does
not fully explain the significance being referred to here. Is a Jew
something different from everyone else? If the answer is that there is
a distinction, what is it?

These biblical narrations may assist us in an explanation of what
we are to understand about a Jewish incarnation. In Shemot
15:22, immediately following the great miracles of the Splitting of
the Red Sea and the Ten Plagues, the Bible says Moses lead Israel

onward from the Sea and then he went out into the wilderness of Shur. Three days in the wilderness, they found no water, yet, when they came to Mara and could drink of the waters, the people still complained. Why should the people complain? If Moses, with the help of the Lord, could split the Red Sea, surely a small feat like manifesting water was not that difficult for him? Yet, the Bible tells us, the Israelites complained. Then, of course, the miracle happened, and water appeared. In many other incidents in the Bible, the Israelites complained. In fact, according to the Bible, the habitual complainer is the Israelite. This pattern continues through the Book of Shemot to the Book of Bamidbar.

It would take many pages just to reiterate the many grumbles and grievances the Israelites leveled at Moses, which began with this generation called the Dor Dea (Generation of Knowledge). These people were even more brilliant and in tune with the Light than we are today. Nonetheless, the day immediately after Korach and the negative people who joined him were swallowed up by the earth, the complaining Israelites blamed Moses for the deaths of those evil people. It is irrational and incomprehensible.

Is this to tell us that being Jewish makes one a complainer who is never satisfied? This seems to be the description from the Bible itself. Is it someone for whom one can completely provide for yesterday yet, if today you fail to provide a glass of water, you will never hear the end of it? This particular nature stems from the generation of the Exodus.

Did nothing more important take place for humankind than the revelation of the Ten Utterances, and what are we told occurred there? In Shemot 19:8, we are told: "All the people answered together and said, 'all that the Lord has spoken we shall do.'" The verse then goes on to say, *na'ase venishma*, "…we shall do and we shall listen." Can you imagine? Who has encountered a whole nation that would reply in this way? This seems to be another kind of description regarding the Israelite—a quality of obedience. On one hand, the Israelites are portrayed as complainers and on the other as obedient: always complaining about the Lord, and listening to Him. How can we reconcile these two ideas?

The Talmud says that, just prior to the Israelites receiving the revelation of the Ten Utterances on Mount Sinai, "the Lord bent over the mountain," meaning He lifted the mountain over the heads of the Israelites and told them, if they do not accept the Bible, this would be their burial ground. If they were obedient people, as the scripture indicates, why then was it necessary for God to threaten them?

From the Bible itself we are given a negative picture of an Israelite, as well as the complementary image of a very obedient people. We also have the Talmud telling us that the Israelite's declaration "we shall do and we shall listen" was not the whole story. Are these two vastly different portraits reconcilable? We are still left with the dilemma surrounding what a Jew actually is.

As always, we will turn to the Zohar for clarity. Studying what the Zohar and Rav Isaac Luria (the Ari) reveal for us provides understanding. The Zohar, in discussing the portion of Genesis I, states that there are five different kinds of *erev rav* (literally translated this term means "mixed multitude"). Who are the mixed multitude? Concerning the exodus from Egypt, the Zohar says that only one fifth of the people who left Egypt were original Israelites and that the remaining four fifths of the people who emerged were people of other nations who had converted, known as the *erev rav*. At this time, God warned Moses not to make a mistake and accept these converts because they would bring trouble. Moses said he knew exactly what he was doing, and accepted all the people. It is difficult to imagine such a conversation taking place between God and Moses.

The Zohar says that the first kind of *erev rav* is Amalek. We read about the nation of Amalek in the portion of Beshalach in the Book of Shemot: Shemot 17:8-16 that says:

> Amalek came and attacked the Israelites at Rephidim. Moses said to Joshua, "Choose some of our men and go out to fight Amalek. Tomorrow I will stand on top of the hill with the staff of God in my hands." So Joshua did what Moses told him, to fight the Amalek, and Moses, Aaron and Hur went to the top of the hill. As long as Moses held up his hands, the Israelites triumphed, but whenever he lowered his hands, Amalek triumphed. When Moses' hands became heavy, they took a stone and put it under him and he sat on it. Aaron and Hur held his hands up—one on one side, one on the other—so that his hands remained steady till sunset. So Joshua overcame Amalek and its people by sword. Then the Lord said to Moses, "Write this on a scroll as something to be remembered and make sure that Joshua hears it, because I will completely blot out the memory of Amalek from under the heavens." Moses built an altar and called it Adonai Nisi. He said, "For hands were lifted up to the throne of the Lord. The Lord will be at war against Amalek from generation to generation."

The Bible says Joshua weakened Amalek with the edge of a sword but he did not destroy him and because of this incident, every generation will war with Amalek. Although we do not hear much about Amalek today, there is a special section in the Bible called Zachor, which is read on the Shabbat before Purim. Every man and woman is obligated to hear the reading of these verses from Devarim 25:17-19:

"*Remember* what Amalek did to you on the way as you were coming out of Egypt; how he met you on the way, and attacked your rear ranks, all that were enfeebled in your rear, when you were tired and weary; and he did not fear God. Therefore, it shall be, when the Lord, your God, has given you rest from all your enemies around, in the land which the Lord, your God, gives you for an inheritance to possess, that you shall blot out the *remembrance* of Amalek from under Heaven; *you shall not forget.*"

It was not enough to be told remember twice, the verse then concludes with the final two words, lo *tishkach* (do not forget). How many times must Moses repeat this? It appears from this that the Israelites have short memories. A close study of the entire Book of Exodus conveys the short memories we possess, therefore Moses has to repeat his admonition—twice to "remember" and once "not to forget." Forgetfulness will happen to us today as well. This is the real meaning of the Amalek story. Be mindful of our short memories especially regarding those who have done good things for us.

Bilaam and Balak are Amalek

Who then is Amalek, and why did Joshua not destroy him? The Zohar tells us Amalek is Bilaam and Balak. How can it be two people? Moreover, the incident with Bilaam and Balak happens much later on in the Bible, and it seems there was a waging of war with Balak and Bilaam. The Bible does not state anywhere that Bilaam and Balak are Amalek. Only the Zohar asserts that these two people represented the force known as Amalek. We are not discussing here a nation or tribe called Amalek. In other words, the Zohar reveals for us that we should not take everything stated in the Bible literally.

The Zohar says:

> Balak and Bilaam tread exactly the same path, THAT OF
> SAMA"EL AND HIS RETINUE and we learned that they
> formed an evil partnership. They said, Amalek IS SPELLED
> *am-lak*, meaning "a nation" (*am*) that "smote" (*lakah*) them,
> like a snake that strikes with his tail. They figured that we
> are more THAN THEY ARE, because Balak IS SPELLED
> *ba-lak*, meaning "came" (*ba*), "he who smote" (*lakah*) them
> as he wishes. Bilaam consists of the letters *bal-am*, meaning
> there are no (*bal*) people (*am*) and no shepherd. Our name
> will cause their destruction and uprooting from the world.
> —Zohar, Balak 21:276

Amalek does not refer to the nation of Amalek but rather it refers
to the force of Amalek, which was the essence of Bilaam and Balak.
Rav Shimon explains that when you take the last two letters of
Bilaam—*Ayin-Mem* (בלעם), and add the last two letters from Balak,
Lamed-Kuf, (בלק) you create the word *amalek* (עֲמָלֵק).

Bilaam and Balak were the *erev rav*. The Zohar says, in many places,
that Amalek is the evil instinct found in all of humankind. We
now understand why the verse in Exodus says that he weakened
Amalek. Had Moses finished off Amalek—meaning finished off the
evil inclination within all of us—then he would have completed
the *tikkun* (correction) for us, leaving us with no work to do? There
would once again be no such thing as free will. Moses accomplished
for us the same feat he accomplished with the middle kingdom.

At the time of the exodus, Moses broke the metaphysical power
of the Middle Kingdom. The rule of the Middle Kingdom was
broken, nonetheless Amalek was not broken because Amalek exists
within everyone. The Bible, in the portion of Noah, says we are all

born with an evil inclination and the purpose of our tikkun is to
overcome the evil inclination.

Where are these five types of mixed multitudes today? They are right
within the individual. They do not live in in places where the world
faced atrocities or expulsion. To give us a clearer description of
the mixed multitude, Rav Isaac Luria (the Ari), in *Sefer haLikutim*
("Book of Compilations"), says the following and I am not making
any declarations or statements here that are my own:

> "Anyone who has an evil desire or evil thought, whether he
> is Jewish or not Jewish, is *erev rav*."

Therefore, anyone who harbors evil thoughts against his or her
neighbor is the seed level of this essence and is from the mixed
multitude. Hatred is not part of any inheritance; hatred is not
genetic, it is part of individual *tikkun* (correction). Even in the
case of two brothers, one can be from the *erev rav* and one may
not. This can happen even with twins. What emerges from the
Ari's explanation is that the human soul and the behavior of the
individual will indicate where he is coming from whether they are
from the *erev rav* or not. The Ari simply observes that anyone with
hatred in his heart, or possessing evil thoughts is unquestionably
from the *erev rav*.

Thus, Amalek is found among the Israelites, and now we can obtain
a very small glimpse into what Balak and Bilaam are about. Bilaam
was part of the *erev rav*, and he was a channel. He was an evil
channel nonetheless.

This is one type of *erev rav*; there is another kind of *erev rav*. Who
are they? Says the Zohar, they built Synagogues, Temples and houses
of study. They even provided the world with Torah Scrolls. These
are good actions, so why does Rav Shimon describe this group in

such a negative manner? The Zohar asks and answers regarding the purpose of these actions. At the end of the biblical portion of Noah, we encounter the Tower of Babel. In this section, we learn that this great tower was built by an evil people who sought, according to the Bible, to make "a name for themselves." According to the Zohar, these people were so sophisticated they had the knowledge to construct a building one thousand stories high. Scripture says, they built a skyscraper that reached up into the Heavens, and that is evil.

The Zohar tells us like the generation of the Tower of Babel, the *erev rav* are not engaged in building houses of worship or in presenting Torah scrolls for the sake of enlightenment—they performed these actions for their own aggrandizement and edification. This does not, of course, mean that all people who build houses of worship and donate Torah Scrolls do it for negative reasons. This is specifically discussing a type of *erev rav*.

To conclude the Zohar's revelation concerning the *erev rav*, the fifth type of the *erev rav* are those who denigrate or look down upon others. Who do they look down upon, specifically? They are the religious-minded people who particularly disparage spiritually minded people. In other words, these *erev rav* are the people who cheapen or denigrate the spirituality of the Bible, such people fall under the fifth category of the *erev rav*.

Rav Shimon says that these *erev rav* are the ones who are responsible for returning the world to a wasteland; its condition before fruition. They were the ones who were entirely responsible for the destruction of the Holy Temple.

Before reading the Zohar, like many other people, I had been under the impression that the responsibility for the destruction of Jerusalem's great Temple lay with the Romans. The Zohar, however tells us the Romans were not responsible for the destruction of the

Holy Temple—it was destroyed by the *erev rav*. And this is, in fact, corroborated by the Talmud that agrees that the destruction of the Holy Temple was caused by hatred for no reason, which in Hebrew is *sinat chinam*. The Holy Temple was not destroyed because the people did not observe the precepts and did not keep the Shabbat, the Holy Days or the dietary laws. Those who hate for no valid reason are the fifth category of an *erev rav*.

Because of this kind of *erev rav*, the Zohar maintains, the world returned to being a wasteland. All that we experience today throughout the world in the form of terrorism, destruction, inhumanity, suffering and chaos, can be attributed to this category of the *erev rav*.

The Temple was the center point of drawing down and connecting with positive Lightforce of God—which benefitted all of humankind. This beneficence existed for as long as the Temple stood.

When the *erev rav* brought about the destruction of the Temple in Jerusalem, they also returned the Earth to a state of wasteland. Therefore, the chaos and destruction we experience today is a direct result of those very *erev rav*. It was not the Romans who were responsible, it was the *erev rav* who were intermingled with the nation of Israel—they are not separate and distinct.

The Zohar concludes that redemption does not depend on the coming of any Messiah, or standing up to and eradicating any external evil in the world. Redemption depends solely upon banishing this innate characteristic of the *erev rav*. Is this saying that were we able to rid the world of all dictators and totalitarian states, we would return to a Garden of Eden? To this, the Zohar says, "No." The redemption or peace on Earth and good will towards man does not depend upon the challenging of other nations but solely on the *erev rav* within each one of us. The different aspects of *erev rav* are different aspects of evil inclination within all of humankind.

Now we shall return to the question of why Moses took in the *erev rav*. Tana Rabbi Meir was one of the great spiritual giants during the time of the destruction of the Second Temple. He was a saint whose lineage was of converts to Judaism. In the Talmud, Tractate Shabbat, regarding the revelation that was to take place on Mount Sinai, Moses pleaded with the Lord to have himself removed of the position as leader of the nation of Israel and the channel by which the revelation of the Bible would take place. Moses said "There is a soul on a much higher level than I, choose him as Your faithful servant." Moses was speaking about Rabbi Akiva, who came from a line of converts.

The Talmud felt sure in declaring that it was only Elijah the prophet, that could and would ultimately determine who is Jewish and who is not. Nonetheless, there is the principle doctrine that states if a mother is Jewish then her offspring are Jewish despite the fact that the father was not Jewish there would still be a continuity.

Why is there this kind of channeling of souls like Balak and Bilaam and like Rabbi Akiva? What would have been lacking if Rabbi Akiva came of a lineage of Jewish parents? What would have been wrong if Rabbi Meir did not descend from a line of converts? Rav Isaac Luria (the Ari) says if one really wants to understand the Torah one would ask the question. Abraham, is considered the first Jew and yet his father was an idol worshipper. Why did Abraham have to come from this kind of union? The answer about Abraham is that high souls have their particular battles that are waged on a metaphysical level. The Ari said when a higher soul is destined to reach this terrestrial plane all of the evil forces in the world make every effort to attach themselves to this kind of soul. A high soul means a high channel of energy. And obviously, the *shedim* (demons) or *klipot* (evil shells), as they are referred to, must receive their sustenance and only receive this sustenance from a channel of energy, therefore they would latch on to, for example, a soul of Abraham. In simple terms, the Ari says that Terach was a ploy to permit this kind of high soul to be able to descend into a terrestrial realm.

Some souls have to come via a particular direction because if they came through the normal channels, Satan and all of the demons would be there as this is the area from which to draw some of this positive energy from these souls.

Getting back to the discussion concerning the Revelation at Mount Sinai, in the Book of Shemot, the Israelites said, "We shall do and we shall listen." The Zohar raises some very beautiful questions concerning Revelation. The first question it raises refers to a verse from the Book of Judges, "When the Lord wished to give the Bible to the Israelites, He first went to other nations of the world." This awakens us to a question we should raise when we read from this section of the Bible: Why was the revelation not given to the other nations of the world? Why only to the Israelites? Is it because we are referred to as the chosen people? Why are we called the chosen people? It is certainly not from the description of the Bible itself. How can there be an assumption made that this is a chosen people, if anything, these Israelites are the opposite of chosen, rejecting and rejected. These are the questions the Zohar raises.

What does the Zohar and Rav Isaac Luria explain about the Israelite and what does the Bible itself, in its description of the Jewish nation indicate? The Bible is a cosmic code and the Bible will provide the code by which we can understand what is happening since the first man, Adam, came into existence. In Bamidbar 14:1, there is a very peculiar expression, describing the familiar Israelites that lifted up their voices and wept. In a previous section, when the spies returned

from the land of Israel and gave their terrible report, and the people
began crying, and again complained about Moses and Aaron. All
of the nation of Israel said to Moses and Aaron—in fact the words
are repeated twice *kol ha eda*, meaning make sure "all of Israel
understands".

After they receive this terrible report, the nation complains once
again and Moses pleads with them. Finally, in Bamidbar 14:11, it
says—and I will first quote the English translation because it is not
as disconcerting, the original Hebrew is astonishing: "And the Lord
said unto Moses: 'How long will this people despise me?'" The word
used in the Hebrew is *yena'azuni*, which comes from the root word
nazi. And Bamidbar 14:22-23 says: *Vechol me na'azai*. This means
anyone despising the Lord. The Lord said, "...none of these people,
(meaning these *erev rav* among the Israelites) shall ever see Me."

We thus return to the question rightfully raised by the Zohar:
Why was the Revelation given to the Israelites and not to the other
nations of the world? The answer to this is stated as: God went to
other nations, and they did not accept it. The Bible says, God came
to Edom, who was agreeable. However, one the Utterances is *Lo
tirtzach* (Thou shall not kill). And Edom said, "Go to Israel." What
did the Bible mean by "go to Israel"? The Zohar says that this was
the way they would prevail over Israel. And all of the nations were
in one unified decision: "give it to the Israelite." Imagine that? I bet
the nations of the world never got together on any singular point
like they did on giving the Bible to the Israelites. Now, this is not
what we learned in Yeshiva or in Sunday school. This description of
the Revelation on Mount Sinai is far from the understanding that
most of us have had, nonetheless this is what it says.

And the Lord came to the Israelite, and they said *na'ase venishma*
meaning we will do and we will listen," Yet, even with this, we still
do not have a full description of what is a Jew. We do have what

seems like a lot of confusion about the nature of the Israelite. What are we meant to understand from it all? In Beresheet I, on the sixth day of Creation, in Chapter 1, God says, "Let us make (na'ase) man in our image," the same word na'ase appears in this verse also, but with a translation of the word na'ase that does not fit with the use of the word in Shemot. In Shemot, na'ase means "we will do" and therefore the question raised is that this seems in contradiction to the Israelite that complains all the time. How then do they immediately say we will do, when God comes to them and wants to give them the Bible?

The clue to this conundrum is found in another verse where the same word na'ase is used to mean "we shall make." In other words, na'ase venishma does not mean "we will do gladly" as has been the interpretation we have been given, rather the word na'ase means "we shall make," not "we shall do".

What is interesting is that the Zohar found it proper to include this information in the section of the Zohar that discusses Balak instead of in the section that explores the Exodus and the Revelation at Mount Sinai, where all of this takes place. Why did the Zohar wait until the portion of Balak to reveal the coded meaning of Revelation? The answer is that it has to do with Balak and Bilaam—amalek.

At the moment when these people became Israelites (or Jews), they were transformed into another kind of people. The Bible calls them am segula. And this is where the confusion and corruption of the translation arises regarding the term "Chosen People." There are many references to the Israelites in the Bible as Am Segula, for example in Shemot 19:5, and also in Devarim 4:6. "Chosen People" would translate to Am haNivchar. The word "chosen" in Hebrew is nivchar and not segula. The word segula is also translated as "a treasure," which is yet another corruption. How does the word segula come to mean "My treasured people"? The truest definition of segula comes from the term segol. Segol is one of the vowels of the Hebrew language (•̣•); it is the three-pointed vowel identifying the Three Column system.

When the Israelite was transformed, when there was *na'ase* (something made), the Israelite received the composite of the most profound, intense energy and could handle all the beneficence the Creator was prepared to bestow upon them. An analogy comparison that might help explain this is the difference between a five watt bulb and a two million watt bulb. One has a greater capacity of drawing energy than the other. When the Israelite was made (*na'ase*), they were transformed into another kind of people—a people reborn with an added dimension to now be a channel to receive energy. This applied to all Israelites for all time—all the souls even those not yet born.

All were present on Mount Sinai so as to permit the total abundance of the Creator to become manifest in this world as it depends on the amount that the channel can handle. If a channel can only handle a small quantity; the Creator, Who was bestowing an infinite flow of energy, required a Vessel of an equally infinite magnitude. Thus, the Israelite on Mount Sinai was converted into another kind of a Vessel.

The Israelite did not act out of obedience when they said *na'ase venishma*. The Talmud states that the Creator opened the mountain, put the Israelites inside, and the Creator then bent over the mountain and said, "This will be your burial ground." What the Creator was in effect saying was that "should you choose to not operate on the principle of *Segula* (*Segol*)—meaning by the principle of the Three Column System of Right, Left and Central, the most significant responsibility of the Israelite (Jew), who would have to set the example of restriction—they will burn up not only themselves but the whole world along with them. As it is completely elaborated upon in the Bible, and if the Israelites forget and there is no restriction (for example they forget the miracles and complain that they needed water or whatever else they need at that moment), they will bring the world to chaos.

When the nations of the world said, "Give it to the Israelite," it was because this was one way to cause them to restrict as no restriction is the intrinsic nature of the Israelite who wanted everything. In this way, they would have to work on restriction. There is a price for everything we want. Nothing comes without restriction. The Lord bent over the mountain and said, "Look, you are now capable of acting as a channel for the infinite beneficence that I want to bestow upon this whole world, not only for you but for all nations of the world. Remember, if you do not adhere to the principles of restriction, this will be your burial site, you will burn up immediately. There is no saying 'I'm sorry.'" It is like the generator where the filament did not operate; an apology from the filament will not keep the building from burning down, as was the case with the destruction of the Temple. Whether it was the destruction in Germany or something else, in all cases of destruction, the whole world suffers chaos.

The nations of the world knew this in advance; they felt and suspected that the Israelite could not restrict because they could not handle their enormous Desire to Receive. Therefore, the nations of the world said, we are satisfied with our Desire to Receive, do not change us, do not give us a new physicality."

"Israelite" means that physicality must reconcile itself with the soul. It could have been any nation. We have learned from the Ari that souls are interchangeable between Jew and non-Jew. We have also learned this from the Zohar as Balak and Bilaam represented *erev rav*. We have learned from the Zohar that there are Jews who build houses of worship not for the purpose of spreading spirituality but for the sake of creating their own edifices. It is clear from both the Zohar and the Ari that this is what a Jew is—an enormous Desire to Receive—and if the Jew does not conform to this principle of restriction, chaos is the result. What the Talmud states is that being "buried" was not a threat to the Israelite, it was an illustration, a parable, that this is what will happen. "Now that you have agreed to *na'ase*, you have prepared yourself to be this kind of channel and there is a price for this—if not, you will be buried with it."

This very same principle of revelation required a transformation, a rebirth of that nation and along with it came the principle of filament, Central Column—restriction. Consequently "accept the Torah" was no longer interpreted as a threat, so they did this immediately; as soon as they heard what it was all about, of course they accepted it. Who does not want infinite beneficence? They wanted it all, so they said immediately, "Yes."

The other nations might well have been smarter, wanting less Desire to Receive so that they would not burn up completely. However, when something blows up it affects everyone. They were not speaking in terms of intelligence or of knowledge but rather in terms of an inner hatred for whatever it is, which is natural. Antisemitism, hating Jews, is an unnatural development in history. There is such an insignificant number of people who exist in the world that hate others who are greater in numbers.

With this knowledge we can begin to understand what is meant when we say that the souls present on Mount Sinai were transferred. The dispute between Moses and the Lord was that Moses realized that the *erev rav* meant those souls, who were Jewish souls but had fallen into what we call the *klipah* of the Desire to Receive for Oneself Alone. Moses knew ultimately that these souls would have to make their *tikkun* (spiritual correction). He knew that without the correction of the *erev rav* (the evil Jew)—there would be more hatred among Jews today as it had been at the time of the destruction of the Temple, where Jews hated each other.

We understand now the reason why souls have to come down to the physical world in this way because in addition to being Jewish there would be the work to correct the aspect of that kind of *erev rav* involved, especially if there was a high soul involved. Therefore Moses' father had to be Terach. This is the same reason Moses felt, and there was no dispute here, that all *erev rav* Jews have a spark in them, which is why Bilaam had to be ultimately incarnated into a Jew because the *tikkun* must be given the opportunity to be actualized. It may be painful, but it must come about. When Moses insisted on including the *erev rav* it was because he wanted to speed up the process of correction and God told Moses, "I do not think the process can be speeded up; it has got to take its toll." Therefore, there was not really an argument but Moses was probably right because look how close we are to the end. The Zohar says that the end will come either through a ball of fire putting an end to the whole show or we all do the right thing and bring the Messiah. Nevertheless, we are the ones who will bring Messiah; not he will come by his own virtue.

Therefore, Moses realized; he could see ahead and he was shown. In fact, the Zohar in a previous portion says, the Creator showed Moses all the heads of the Israelite Nation. Moses probably felt (and this is my own interpretation; you can give any that you prefer) that with these kind of people leading the Israelite Nation in the Age of Aquarius there will be such chaos by these rabbis and religious leaders. The Zohar says that Moses said, "Why do we have to wait 3,000 years the same chaos that will be there? At least let the ones that maybe can do it, get it done quicker. And the ones who will be creating chaos will create chaos throughout every generation…" as it was and as it still is. The most rebellious and most negative

attitudes toward the rebirth of spirituality in Judaism stems not
from the people themselves but from the leaders. This is what Moses
saw when God showed him the leaders, and so therefore he said,
"Why wait? Whatever is going to happen later is going to happen
now." And by that process, Moses thought that he could bring it
about immediately.

Understanding Conversion

Without getting into the politics of conversion—a spiritual
person never enters into politics because spirituality has no place
in the realm of politics and politics has no place in the realm of
spirituality. However, the Zohar makes the statement, a statement
that many would not like to declare: that in the Age of Aquarius
converts (*gerim*) will be like plague unto the nation of Israel. What
does this mean? A plague is what it says. Yet the Zohar does not
deviate from our previous discussion that *gerim* have existed. Rav
Isaac Luria (the Ari) has demonstrated it and has explained why
certain souls must come through that way—they could not come
into physicality any other way.

The Ari says that true *geriem* always begin with a higher level of
consciousness of spirituality. There are three levels of consciousness:
there is the lowest level Nefesh, then Ruach and the highest is
Neshamah and because of its level of consciousness, no convert
ever begins on the level of Nefesh; they immediately come into
this congregation of Israel, which we now have explained to
some extent, as Ruach because they are always of a higher level of
consciousness and feel the necessity of taking on this rebirth. It is
considered a rebirth because there are certain physical doctrines
and laws that the convert must pass through. Nonetheless, the soul
of a non-Jew, like Rabbi Meir understood and felt, beyond any
shadow of a doubt, that he was an Israelite soul that was not able

make it in the last life time, could not even make it now, so his soul was sent into this physical plane as a non-Jew to become a *Ger Tzedek*—a True Convert. If one is a true convert, this means that they were Jewish in a prior lifetime and could not perform the role of managing the Desire to Receive, therefore the soul returned to physicality with a lesser Desire to Receive. When a person feels an awakened desire to convert, this is an inner expression. It is not in response to family pressure. This is not what we are talking about. There has to be a genuineness that comes from an internal aspect. This, we should understand, is what the Zohar and the Talmud are referring to as *Ger Tzedek*.

When the Zohar says, we can have the other side of the coin, where there are converts who become so religious that everyone else is *pasul*—there is no one as holy as them, the Zohar is addressing this kind of convert that in the Age of Aquarius will be like plague unto the nation of Israel. We have got enough enemies, we can do without this kind of Jew, right. This is what the Zohar says can also happen; that he falls down again, in the same way he did in a prior lifetime. He/she was a hateful individual in a prior lifetime, so the soul is sent back with a lesser Desire to Receive, which constitutes the difference between Jew and non-Jew.

In this current life the individual may feel the need to become Jewish, meaning he/she feels they wanted this conversion, which is not about accepting one religion, it is about rebirth. There is a spiritual and physical rebirth of the individual. And I hope with this understanding things will become even a little clearer as to "who is Jew."

Bilaam as a Prophet

It is important to understand that Bilaam was a prophet. Everything he said was with prophetic power. Bilaam truly saw that the Creator did not want him to go with the emissaries of Balak. Nevertheless, he mounted his donkey and followed them. To stop Bilaam, the Creator sent an angel who was revealed to only the donkey, and not to Bilaam. Furthermore, it is written that the she-ass spoke to Bilaam, and they engaged in a very strange conversation. How extraordinary it would be to have such a conversation! The donkey asked Bilaam why he was whipping her. How many times did Bilaam whip her? According to the English translation, it was three times, but the Hebrew word *shalosh regalim* (שלש רגלים), used in the Torah translates as "three legs." The translation of the word *regalim* is not "times" because the word for "times" is *pe'amim* (פעמים).

Therefore, we ask ourselves what the Bible really means when it says three legs. The Hebrew word *regalim* literally means "foot" and refers to the pilgrimage that the children of Israel would make by foot to Jerusalem three times a year—on Passover, Sukkot, and Shavuot. The next question one might ask is: would it not count if someone came to the Holy Temple on a donkey? The Torah is teaching us the significance of the Central Column, which balances the receiving energy of the Left Column and the sharing energy of the Right Column. The power of the Central Column is resistance or restriction, and it is only found in Kabbalah. Other religions or spiritual paths only have the two columns.

Bilaam and the Negative Side

Balak was a very powerful person who knew how to tap negative energy. He knew the Israelites were strong and capable of releasing themselves from the shackles of chaos. Very few people can do this. Balak did not think he could overcome the nation of Israel by himself, and therefore sought out Bilaam to help channel this negative energy. Both men united to place a curse on the Israelites. To further embellish the drama, there is the seemingly ridiculous story of the donkey Bilaam was riding. The Zohar tells us that it was the same donkey Rav Pinchas Ben Yair, the father-in-law of Rav Shimon Bar Yochai, rode 1,400 years later. Are we expected to believe that a donkey could reach virtual immortality? This donkey could also, of course, see angels. How is it that a donkey was more aware than Bilaam, one of the most elevated people? It was because Bilaam was so focused, he could not see, he had already decided what to do.

Every child, until the age of three, is able to see angels. Since we were deprived of reading the Zohar while we were growing up, we were also deprived of the ability to see angels. Each morning, and three times on Shabbat, however, with the help of a special prayer, we have an opportunity of learning to deploy the real technology of Kabbalah, and thereby attune ourselves to the presence of angels. This donkey saw the angel of God standing in the path of Bilaam.

It is written that there will never be another prophet to rise up equivalent to Moses among the Israelites but that among the other nations someone of that consciousness would rise up—and that person was Bilaam, who achieved the ultimate tapping of the Negative Side, the energy to create chaos in the world. Kabbalists say if you have any hatred for no reason—*sinat chinam*—in your heart, you are not an Israelite.

If we can keep the level of consciousness of treating everyone around us with human dignity, no matter what an individual has done to us, this allows us to be Israelites. If we cannot do this, we are on a different level, a sub-level.

Certainty

As has been previously noted, the last two letters of Bilaam and Balak spell amalek, which has the same numerical value as the word *safek* (240), which in English is "doubt" or "uncertainty." The root of chaos is *amalek*, uncertainty, a tool of Satan. We cannot remove chaos from this world if we permit uncertainty to be part of our lives. The Zohar explains that as long as we succumb to uncertainty, we will be ruled by chaos. The Zohar provides us with a tool to counter uncertainty with the word *vadai*, which is spelled *Vav, Dalet, Alef, Yud* (ודאי)—certainty.

A theory exists in the business world that if we focus on certainty unwaveringly we will achieve all our objectives. Most of us can accept this for business, yet we have difficulty implementing it in our personal lives.

The portion of Balak is a prelude to the portion of Pinchas, and what we will find in that portion is certainty. The information has been there, concealed for thousands of years. Bilaam was the master of tapping into the Negative Side. He and Balak wanted to inject into the world the consciousness of uncertainty. Even those who study at the Kabbalah Centres can find themselves thinking that if things get rough and tough, maybe the wisdom and technology is not really working, and once we think something is not working, uncertainty enters and the result is chaos.

We need to inject certainty, and keep that certainty until we reach the end of chaos. As we raise the Torah Scroll, we can connect to the curse of Bilaam that was transformed into a blessing. With this we have this opportunity to transform all curses in our lives into blessings, and convert the energy of uncertainty into certainty.

The Donkey's Insight

Bilaam was obviously a brilliant man to be compared with Moses. So what happened here? Why is it that only after the pleading of the donkey are Bilaam's eyes opened so he can see the Angel of God with a sword standing in the way? The angel then reminds Bilaam that he has beaten his donkey three times, when the donkey had seen the Angel standing in its way. What does the Bible want to teach us with regards to the Angel being visible to the donkey at first and not to Bilaam? Moreover, what is significant about the three times that Bilaam beat the donkey? This is a very special donkey.

What is special about a donkey? It works hard, harder than any another animal. You can load a donkey up many feet high with stuff on its back and the donkey does not say a word. The donkey can lock its knees, like a solid piece of steel giving it the ability to carry this weight and not buckle under the load like other animals might. You do not want to block his way, nonetheless a donkey goes it accepts its burden.

There is an expression in the Zohar and Talmud that says we are to accept all yokes, (*Kabbalat Ol Malchut Shamayim*), that this world does not work by chance or coincidence. It is a burden to be with the Light because the Desire to Receive for the Self Alone becomes comfortable. Until the age of 13, we are in good company with the Satan, having no responsibility and being very playful. Then at the age of Bar/Bat Mitzvah, we have to assume the responsibility to share and accept that we did not come into this world to be with the Satan but instead to accept the burden of transforming our nature and the feeling of freedom without responsibility. This is how the world began for us, is this how it is supposed to finish? No, we came here to be like a donkey; to assume that responsibility, that burden. Some of us still believe that we came into this world to have a good time; to continue to live like this world is a bed of roses that looks nice and smells nice. It does not work this way. We do not consider until 12 for a girl or 13 for a boy why things are happening to us, that we came here to accept the burden.

This is the reason Bilaam could not see the angel, even though his donkey did. Bilaam did not know why we came to this physical plane. He thought he came to live a life of honor. Is there responsibility to come into this world to reap the rewards of honor? Brilliant people often think they are entitled, not that our intelligence or money is given to us. What is our contribution? There is little sense of responsibility. Instead we have to be more like the donkey. Yes responsibility gets heavy at times but what is responsibility if it does not get heavy?

36 And when Balak heard that Bilaam was come, he went out to meet him at Ir-Moab, which is on the border of Arnon, which is in the utmost part of the border. 37 And Balak said to Bilaam: "Did I not earnestly send to you, to call you? Why did you not come to me? Am I not able to promote you to honor?" 38 And Bilaam said to Balak: "Look, I have come to you; now have I any power at all to say anything? The word that God puts in my mouth, that shall I speak." 39 And Bilaam went with Balak, and they came to Kiriath-Huzoth. 40 And Balak sacrificed oxen and sheep, and sent to Bilaam, and to the princes that were with him. 41 And it came to pass in the morning that Balak took Bilaam, and brought him up into Bamoth-Baal, and he saw from there the extent of the people.

The Evil Eye

This section is here to teach us that once Balak (the Satan) has entered our consciousness we become not so smart. Why did Bilaam really go? Was he a fool? No. He was a great sorcerer. With all of his intelligence and with all that had happened—the angel spoke to him, God spoke to him and still he went with Balak? This does not make sense.

The moment the evil eye enters, a person cannot see what those around him can see. How is it possible that everyone else can see what the individual cannot? This is Bilaam. The moment a connection with Satan has been formed, either by means of the evil eye or as in the case of Bilaam, who was the embodiment of Satan, the individual has effectively been blinded. Even if the Creator tells us directly, "Do not do it," if the power of Satan is within us, nothing helps.

Bamidbar 23:1 And Bilaam said to Balak: "Build seven altars for me here, and prepare for me seven bullocks and seven rams." 2 And Balak did as Bilaam had spoken; and Balak and Bilaam offered a bullock and a ram on every altar. 3 And Bilaam said to Balak: "Stand by your burnt-offering, and I will go; perhaps the Lord will come to meet me; and whatever He shows me I will tell you." And he went to a bare height. 4 And God met Bilaam; and he said to Him: "I have prepared the seven altars, and I have offered up a bullock and a ram on every altar." 5 And the Lord put a word in Bilaam's mouth, and said: "Return to Balak, and thus you shall speak." 6 And he returned to him, and there he stood by his burnt-offering, he and all the princes of Moab. 7 And he took up his parable, and said: "From Aram Balak brings me, the king of Moab from the mountains of the East: Come, curse me Jacob, and come, denounce Israel. 8 How shall I curse, whom God has not cursed? And how shall I denounce whom the Lord has not denounced? 9 For from the top of the rocks I see him, and from the hills I behold him: look, it is a people that shall dwell alone, and shall not be reckoned among the nations. 10 Who has counted the dust of Jacob, or numbered the stock of Israel? Let me die the death of the righteous, and let my end be like his!" 11 And Balak said to Bilaam: "What have you done to me? I took you to curse my enemies, and, behold, you have blessed them bountifully." 12 And he answered and said:

"Must I not take heed to speak that which the Lord puts in my mouth?" 13 And Balak said to him: "Come, I pray you, with me to another place, from where you may see them; you shall see but the utmost part of them, and shall not see them all; and curse them for me from there." 14 And he took him into the field of Zophim, to the top of Pisgah, and built seven altars, and offered up a bullock and a ram on every altar. 15 And he said to Balak: "Stand here by your burnt-offering, while I go toward a meeting over there." 16 And the Lord met Bilaam, and put a word in his mouth, and said: "Return to Balak, and so shall you speak." 17 And he came to him, and he stood by his burnt-offering, and the princes of Moab with him. And Balak said to him: 'What has the Lord spoken?" 18 And he took up his parable, and said: "Arise, Balak, and hear; give ear to me, you, son of Tzipor: 19 God is not a man that He should lie; neither the son of man that He should repent: when He has said, will He not do it? Or when He has spoken, will He not make it good? 20 Behold, I am bidden to bless; and when He has blessed, I cannot call it back. 21 None has beheld iniquity in Jacob, neither has one seen perverseness in Israel; the Lord, his God, is with him, and the shouting for the King is among them. 22 God who brought them forth out of Egypt is for them like the lofty horns of the wild-ox. 23 For there is no enchantment with Jacob, neither is there any divination with Israel; now is it said of Jacob and of

Israel: 'What has God wrought!' 24 Behold a people that rises up as a lioness, and as a lion does he lift himself up; he shall not lie down until he eat of the prey, and drink the blood of the slain.'" 25 And Balak said to Bilaam: "Neither curse them at all, nor bless them at all." 26 But Bilaam answered and said to Balak: "Did I not tell you: All that the Lord speaks, that I must do?"

Certainty and the Tree of Life

Amalek is an internal matter. The word *amalek* (עֲמָלֵק) has the same numerical value (240) as the Hebrew word *safek* (סָפֵק), which means "doubt," therefore *amalek* is the internal doubt, uncertainty, that we must put to an end. For example, a thief steals because he does not have confidence the Creator will supply him with all his needs—a thief has doubt in the Creator.

In our generation, even some of the greatest scientists have reached the conclusion that the whole universe operates according to the principles of uncertainty, which is why Rav Ashlag started promoting Kabbalah; Rav Ashlag introduced Kabbalah as a teaching to connect people to the awareness of certainty.

All the erroneous opinions arise as a result of uncertainty in the Light or a general doubt. If a person is sure that tomorrow will be all right, then it must be all right now; and the converse is also true, if it is not all right now, then a person surmises that tomorrow it will also not be all right. The whole issue of separation, which is Satan consciousness, is caused only because of this doubt.

The only free choice we have while in this physical world is the choice between the Tree of Life Reality and the Tree of Knowledge Reality. What does Bilaam mean by the statement: "The word that God puts in my mouth, that must I speak." We are much like robots while in this world, and if we pay attention to the way we speak, we can see that we do not control speech; speech continues by itself without self-control. It is as if there is a cassette within us that is running, however most of the people with a strong sense of self-love think they control their life. What motivates a person to speak good or evil? And if it is only the cassette, are we at all to blame? When we enter into the Tree of Life Reality, we continue to be a channel, only now we are a channel of the Light and therefore the cassette from which we speak is actually from the Light.

When an individual becomes a channel for the Light, no matter who the person is, the Light speaks through them. All we have to do is exercise our free will and choose the Tree of Life Reality; from this state of consciousness, everything works correctly. If something is not working correctly, we have not selected the Tree of Life.

This portion deals with doubt, which we must uproot because it is the greatest obstacle to being with the Light.

27 And Balak said to Bilaam: "Come now, I will take you to another place; perhaps it will please God that you may curse them for me from there." 28 And Balak took Bilaam to the top of Peor that looks down upon the desert. 29 And Bilaam said to Balak: "Build seven altars for me here, and prepare for me here seven bullocks and seven rams." 30 And Balak did as Bilaam had said, and offered up a bullock and a ram on every altar.

Bamidbar 24:1 And when Bilaam saw that it pleased the Lord to bless Israel, he went not, as at the other times, to meet with enchantments, but he set his face toward the wilderness. 2 And Bilaam lifted up his eyes, and he saw Israel dwelling tribe by tribe; and the spirit of God came upon him. 3 And he took up his parable, and said: "The saying of Bilaam the son of Beor, and the saying of the man whose eye is opened; 4 The saying of him who hears the words of God, who sees the vision of the Almighty, fallen down, yet with opened eyes: 5 How goodly are your tents, Jacob, your dwellings, Israel!

Goodness and the Letter Mem

There are six places in the Torah Scroll where the column does not begin with the letter Vav and rather begins with a different letter. In Bamidbar 24:5, the letter Mem begins the top of the column with the word *Ma* (How). The letter *Mem* (מ) is formed by two letters—*Kaf* (כ) and *Vav* (ו), which add up to a numerical value of 26, which is equal to the numerical value of the Tetragrammaton—*Yud, Hei, Vav* and *Hei*—Tree of Life Reality. The word ma has a numerical value of 45, which is the same value as the word *adam* (אדם) the Hebrew word for "man".

Bilaam attempted to curse the Israelites and failed; he then tried in another location and still failed. Whoever is connected to the Tree of Life Reality—the Tetragrammaton (26)—can help himself out of the dirt, which is why this verse says, "How good (*ma tovu*)..." which is the Tetragrammaton.

When we are connected to *ma*, there are no problems. We fall when we forget and leave the place of certainty. When a person internally questions expressing the complaint, "Listen, Creator, don't you see I did everything I was supposed to, all the communications, and yet I'm still in the same place I was before." This is Satan. Why? Because the Creator wants to help, it is our responsibility to make the connection. This is the power of the letter *Mem* at the top of the column.

Through the letter *Mem* in this section we can connect to the energy and support of certainty that can allow the healing nature of the Light to do its work. With certainty we can enhance our immune system to repel disease.

Bilaam's Prayer

When, at the request of Balak, Bilaam went to curse the Israelites and make no mistake that was his intention, he somehow gets lost in his objective and he praises them instead, saying, "How goodly are your tents, Jacob, your dwellings, Israel!" (Bamidbar 24:5)

This verse is recited by every congregant who enters the Kabbalah Centre War Rooms indicating that this verse has some enormous power as it should be recited at the very beginning of all prayers. Yet, this same prayer was uttered by the great archenemy of Israel, Bilaam. How do we reconcile these to pieces of information?

6 As valleys stretched out, as gardens by the riverside; as aloes planted of the Lord, as cedars beside the waters; 7 Water shall flow from his branches, and his seed shall be in many waters; and his king shall be higher than Agag, and his kingdom shall be exalted. 8 God who brought him forth out of Egypt is for him like the lofty horns of the wild-ox; he shall eat up the nations that are his adversaries, and shall break their bones in pieces, and pierce them through with his arrows. 9 He crouched, he lay down as a lion, and as a lioness; who shall rouse him up? Blessed be every one that blesses you, and cursed be every one that curses you." 10 And Balak's anger was kindled against Bilaam, and he smote his hands together; and Balak said to Bilaam: "I called you to curse my enemies, and, behold, you have altogether blessed them these three times. 11 Therefore now flee you to your place; I thought to promote you to great honor; but the Lord has kept you back from honor." 12 And Bilaam said to Balak: "Did I also not speak to your messengers that you sent to me saying: 13 'If Balak would give me his house full of silver and gold, I cannot go beyond the word of the Lord, to do either good or bad of mine own mind; what the Lord speaks, that will I speak?' 14 And now, behold, I go to my people; come and I will announce to you what this people shall do to your people in the end of days." 15 And he took up his parable, and said: "The saying of Bilaam, the son of Beor, and the saying of the

man whose eye is opened; 16 The saying of him who hears the words of God, and knows the knowledge of the Most High, who sees the vision of the Almighty, fallen down, yet with opened eyes: 17 I see him, but not now; I behold him, but not near; there shall step forth a star out of Jacob, and a scepter shall rise out of Israel, and shall smite through the corners of Moab, and break down all the sons of Seth. 18 And Edom shall be a possession, Seir also, even his enemies, shall be a possession; while Israel does valiantly. 19 And out of Jacob shall one have dominion, and shall destroy the remnant from the city." 20 And he looked on Amalek, and took up his parable, and said: "Amalek was the first of the nations; but his end shall come to destruction." 21 And he looked on the Kenite, and took up his parable, and said: "Though firm be your dwelling place, and though your nest be set in the rock; 22 Nevertheless Kain shall be wasted; How long? Asshur shall carry you away captive." 23 And he took up his parable, and said: "Alas, who shall live after God has appointed him? 24 But ships shall come from the coast of Kittim, and they shall afflict Asshur, and shall afflict Eber, and he also shall come to destruction." 25 And Bilaam rose up, and went and returned to his place; and Balak also went his way.

Doubt and Uncertainty

Because of lack of kabbalistic knowledge, many people in the world who read this portion of the Bible think it to be an inappropriate source of the Bible. Why then would we come to listen to the reading of Balak on Shabbat? We do so because it is the instruction on how to heal oneself from all forms of illness.

Says the Zohar, Bilaam and Balak are metaphors for doubt and uncertainty. The last two letters of each of their names forms the word *amalek*—a coded instrument that remains abtruse and shrouded in secrecy and does not appeal to the rational consciousness. The entire Bible is filled with codes and messages that have to be deciphered and the code breaker is the Zohar. The Zohar tells us that the singular root of the chaos that we all experience, whether it is illness, financial failure, social ills is in the word—*amalek*. The Zohar explains that the war between the nation of Israel and the nation of Amalek in Exodus is merely a metaphor. *Amalek* has the same numerical value as *safek*—doubt. The cause of all dis-ease is uncertainty.

As Rav Ashlag began to manifest the Zohar in the 20th century, the force of Satan knew this would be the demise of its power. So Satan brought a thought to the great minds of science and a new principle—the uncertainty principle, was born. No matter how positive the test results, one will still experience an uncertainty. Even with the appearance of new drugs doctors are still unsure, as a drug that can help heal a person can also kill the individual.

Themes of doubt and uncertainty are found throughout the Bible. After all the miraculous events the Israelites witnessed: Ten Plagues, the Parting of the Red Sea and Manna falling from Heaven, the people still doubted. All of these events defied the laws of nature. Yet, when Miriam passed away, and her well ceased to provide a source of water, what was the first reaction of the Israelites? They complained to Moses. It was not as if a long time had passed and they had forgotten, it was 24 hours later. We are no different today. The minute something appears to turn, we believe it is all over with.

The wisdom of Kabbalah that helps us to understand the workings of the spiritual dimension and the tools that expand our consciousness, also help us remove uncertainty. Yet if we cannot bring our consciousness to a level of certainty then, during times when something challenges us, we will fall back into the realm of doubt. If we are still molded in the framework of uncertainty nothing can help us. We have codes—the letters *Vav, Dalet, Alef, Yud*, which spell the word *vadai* (וד‎אי)—certainty. The letters of the Zohar give life; this is why Kabbalah has survived for four thousand years. The force of Satan is aware that this is the final card to play, Satan knows this is his last stand, which is why, when entering this century, we were already prepared for immortality. The twists and contradictions; everything we see that is on the physical level is just a blip on the screen. Satan has been playing one game with people: religion.

Rav Isaac Luria (the Ari) knew all the languages of the birds, fish, animals—they speak the way we do but we have lost the ability to understand them. A person may understand little about the computer, while still being able to use one. Similarly, we may not understand why and how the language of the Hebrew letters was assembled in the Torah scroll, yet one day that veil will be lifted and the world will discover that everything is very simple.

We came here to listen to the reading of the Torah Scroll so as to remove uncertainty and to affect our destiny. When Bilaam said, "*Ma tovu...* ("How beautiful are your tents, Jacob, your dwelling places, Israel.") (Bamidbar 24:5) Balak asked him why, if they had both come there to curse, he was blessing the people. There are indications over the past four thousand years that they have been right. When you want to receive a magic bullet that can destroy cancer, you have to include the cancer itself. The Bible is telling us here that we cannot cut out a cancer cell because one percent, which may represent a billion cancer cells might still be there. We do not take out that cancer cell but we have to go back to the root and take out that part we do not see. Cancer means confused; the body is in a confused state. This is our opportunity to remove the confusion. We have the same tools that were given to the Israelites—except that the day that they believed they had no water was the day they got confused. It was not there in physical form as it was at Mount Sinai. So we must go back. It is never the physical challenge, it is the confusion. If we removed the physical problem it does not solve the problem. Without certainty, we cannot make it, no matter what happens. This is the blip on the screen; this is not the way the universe was structured.

Through the letter *Mem* (מ) of the word *Ma* in Bamidbar 24:5, we have the opportunity to connect to the energy and support of certainty that can allow the healing nature of the Light to do its work. With certainty we can enhance our immune system to repel dis-ease.

Bamidbar 25:1 And Israel stayed in Shittim, and the people began to commit harlotry with the daughters of Moab. 2 And they called the people to the sacrifices of their gods; and the people ate and bowed down to their gods. 3 And Israel joined himself to the Baal of Peor; and the anger of the Lord was kindled against Israel. 4 And the Lord said to Moses: "Take all the chiefs of the people, and hang them up to the Lord in the face of the sun, that the fierce anger of the Lord may turn away from Israel." 5 And Moses said to the judges of Israel: "Every one of you slay his men who were joined to the Baal of Peor." 6 And, behold, one of the children of Israel came and brought to his brethren a Midianite woman in the sight of Moses, and in the sight of all the congregation of the children of Israel, while they were weeping at the door of the Tent of Meeting. 7 And when Pinchas, the son of Elazar, the son of Aaron, the priest, saw it, he rose up from the midst of the congregation, and took a spear in his hand. 8 And he went after the man of Israel into the chamber, and thrust both of them through, the man of Israel, and the woman through her belly. So the plague was stopped from the children of Israel. 9 And those that died by the plague were twenty and four thousand.

Pinchas and Immortality

Pinchas took a spear and slayed two people and this action ended the plague where 24,000 died. Pinchas provides us with the opportunity to heal ourselves completely but unfortunately, we get in our own way.

Following the incident when Bilaam's curse transformed into a blessing and he was unable to curse the Israelites because of the protective shield around them, Bilaam felt the only way to grab the consciousness of the Israelites was to tempt them to cause a breach in their protection so he sent in the beautiful women of Midian. Cozbi, the most beautiful of the Midianite women was instructed to approach Moses and seduce him. Asking how she would recognize Moses, she was told to look for someone surrounded by people. Seeing the chieftain of the tribe of Shimon, Zimri, she mistook him for Moses, and proceeded to seduce him instead. The result of this act was an outbreak of plague where 24,000 Israelites perished.

Pinchas, the son of Elazar, grandson of Aaron the High Priest, stood up and took a sword, or whatever instrument, and slayed these two people. From this verse, Jewish extremists have found their refuge and their validation to kill in the fact that Pinchas was rewarded with the position of the High Priest. If taken literally, this seems to be the conclusion that can be derived from this story—killing for good reason. Nonetheless, murder is murder. With this story and others like it, religions can surmise that murder for the benefit of God is okay. Thereby Rav Shimon asks, "So then does the Bible sanction murder?" Murder is murder and a priest who murders is invalidated even if is the action is for all the good reasons.

This creates a true dilemma—why was Pinchas rewarded? Is the Bible providing validation for such actions? Rav Shimon says, "No." The Zohar explains that as Pinchas was a murderer he was invalidated as a High Priest. When the tribe of Shimon saw their chief slain, they all came upon Pinchas to kill him. The Zohar tells us that he died of fright. However, two new souls entered his form, which was reborn. Here we have the first instance in the Bible of a physical immortality. The Zohar says that what happened here is a clinical death. Pinchas was reborn.

The portion of Balak is the prelude to the portion of Pinchas. We thus ought to be very concerned with the regeneration of our own lives. Pinchas knew that murder is murder, and he was prepared to sacrifice himself—his life and his position—for the benefit of the nation.

Connecting to the portion of Balak can help us rid ourselves of the cesspool in our head, which results in a complete regeneration of our bodies and our minds.

According to the Halacha (Laws) if a priest murders or commits some other transgression, he cannot be a priest. Pinchas transgressed "Thou shalt not kill," which is explicitly stated in the Bible. Therefore, how did he know that to kill the chief of the tribe of Shimon, was the right thing to do? How did Pinchas know that killing the chief of the tribe of Shimon would be what could stop the plague? In truth it seems that we do not know how Pinchas knew the answer to this. However, if we make a thorough investigation of the Bible we find out that Pinchas knew. Although his life was threatened by the people of the tribe of Shimon, Pinchas did not care. He did what he did because he understood that it was good for the community, and this is the secret Pinchas wants to teach us.

Light as a Cure for Chaos

In the Zohar section of the portion of Balak, there is a story of Tzalyah (צליה) who was able to fly in the sky and chase Bilaam and his two sons.

> *"Tzalyah, a member from Dan's tribe, rose and took charge of the powers that are dominant over witchcraft, and flew after him. When the wicked one noticed him, he took another course in the air and penetrated five other layers of air in that course. He rose higher and disappeared from eyesight...."*
> —Zohar, Balak 176

Here the Zohar is talking about actually flying in the physical sky. It was not George Lucas in Star Wars who invented a war in the sky. Both the Bible and the Zohar 4,000 years ago describe Bilaam as flying in the air like a bird. The Zohar is teaching us with this story that everything that happens takes place not only in the physical dimension, but also on the metaphysical level, even if we cannot see it. This is because the Light cannot be seen or felt. The curse of Bilaam was to interrupt the connection between the Light and the physical world.

Hence, we learn in Kabbalah that to control our problems and avoid short-circuits of energy is to take care of the root of the problem. Doctors today who treat cancer as an effect are only looking at the physical. Rather we know that the problem is a short-circuit and that we can and should address the metaphysical problem at the root level, using Tikkun haNefesh, Ana Beko'ach and the Zohar.

The Light is shining and chases away the darkness. We must have certainty that if there is a problem in our life, health or otherwise, when we have pain and troubles there is a pool of Light. It is exactly as with a dark room. In a place where there is no light one can stumble on the furniture, but the second we flip the switch, the darkness disappears.

When we meditate with certainty on the healing Name of *Mem*, *Hei*, *Shin* (מ.ה.ש) on Shabbat, we have flipped a switch creating the connection between the Light and the problem. We have bridged the Light and the problem and with that, the darkness disappears. No one cares where the darkness has gone, as long as, when we enter the room, the Light is there.

The Zohar explains that Bilaam and Balak knew how to draw the Light, which means they did not have a unique physical power to curse. The words themselves have the power. So what does it mean to curse the children of Israel with such force that it can destroy them?

The Bible tells us that within the nation of Israel there was no greater prophet in the Pure System other than Moses. Conversely, in the Impure System there was no greater prophet than Bilaam. The Impure System is one analogous to short-circuitry, causing a separation between the Light and us, thereby preventing the Light from influencing the universe. This was the desire of Bilaam and Balak; they wanted to curse the Israelites and cause them to become separated from the Light. As it is with electricity, if the circuit of energy breaks there is no light—there is only darkness.

In discussing the Pure and Impure Systems, we are not dealing with religion, which has been steeped in corruption for the past 3,000 years. In simple terms, the Pure System means that there is circuitry of energy—an unbroken connection—with the Light, whereas with the Impure System that connection is broken. The only way to understand these systems is to study Kabbalah.

The trick is to find the means to bring the Light into the places that lack the Light. It is a lack that causes cells to "go wild," get crazy and lose control. These cells were normal and all of a sudden, they change. This can be likened to a person that for 20-30 years is normal and one day he kills for no reason. How does such a thing happen? Maybe the individual drank water that had a *dibuk* (negative soul that entered him) of a killer and it influenced him. The problem is that once doubt arises, we forget that not everything is visible to the eye.

This is the reason we come to hear the reading of the Bible. We have tools today that were not available or accessible 20 years ago. Even the Zohar that was published 60 years ago, for most people was not to be read or studied, nor did the general public understand its power. People would say, "It is too holy and lofty for us to study because we are in a very low level, and we are not clean and should not even touch it." Only through the understanding given by the Zohar can we connect to and understand the energy of this portion of Balak.

Rav Ashlag, in his *Sulam* commentary of the Zohar, explains that the reference to the name Balak son of Tzipor (*tzipor* means "bird" in Hebrew) is a code for the Upper Three Sefirot—Keter, Chochmah, Binah. Magicians draw energy in the Impure System in the same way we draw energy in the Pure System from Keter (the Upper Sefira) in the Amida prayer of Musaf. We want to eliminate Tzipor (not Balak's father) but the negative level of it. Balak knew how to draw this Light from the Upper Three Sefirot of the Impure System. This is why the Zohar says there was no prophet like Moses to the Israelites because Moses knew how to draw the Light from the Pure System. Moses was connected to this level on the Pure System and wanted to connect the Light to our world. In contrast, although Bilaam also knew how to draw the Light, he was connected to the Impure Side.

With the portion of Balak we are given the knowledge of how to connect and bridge between the Light, which is metaphysical, and our physical world. The power we receive from the Torah reading on Shabbat involves how to remove all varieties of negative forces and curses. Without this power we will not be able to do it. Thus, the words of the Torah are our bridge between the physical world and the Light.

Soon we will see that once death is removed permanently—*bila hamavet lanetzch*—we will be capable of many spectacular deeds, such as flight. Anyone wishing to attend Shabbat in Israel could be there in a moment. Such is the power of the Zohar. Without the Zohar this portion is incomprehensible. None of the commentaries speak about the fact that a physical person can arrive unaided in Israel in two minutes. It is all a question of consciousness, Balak and Bilaam knew this—they knew how to veil the entire world and make us blind.

Overcoming the limitations of time, space, and motion, as well as the force of gravity here on Earth, should be in our consciousness when we listen to the reading the Bible, so that we can experience no trouble travelling from Israel to Los Angeles in a few seconds. Many of us may say, "It does not make sense." Where is the logic that if with a very small minor flip of a switch we bring in the light and the darkness is gone? Yet once we control gravity on this Earth, it will disappear, along with the limitations of time, space and motion.

We must remember that all energy is a force. Where did the Nazis get their power to kill 50 million people? Evil is a force. They drew the Light for themselves, and they could do it because they received their energy as an outcome of our behavior. When people are sharing one to the other, Satan transfers the Light to the Pure Side. Everything in this universe has Light—the Light is the cause of everything—the only question is whether it is in the Pure or Impure System.

We know that when Bilaam started to curse, he said, "*Ma tovo* ..." it became a blessing instead. This means that the power of Moses was so strong that he could move the same amount of Light over to the Pure Side to remove the Impure Side of Bilaam. Moses transformed what was supposed to be a curse into a blessing.

We read in the end of this portion that "*Vayakam Bilaam*... (And Bilaam got up...)" and if we take the last two letters of names Balak and Bilaam and put them together, they spell *amalek* (עמלק) "doubt," the root of all the problems in the world.

One should be with certainty for the good. Mind over matter. The scientists today do not understand why mind over matter is not happening. The answer is *amalek*—doubt, no certainty. We use the name *vadai* (ודאי) "certainty" to remove doubt. When we have certainty, the doubts are eliminated. Today, many people around the world are aware of this fact—the importance of overcoming the doubt.

The Bible does not mention when the plague began, and that the Israelites went with the women of Moab. This resulting plague killed 24,000 people until Pinchas stopped it.

Pinchas died once he had speared Cozbi and Zimri. Pinchas experienced a clinical death, and he came back to life with the souls of Nadav and Avihu. This is the power of immortality. We speak about immortality as if it is something out there in Heaven, yet Rav Shimon and all the sages could restore the dead to life. The establishment would like us to believe that immortality is not available to us because we are low and not at that level. We may be on a lower level but this does not mean we cannot experience immortality. At the time of Moses, the people were also on a low level; and many years have passed since then and we have undergone spiritual cleansing therefore, who knows, perhaps next week we will have immortality. The scientific world does agree that immortality is happening and people are "coming back from the dead." This day is not so far off.

Bilaam Did Not Listen to God

God told Bilaam not to curse the Israelites but he tried to anyway. Why did Bilaam, the second wisest man of his time not understand? Is it like us, in that sometimes we do not understand that it is God speaking to us? We may see signs, miracles, and still not know. But Bilaam knew it was God. What is the difference? How do we fall into the same trap? This portion teaches us how to survive. But if Bilaam could not, nor could the people of the desert, then why today would it be any different? Two thousand years ago they did not have the tools. Yet the Israelites in the desert had all the tools and understood them so could they not have survived? Why did they not rise above the illusion and stop complaining? They forgot about yesterday.

How can we know? I am sure everyone at the Kabbalah Centres, at one point thought, "Maybe this is not for me." I, too, experienced this as a student. I was much younger. I even disagreed with my teacher Rav Brandwein. Some people did not like my teacher and I was disturbed by it and I thought: *Who needs all this. I think I am going to leave the whole thing.* Our children will not have to go through this because they come from a whole different background. But how can we be safe? Bilaam still went to Balak even though God told him not to. He went against everything and eventually Pinchas killed him. How long does it take to learn the lesson? We too make the same mistake over and over again.

How should one think when confronted with this kind of situation? The Torah is telling us that Bilaam never gave up. How vast is the playing field of Satan? Is it just in the desert or all around the world? The truth is that Satan is global. When one decides to take control and you take control of a little piece, then the price is small. If you want to control it all, the price is global. It is as difficult as the reward is incredible. Because Bilaam was of such a high state, he was out for the biggest prize—the whole world. He wanted total control, to embrace the whole world with chaos. If you do not want to affect the whole world and you are in the Kabbalah Centres, you are in the wrong place. We are global and we are one, unified.

Whether you understand or not, whether we will save the planet from chaos or not, know that the Kabbalah Centre gives us the potential to eliminate chaos—at the very least in our personal life.

The Zohar says Bilaam and Balak's names combine to give us the word *amalek*, which has the same numerical value as the word *safek* meaning "doubt." Whether it is doubt about the Kabbalah Centres or more general doubt about life itself, the worst thing is this kind of uncertainty. The most important rule and tool, is to always follow certainty because without certainty you are left with a life of one day this and one day that—it is all chaos. If you are not certain about anything in your life, the route to take is to pray for certainty. Do not begin before you take care of the certainty: *I am sure the Light will take care and lead me to where I want to be.*

Conclusion

The portion of Balak refers to the separation of the men from the boys, girls from the women. While we all consider ourselves adults, the children among us are probably on a higher level because adults are already adulterated, and it is more difficult for us to see things as they really are.

There are very few people in the world who can claim to have seen what they go through each and every single day. This concept is what the portion of Balak is all about. It is a cure that certainly exists because we do not believe that the Lightforce of God would have created this kind of chaos without providing us with the cure at the very same moment. Balak is really all about the playing field of Satan, nothing more. Balak is all about uncertainty, and this one word is what brings chaos into the lives of every single person who exists in this universe, making the overcoming of uncertainty virtually impossible. Anyone saying they have the consciousness of certainty in their life, and yet chaos still exists in it, is fooling themselves. Certainty does not coexist with chaos. Opportunities, uncomfortable moments in life will arise but irreversible or constant chaos without respite cannot co-exist with certainty.

We are on Satan's playing field, yet how do we know this? One word: Electronics. Everyone around the world now operates a computer, a highly sophisticated piece of equipment. This is, of course, not what electronics is; the application of electronics ultimately develops into a computer. Electronics means one thing, Left Column energy, the Desire to Receive. If you know anything about microchips, there is one basic problem: the more processing that goes into a chip, the hotter it becomes—this is why it will always be limited.

The Centre is intent upon changing this consciousness of the world from electrons and electronics with photons and photonics. This is so profound, to literally take the word electronics out of the lexicon of this entire universe, beyond a comprehension by any individual, including myself. This is where we are. Changing the entire world from the concept of Satan's playing field—electronics (Desire to

Receive)—into photonics (Desire to Share). Yet there is a problem; we are so governed by uncertainty, as science has given us this false impression of the universe, with the uncertainty principle. If a person is uncertain and has to protect themselves, they cannot think outwardly. How can we think of going beyond on behalf of others if we are in a state of uncertainty?

The level we desire to achieve is that of changing the universe from electronics to photonics, sharing, which obviously is the cure for all of the ills in technology. All of the problems that technology faces is because of that one term—electronics. For those who do not know what I am talking about, take a look at a light bulb that provides us with 10% light and 90% heat. Why can we not get 100% light? We cannot because Satan controls this world. He will give you a little pittance, and make you think you control it.

All are within this one portion of Balak: certainty and everything that goes with it, and aggravation, involving the chaos that would normally come into our lives. We will not succumb, we have the certainty that the Light provides us with everything we will ever need, even those things we cannot yet dream about in the future. We need to understand that, as long as we eat and breathe electronics, we are in the playing field of the Satan, waiting for the time he will snatch away everything we have. Satan's time is over. By making use of the tools of Kabbalah, and the portion of Balak, we will receive the energy we need to take control of our birthright to be the determinators of this world.

BOOK OF BAMIDBAR:

PORTION OF PINCHAS

PORTION OF PINCHAS

Bamidbar 25:10 And the Lord spoke to Moses, saying: 11 "Pinchas, the son of Elazar, the son of Aaron the priest, has turned My wrath away from the children of Israel, in that he was zealous (jealous) for My jealousy among them, so that I not consume the children of Israel in My jealousy.

Murder the High Priesthood and the letter Yud

Every Shabbat provides us with a specific dimension of Light directed toward a particular need of humankind—to avoid the chaos that seems unavoidable. Therefore, listening to the reading of the Torah Scroll on Shabbat is a universal technology for achieving the opportunity of removing chaos for the coming six days. Moreover, we can make use of this instrument every single week.

The Bible is not the exclusive right of the Jewish nation. The Talmud and the Zohar repeatedly state that the entire Torah was translated into 70 languages. It is an instrument for all nations to remove chaos from their lives. So what does this discussion of Pinchas have to do with manipulating chaos into a positive energy force to serve and benefit us? Why was the portion Pinchas chosen as the healing portion for every conceivable illness that can befall humankind?

To provide a background of what Pinchas accomplished, we must refer back to the previous portion of Balak where, without going into detail, a plague broke out among the children of Israel because of their negative activity. Twenty-four thousand people died within moments. It does not make a difference whether it was in moments or over years, the sum of 24,000 people nevertheless represents a plague.

Pinchas performed an action that brought an end to the plague, and because of this action he was rewarded. However, his action involved the death of two people, and yet he was rewarded with the Priesthood. The Zohar questions the Torah as to why Pinchas was rewarded with the priesthood when it appears that, for all the "good reasons" he nonetheless violated a universal law and perpetrated an offense against another human being. There is no question that it was for good reason. His actions brought about the end of a plague that could have consumed all the nations of the world, which indeed makes it a noble act. There is no disagreement in this, except perhaps from the perspective of the two people who were "victims."

However, when a Priest (Kohen) commits a murder, he invalidates his service as the High Priest. This indicates for us that when we treat others with less than human dignity, we invalidate our spiritual work, even if it is for all the right reasons. All the nations that have waged war on other nations thought they did so for all the right reasons, irrespective of the feelings of the oppressed. By virtue of the Zohar's question we learn that Pinchas should have become invalid.

When Pinchas slew those two individuals—Cozbi and Zimri—the nation rose up and demanded he be punished. Although he had stopped the plague, nevertheless he was a murderer. The tribe of Shimon descended on him and out of the fear that overcame him, he died.

In the Bible it is written, "Pinchas the son of Elazar, the son of Aaron." The Zohar explains that the repetition of the term "son of" indicates Pinchas experienced a clinical death. He died but was immediately restored as a new Pinchas. The old Pinchas could not have continued to serve in the priesthood. His soul left and his body was now imbued with the souls of Nadav and Avihu, the highest souls to ever enter into this world and thereby the physical body of Pinchas and the combined souls of Nadav and Avihu, earned the reward of serving as High Priest.

Three very unique aspects are found at the very beginning of the portion. These important instruments found within the Torah were God-given for all humankind.

First we find a small *Yud* (י) in the name of Pinchas. In the universal alphabet of Hebrew, the letter Yud is the smallest letter of the 22 letters. When scribed in the name Pinchas in the beginning of this portion, the *Yud* is further reduced to almost a dot. This further reduction of size is there to indicate that the physical aspect of this letter is the nature of Pinchas.

The Bible states that God said to Moses: "Pinchas returned my anger from the children of Israel when he avenged (*nikmot*) this crime. The Hebrew word for avenged comes from the word that means zealously (*kin'ati*). Was God jealous because something took place against His will?

From the study of Kabbalah, we know that the terms: jealousy, anger, hatred, insensitivity, intolerance, are not words that can be applied to God. The God image that we understand is not discussing God, but rather the Light that emanates from God. And the Light force of God is positive; there is no negativity in God. Therefore how can the Torah talk about a revengeful God? How could it be that Pinchas satisfied this desire on behalf of God to avenge this crime? How and from where could there emerge a feeling of revenge and hatred within God? The energy force that emanates from God is nothing but a positive. Therefore we want to arouse the Godlike feature within ourselves.

It says in both the Talmud and Zohar that our soul is a part of the Light of God, however, we can take that same aspect of the Lightforce within us, and by our choice, use it as a force of construction or destruction. Like the atom—a powerful force in this universe—that we can turn into a constructive or a destructive force. The choice is ours. If we are proactive, as is described in the study of Kabbalah, and follow the spiritual rules of the universe, we are like God. If not, then we are the opposite of God, and therefore must become and remain victims, thinking that God punishes us. God never punishes.

The word *kin'a* (zealously) appears three times in this verse. Jealousy regarding what? This is a perfect example of how we cannot possibly accept the Bible as a literal document. The Zohar explains that the word *kin'a* is derived from the Hebrew word *nika* (cleanse), and it has the same numerical value as the word mikveh, which is 151. What is the relationship between jealousy and spiritual cleansing? We have learned that everything in life has a positive and negative aspect—nothing is totally good or bad. It is the same with the word *kin'a*, which has the same numerical value as the word *mikveh*. Jealousy is not an action it is something internal. The Bible wants to teach us that if we want to be Godlike, we must become proactive. We cannot experience jealousy. This is why this verse revolves around the word *kin'a*—as if God is vengeful and seeking revenge against infidels.

This is not the case. By what he did, Pinchas transformed the energy of these two individuals—the Light they revealed—to one with a positive nature. Pinchas cleansed the impurities that prevent us, within our own selves, from manifesting a Godlike nature. The physical reality of chaos and negative activity are what prevent this nature from being realized. What Pinchas did was to cleanse the entire world's total atmosphere and thereby, he removed the plague.

The Zohar says that Pinchas created a condition with his action whereby, although he knew he faced certain death, he was immediately reborn with the souls of Nadav and Avihu, the two sons of Aaron who had died, and who encompassed the entire Light of all Israel within themselves. All of us embody a certain aspect of the Light but Nadav and Avihu embody the Light of an entire nation. When Pinchas died, the moment his body separated from his soul, he was reborn with a dimension of the most Light, which is indicated by the diminution of the letter Yud.

Rav Shimon declared that the entire Torah—everything that we read and translate is coded; the letters, words, and phrases deliver a message. The word used in this portion to describe God's vengeance and anger—*kin'a*—actually refers to cleansing.

What the Zohar wants to teach us from the character of Pinchas is that if we want to be like God, we have to become proactive. We cannot have hatred inside us even for all the right reasons. This is why the word revenge or jealousy is used here. God does not seek revenge against these infidels. By his action, Pinchas transformed the negative energy of these people who caused a disaster that could have spread throughout the entire world. He turned the Light to one of a positive nature.

Pinchas took this action, knowing full well that he would invalidate the opportunity to be the high priest. Nevertheless, he was prepared to give up everything of himself so that the world would not succumb to this plague. He was reacting to the opposite of himself; he was proactive. The small Yud in the name Pinchas shows us that he thought nothing of himself. The small Yud indicates that to achieve this level of connection with the Light requires that, no matter the reason, we place into our consciousness that we are prepared to do away with our reactivity. Even if we do not care for another person, nonetheless in spite of this feeling, we do not withhold the quality of human dignity.

The letter Yud and physicality

The *Yud*, which is the first letter of the Tetragrammaton, includes everything that follows it. Just like a seed of a tree incorporates every aspect of the tree, every different level is already incorporated in that seed. The *Yud* is the smallest letter of the Hebrew Alphabet. Science has begun to learn only recently what the Zohar has been revealing for 2,000 years, which is: what is more in the physical dimension is less and what is less is more. Physical reality is but a blip on the screen. Everything of a physical nature represents an interference. In this portion, the smallest letter is further decreased in size and is presented in a smaller form than the size of most of the letters in the Torah. Before Kabbalah, I would not have known this. The Zohar makes a point to stress that this small *Yud* inside the name Pinchas, which is almost not recognizable as a letter, is there to indicate the priestly ability to penetrate beyond the physical environment. The letter in the scroll is so small we will literally have to strain our eyes to see it in the name of Pinchas.

This little *Yud* gives us the power to reduce the influence of physicality on our consciousness. One of the goals of the Kabbalah Centre is to remove the limitations of physicality. Everything in the four Kingdoms: Human, Vegetable, Animal, and Mineral (Inanimate) is governed by the limitations of physical reality. However, it is only the physical realm that has the limitations of time, space, and motion.

Pinchas and the Souls of Nadav and Avihu

The Zohar discusses the additional Hebrew letters added to the names of both Joseph and Pinchas, which are *Hei* (ה) and *Yud* (י) respectively. It further highlights the difference between them.

Joseph received the letter Hei to indicate the level of Malchut because his action of restriction was only between him and the wife of his Egyptian chief, Potiphar (Pharaoh's official and the captain of the guard).

Pinchas received a higher letter than Joseph, the *Yud*, which is the level of Chochmah, Right Column energy, corresponding to the level of the Kohen or priesthood, because his restriction was for everyone.

Pinchas received the eternal priesthood, the same title that Aaron received, even though he killed the head of the tribe of Shimon. The Zohar explains that, although he died on the inside, meaning his soul left the physical domain, at that same moment the souls of Nadav and Avihu entered into Pinchas' physical form. Therefore, his physicality did not die since his body instantly received the souls of Nadav and Avihu.

The Zohar says that even before Pinchas killed Cozbi and Zimri, he had received the eternal priesthood, and was meant to lose it when he killed them. However, God could see that Pinchas would regain his merit, and therefore Aaron remained the eternal Priest. The priesthood was also lost when Nadav and Avihu lit "strange fire" in the Tabernacle and consequently, they died. What Pinchas did was bring back the priesthood to Aaron retroactively; he became Chesed in that moment and restored Nadav and Avihu. This is why the Bible says, "the son of Elazar, the son of Aaron."

The Nature of God

The Bible says that God told Moses that Pinchas had turned His wrath away and for this reason, God would not consume the Israelites in His jealousy. As we mentioned earlier, the Lightforce of God is only positive, so what does the Bible, which is a coded message mean here? We should be in a position to perform the miracles we seek each and every day but somehow we "depend" on God, Whom we feel does not respond to our needs. From this, we learn that we need to arouse the Godlike feature within ourselves for we are all God. God told us: "I gave you the tools to act like Me, for you are Me."

Proactivity, Jealousy, and the Sons of Aaron

By the essence of this little *Yud*, Pinchas converted the Desire to Receive for the Self Alone and reduced it to almost nothing. The little *Yud* is there to teach us that what we are will last forever for it is out of the domain of the physical. It is physical in a sense, but it is not governed by the physical reality as we know it.

Pinchas took that step, fully prepared to give up everything he had, everything of himself, so that the world would not fall victim to the plague. He wanted nothing for himself. This connection requires us to be prepared to do away with our reactive nature.

Pinchas transformed the energy of these two individuals—the Light they revealed but gave to the negative side, into one of a positive nature. Pinchas cleansed the impurities that prevent us, within our own selves, from manifesting a Godlike nature. The physical reality of chaos and negative activity are what prevent this nature from being realized. What Pinchas did was to cleanse the entire world's total atmosphere, and thereby he removed the plague. This bears repeating again and again.

As the Zohar says, Pinchas created a condition with his action whereby he was immediately reborn with the souls of Nadav and Avihu, the two sons of Aaron who had died, and who also encompassed the entire Light of all Israel within themselves. All of us embrace a certain aspect of the Light but Nadav and Avihu embraced the Light of an entire nation. When Pinchas died, the moment his body separated from his soul, he was reborn with a dimension of the most Light, which is indicated by the diminution of the letter *Yud*.

The Month of Negativity

In the *Sefer Yetzirah* ("Book of Formation"), Abraham the Patriarch explains why the portion of Pinchas is always read in the month of Tammuz, the month represented by the Zodiac sign of Cancer. It is because the floodgates to the disease of cancer are open during this month. There is no other month where both negativity and positivity are so prevalent. Abraham tells us a cancer cell is a normal cell that becomes confused and then, by multiplying aimlessly, devours everything around it. This is how the disease of cancer functions.

However, our immune system can re-create balance, which is why Abraham designated this month as Cancer. Within this month there are two contrary states we can tap into. We know from our own experience that we can follow the rules of the Zohar and enter into a new reality or we can face the alternative of surrendering to the operating table and to doctors who do their best. Nevertheless the epidemic of cancer persists. We have the tools—the problem is that we are not always ready to accept the responsibility. If we allow Satan to convince us and thus do not participate in our own welfare, imminent chaos will be there instead.

12 Therefore say: Behold, I give to him My covenant of peace; 13 and it shall be to him, and to his seed after him, the covenant of an everlasting priesthood; because he was zealous for his God, and made atonement for the children of Israel."

Yud and Vav

In this section of the scroll, almost at the beginning of the portion of Pinchas, in the word "peace" (*shalom; Shin-Lamed-Vav-Mem*), letter *Vav* is required to be split. If this letter is not scribed in this way, the entire Torah Scroll is invalid. This *Vav* must contain this break. This is an exception, as the rule generally applies that if there is a letter in the Torah with a split, the entire scroll becomes invalid. Yet, here we are told there must be a split in the *Vav*. Not only does this split make the Torah valid, if the letter is not split the Torah would be invalid.

The Zohar explains that the split of the *Vav* is found at the top of the letter making the upper part into the letter *Yud*, and the bottom part into the letter *Vav*.

Why does this happen in the portion of Pinchas and in the word *shalom*? Because the word shalom means "peace" but it also refers to everything that comes without chaos. The same letters that form the word *shalom* also form the word *shalem*, which means "complete, whole." That which is whole is missing nothing. It is such a powerful word. This word *shalom* can handle the removal of all chaos.

The *Vav* in the Tetragrammaton represents Zeir Anpin—the quality of sharing. The *Yud* is the Sefirah of Chochmah, and Chochmah is the first connection of the Light and Vessel. The *Yud* represents Chochmah and the Vav of the Tetragrammaton is another extension of the Light, revealed by the process of the intervention of the Vessel.

In this instance, the *Yud* and Vav of the Tetragrammaton are both found in the one letter of the word *shalom*, which refers to that which is complete where there is no lack, no complaint, no deficit, indeed no liabilities at all. *Shalom* is whole, and that force which is whole and complete can remove all chaos. It really is this simple.

The Zohar is so profound in its revelation of the opportunity provided to us by this small space. When we come to the word *shalom* during the Torah reading on Shabbat, this is the time to tap into the Lightforce available, and bring into ourselves a state of completion, meaning make whole all the broken parts of our lives in whatever way they appear.

The split letter *Vav* in the word *shalom* gives us the opportunity to restore the *Vav* into a whole letter using our consciousness. The Bible is teaching us that, with our consciousness, we can restore anything broken, anything that causes pain and suffering. Thus we can create wholeness and contentment within ourselves. Such is its power—and this does not exist in any other portion.

The Zohar chose the portion of Pinchas to discuss each and every single aspect and part of the body in depth. This is because when we connect to this reading, we can restore and make whole all these individual parts and aspects. But first we must know that it is concealed. The Bible defines our connections to the immaterial as more real than the physical reality. There is far more that exists than just physicality in the vastness of this universe. The physical aspect of our body contains only one percent physicality—the rest is space.

The Zohar explains that we can use the opportunities in this portion to create *shalom*, wholeness, completeness. We can restore a body that may be afflicted with disease, whether we know of its presence or not. Today, the medical profession agrees that all ailments could have begun thirty years before they appear as symptoms. We do not see this because the eye cannot see. King David states in Psalms that we have eyes but do not see. Therefore, we have a great opportunity here to bridge the *Yud* and the *Vav*.

14 Now the name of the man of Israel that was slain, who was slain with the Midianite woman, was Zimri, the son of Salu, a prince of a fathers' house among the Simeonites. 15 And the name of the Midianite woman that was slain was Cozbi, the daughter of Zur; she was head of the people of a fathers' house in Midian. 16 And the Lord spoke to Moses, saying: 17 "Oppress the Midianites, and smite them; 18 for they oppress you, by their wiles, they have beguiled you in the matter of Peor, and in the matter of Cozbi, the daughter of the prince of Midian, their sister, who was slain on the day of the plague in the matter of Peor."

Oppression, Suppression, and Satan

What does the Bible mean with the words, "Oppress the Midianites"? It is to teach us that when there is a problem we do not eliminate it immediately but rather we suppress it, and then the problem appears in another form. If we eliminate one dictator, another will arise. The word *tzeror* (oppress) can also mean "bundle" or "bunch together." That is, to combine together and compress all the evil so it can then be eliminated. We must first identify our Satan and see the negative effect he has on all of our existence, meaning we must acknowledge that the ego exists, rather than the Light. When we relinquish our existence, we become a conduit, and then we can transmit Light.

What is the power of an infant? Most of us think that a baby has little intellect. Nevertheless, since the destruction of the Holy Temple, there have only been two kinds of prophets—fools and infants. Why? Because they are not bound by the limitations that we have—such as a preoccupation with how they appear in the eyes of others, how they appear to be good, or seem righteous, and so on. When we are busy trying to impress, we become blocked from the Light. We can hide all the things that are unappealing, so that no one will know or see our faults. Satan assists us with the image we want to present to others. However, Satan exacts a high price because when we choose to be impressive, we cannot be a conduit for the abundance of Light revealed nor can we be like an infant, who has no limitations. An infant shows us clearly how everything is pure. We sometimes call babies stupid because they do things we might like to do ourselves yet do not dare to because of what people might say about us. The most important quality an infant possesses is innocence. They are pure conduits of Light, for the mind is blocked from an understanding of what seems to be going on. All it takes is one small opening, and Satan is in, God forbid.

Bamidbar 26:1 And it came to pass after the plague [space in the words] that the Lord spoke to Moses and to Elazar, the son of Aaron the priest, saying: 2 "Take the sum of all the congregation of the children of Israel, from twenty years old and upward, by their fathers' houses, all that are able to go forth to war in Israel."

Space and Change

If any verse anywhere in the Torah Scroll has a space in the middle of the sentence the whole Torah becomes invalid. Yet here, in the portion of Pinchas, following the word *magefa* (plague), a space must be included and, moreover if there is no space, the Scroll is invalid. The space is required to be made up of a minimum of nine letters. There can be more letters but not less. Anything less than a space equivalent to nine letters, is not considered a space. This space removes plague—which is why it is placed here. We will not know if it works or not until we reach the point of abandoning the chaotic consciousness of the physical reality. The Tree of Life is a completely different paradigm. It is a realm of no limitation.

The paradox here shows us that everything to which we are accustomed will change. This is the reality of the Tree of Life, an entirely alternate reality—one which makes our minds think differently from the way we are accustomed. We will not know if the Tree of Life Reality exists until we reach the point of abandoning a chaotic consciousness of the physical reality. The Tree of Life is a completely different paradigm. It is a realm of no limitation.

The portion of Pinchas is for healing, and chaos is the root of all illness. Chaos brings about aggravation, nervous breakdowns, and far worse. Chaos brings about all the upsets a person can endure. When we do not go through these episodes of chaos, then we have health, which is a natural result of no chaos. This is why the portion of Pinchas is all-inclusive—it covers every conceivable situation over which the Satan has dominion. Are there infinite forms? No, whether the chaos is a missing tooth, arm or finances, the principle is the same—there is a loss, a lack.

What Cozbi and Zimri did was so negative an act that, in one moment, 24,000 people died. Pinchas stood up and slew them. His action caused the plague—which could have brought about the destruction of the entire nation of Israel—to come to an end as suddenly as it had begun. This space in the middle of the verse indicates there is something unique about Pinchas, a reason why he was so powerful.

The Zohar asks what is more important, the letters of the Scroll or the parchment? The Zohar explains the parchment, the spaces between the letters, words, and paragraphs, represent the Lightforce of God, and the letters are merely a channel. The Lightforce becomes channeled by virtue of the letters into the physical reality, and the black letters are only in a potential form until they manifest the Lightforce of God.

There are plagues in the world right now but they are unlike the bubonic plague, where suddenly thousands of people die in a matter of days. Today, people are dying of the same ailments, being poisoned by radiation or toxic substances, although not always in the same vicinity and not days apart. The Bible is here to teach us that Shabbat has the power to remove us from the possibility of the plague that moves and kills slowly.

The portion of Pinchas is about the ability and the opportunity to remove plague. We do this work in every Kabbalah Centre around the world. The word plague in this portion has white space around it because according to the Torah, the only way we can uproot a plague is with an infusion of Light—to connect the plague to an infusion of Light. Plagues are not a new condition. Rather, a plague is warfare as well as disease. Warfare does not happen when one country embarks on conquering the world, which will never happen because world tyranny is not the enemy. It is the joke Satan plays on us. The truth is, just as we must be participants in our own healing process, so too we must be the creators of our environment.

The Central Column is the immune system. There is no such thing as just Left and the Right. The Central Column is that part that we do for ourselves. There is no one out there who saves us. The entire procedure in Pinchas, that we in the Kabbalah Centre place so much emphasis on, generates this kind of energy. Tools like *VeYitnase*. We are the only ones who can remove the chaos. The physical environment, Satan's playing field, is too hostile for any aspect of established remedial process to remove chaos.

The space designated within the verse, following the word "plague," connects us to the pure white parchment. The white of the Scroll is like an injection of the Lightforce of God that provides us with the force, when plagues beset us—as unfortunately they will these days—to stop them.

Satan does a good job of making us think we do not have plagues today. Though it may seem that there is no plague killing 24,000 people at once, there are still hundreds of thousands dying each year of heart disease and cancer in the USA alone. There are pockets of people in various parts of the world who are dying of some plague—and we only understand the magnitude of this when we put all the pieces together. In our finite minds, we do not see the scope of the epidemic. Statistics say that one in every two males will succumb to prostate cancer, and that one in every three women will get breast cancer. Are we blind? Do we not see that these are all really plagues?

The space in the verse is an opportunity to separate the pain from the Light, the *Oy* (Woe) from the *Ashrei* (Praiseworthy). Even though there is chaos all around us, in the midst of confusion, the Light can shine forth—we can connect to the Tree of Life Reality.

The white aspect, the bare parchment, is the Light. The letters are the way the Light reaches us since the Light is channeled through the letters. The letters are black because they are limited vessels, limited receptacles, and are here to teach us that the plagues are the same plagues as before yet simply defined by society in many varied ways.

With the portion of Pinchas, we can tap into the awesome Light of the Creator within us—we all contain this Light. This knowledge has been concealed for millennia, although it has always been said that we are part of God. Now we have an opportunity to exercise our free will. This unique phenomenon of a space between the words reveals for us that we can tap into the awesome energy of the Lightforce of God, and thereby remove plagues from this world.

Uncertainty and Knowledge

The whole Bible is a code providing us with clues as to how we can deal with daily living. It is not a record of incidents and laws laid down at a time when the Israelites were in the wilderness.

Before the portion of Pinchas, we find the portion of Balak, which deals with the forces of Balak and Bilaam. This story is not just about two nations who waged war and attempted to annihilate the people of Israel. Instead, it teaches us about the root of problems that humanity faces always, everywhere, day in and day out. The Zohar says that the last syllable of the name Bilaam (בלעם) and the last syllable from the name Balak (בלק) form the word *am-alak* (עמלק), and *amalek* (עמלק) is the enemy of not only the Israelites but of all humankind. The word amalek has the same numerical value as the word *safek* (240), which means uncertainty and doubt. The Zohar reveals that the enemy of humanity is not a nation, or a tangible being, or a natural disaster, but rather uncertainty itself is the root of everything that can go wrong with us and for us.

The reason I feel that this particular subject is so important is because, although we hear these words often, for the most part they remain information and never become knowledge in our consciousness. The difference between information and knowledge is that knowledge is something we make use of—it becomes part of us. Whereas information is just something we did not know before. It provides the answers to some of the questions we may have raised. But for information to make a difference, to enhance our lives is another matter altogether. Therefore, no matter how many times we hear something, for information to ultimately become knowledge it depends on the level of our consciousness—in other words, where we are, and how we receive this information. If the information does not turn into knowledge, then it was a wasted experience.

Pinchas and the Plague

At the end of the portion of Balak, the two characters, Bilaam and Balak, realized they could not destroy the Israelites—the term does not refer to the people of Israel but to all people of the world—so they sent Cozbi, the most beautiful woman in Midian, with the intention of seducing Moses. She mistook Zimri, the chieftain of

144

the tribe of Shimon, for Moses and seduced him in error. The Bible says this seduction led to a breakdown in the morality of the world and Pinchas, the grandson of Aaron the High Priest, slayed Cozbi and Zimri—and this action ended the plague that up until that point had killed 24,000 people.

There is no explanation for why the plague began, nor is there a description of the nature of the plague. As always, we turn to the Zohar—because we raise our consciousness by studying its words.

> Rav Chiya began: "'This he ordained in Joseph for testimony, when he went out over the land of Egypt, I heard the language of him whom I had not known.' (Tehillim 81:6) We have learned THAT THE ANGEL taught Joseph seventy languages, AS WERE KNOWN BY PHARAOH, but also in the Holy Tongue HE WAS greater THAN PHARAOH, FOR PHARAOH DID NOT KNOW THE HOLY TONGUE. This is indicated by, 'I heard the language of him whom I had not known' FOR HE TAUGHT HIM LANGUAGES THAT HE HAD NOT KNOWN PREVIOUSLY." HE ASKS, "But, IF THIS IS SO, what is 'testimony?'" HE ANSWERS, "Come and see. When Potiphar's wife took hold of him for the reason, Joseph made himself as one who did not know her language, and so it was each day until the last time, as it is written: 'And she caught him by his garment.' (Beresheet 39:12) HE ASKS, "What is the meaning of 'she caught him'?" HE ANSWERS, "Until that time he had pretended that he did not know her language, BUT THEN SHE SAW THROUGH HIM THAT HE DID KNOW HER LANGUAGE, MEANING THAT HE UNDERSTOOD HER INTENTION. THIS IS THE MEANING OF 'SHE CAUGHT HIM'; THAT SHE CAUGHT THE TRICKERY IN HIM. 'HIS GARMENT

(beged),' IS DERIVED FROM TRICKERY *(begidah)*. And the Holy Spirit, THAT IS, MALCHUT, cried out to him, 'that they may keep you from the strange woman, from the alien woman who makes smooth her words.'" (Mishlei 7:5) HE ASKS, "What is this trying to teach us here?" AND ANSWERS, "THIS IS TEACHING US that everyone who keeps himself from such a thing AS JOSEPH DID is bound up with the Shechinah and holds on to this testimony, WHICH IS MALCHUT. And which is it? This is the *Hei* that was added to him, as it is written: 'This he ordained in Jehoseph for testimony.' Also in our section, a *Yud* was added to the name of Pinchas because he was zealous over the same matter, THE AFFAIR OF ZIMRI, FOR THE YUD HINTS AT MALCHUT."
—Zohar, Pinchas A 5:16

In the portion of Pinchas in the Zohar, Rav Chiya quotes a verse from Tehillim 81:6: "This He established in Joseph as a testimony, when he went throughout the land of Egypt, where I heard a language of him whom I had not known." This Psalm refers to Joseph, and that his greatness originated when an angel taught him the same seventy languages that were known to Pharaoh. However, Joseph knew an extra language, the Holy Tongue, which Pharaoh did not know. King David states that Joseph knew "a language of him whom I had not known." Meaning, no one knew Hebrew at that time.

This is a very difficult passage of the Zohar to understand properly. If we merely look at the words as King David put them down, it says, *edut beYehosef shemo*, which literally means, "witness to the name of Joseph." What does "witness to the name of Joseph" mean? And here the Zohar also adds that there is an additional Hei in the name of Joseph (יוֹסֵף), which is spelled Yehosef (יְהוֹסֵף).

The Zohar continues with the story of Potiphar's wife, who took a hold of Joseph to seduce him (similar to what is discussed in the portion of Balak). Joseph acted as if he did not understand what she was saying to him until the very last moment, when the Bible says she "caught him by his garment." (Genesis 39:12) What is the meaning of "she caught him"? In this instance, the Bible is not insinuating Potiphar's wife grabbed him or took hold of him. "Caught him" is an expression we use when we catch someone in a lie so to speak. The Zohar says the words "she caught him" mean she recognized that Joseph knew the language she was speaking. The Zohar explains the Hebrew word *beged* (garment) is derived from the word *begida*, which means trickery or unfaithful.

The Zohar also relates what we have just described here to the story of Pinchas. It says that, just as the Hei was added to the name of Joseph, so too, a letter Yud was added to the name of Pinchas. These additional letters seem to have some relevance to one another; they are both added to the names of people where there seems to be a violation of the laws of the universe with regard to sexual relations.

What the verse seems to indicate here is a secret regarding plagues and how to deal with them. When Pinchas impaled Cozbi and Zimri, the Bible says the plague was stayed from the children of Israel, and not that the plague ended. The Hebrew words used are, *vate'atzar hamagefa*. The root of the Hebrew word *atzira* is *otzar*, which means "curfew" not "end." The Hebrew word for "end" is *gamar*. A curfew is when the suspension of an action occurs it means that there is a temporary disruption of the norm.

When the Bible says the plague was stayed, it means there was a delay. The Zohar explains that, when the Bible does not tell us what the plague was about, this is the answer to the questions we have raised. What is the connection?

147

What is the difference between an earthquake, the bubonic plague pandemic or the AIDS virus? There is no difference—they all consume people without warning. An earthquake does not tell us when it is coming, neither does a plague tell us whom it will strike. What is the difference? The answer is there is no difference.

From a kabbalistic perspective, a plague, as is indicated in this portion, relates to uncertainty. Where does AIDS come from? What causes it? Medical science tells us that it is the breakdown of the immune system. Nonetheless, does that mean we know the source? Science describes that which can be observed and understood. If we are discussing things that we have no knowledge of or things that we cannot grasp with our five senses, it is not science.

Uncertainty and Illusion

In this portion, what is being discussed is that which can neither be seen of felt—matters that do not relate to what we can relate to. This is why Kabbalah is called mysterious, mysticism, beyond the five senses. Kabbalah deals with laws and principles that cannot be connected directly to each other; where the result/effect cannot be connected to its cause. There is no mystery in science because quantum determined the Uncertainty Principle. Why is it called Uncertainty Principle? Because if, as quantum suggests, a person eating rice in China can affect another person elsewhere in the world to pull a trigger, which is feasible and conceivable under the rules of quantum, then we live in a world of uncertainty because it is uncertain to us what motivated the individual to pull the trigger.

We can no longer ascribe the cause to be that the man who pulled the trigger had a fight with his wife or to the fact that he became temporarily insane or that maybe there is something wrong with him genetically and that in his family are conditions that could be a related reason.

We have been programmed, and maybe rightfully so, to relate cause to effect in the area of our understanding. The moment that we are forced into a situation where we can no longer connect or relate effect to the cause because the cause is somewhere we cannot see, we are in a dilemma. We cannot see that the fellow in China who is eating rice is affecting me as I stand here today, which is incidentally conceivable.

How is it conceivable? This no longer needs to be answered as there is no requirement to find a connection once we apply the Uncertainty Principle. The Bible does not subscribe to this way of thinking and it is the lesson of the story of Pinchas. This is why it begins by quoting the two names Bilaam and Balak. The Zohar says that by examining these two names we are provided with a clue as to the cause, which is essentially the cause for every dilemma, every disruption in our lives. As mentioned previously, the word *amalek* is created by joining together the last syllable of each of these two names. And the meaning of *amalek* is "doubt" and "uncertainty."

Uncertainty is the enemy of humankind. Plagues are not the enemy of humankind; the enemy is that which brings about plagues. What brought about these plagues? Uncertainty. Uncertainty is the root of every conceivable chaos.

What brings about earthquakes? Uncertainty. Do we know when an earthquake will strike? No. Do we know where it will strike? No. Do we know whom it will strike? No. Will everyone become victims? No, there will always be survivors and there will be victims.

Everything in our lives is shrouded by that one word, uncertainty. The Bible wants to draw us into a level of consciousness—which

149

is enlightenment—to understand that everything that goes wrong in this world can be related to the idea of uncertainty. Therefore, uncertainty is the cause.

How is uncertainty the cause? Uncertainty only deals with this physical realm of existence, which Kabbalah refers to as the realm of the Tree of Knowledge Good and Evil. It is referred to as Good and Evil because it is the realm where today things are good for us; tomorrow things are not so good; the following day may be good and the next not so good. For the most part, we exist in this realm. The way we live and behave is always with a consciousness of uncertainty.

However, the objective of the Zohar and the Bible is not to simply show us that uncertainty is the way we live, rather the objective is to have us awaken to the question: How can we remove ourselves from this uncertainty?

Once we remove ourselves from uncertainty, we find we are in the *Etz haChaim*, the Tree of Life Reality where there is no admixture of good and evil, there is only good. In certainty, there is no evil. Evil only exists in uncertainty.

This idea of certainty the Zohar presents to us is not an easy consciousness to achieve, though it is simple enough to understand. As we react and interact with this world, it is difficult not to fall into uncertainty because it is unknown what tomorrow will bring.

The moment we are faced with daily existence outside this room, we are confronted. The moment we have a problem or we meet up with a person and there is a difference of opinion, not an argument—just two people who do not completely agree with each other—the mere fact that we meet up with another person in this world, we will be confronted with an idea that is not completely in accord with our own. And this will immediately have its effect on us and with that we are in the realm of uncertainty.

We may defend our position that we feel it is absolutely correct, thinking that what the other person thinks is not correct. The mere fact that we live in this world means we will meet up with the people, situations, conditions, that will lead us to uncertainty.

Applying the idea that there is another realm known as the *Etz haChaim* (Tree of Life Reality) is one of the most difficult conditions and situations we face. This is why there is a Bible with laws and principles. The fact we achieve a consciousness that the whole physical world, as we observe it, is of an uncertain nature, was declared the first day of Creation as night and day, knowing by and of itself does not lead a person into the world of *Etz haChaim*, the World of Certainty. To connect with the World of Certainty requires effort, study, performance, meditation.

For us, at least for today, our first step is to achieve a consciousness, a constant awareness that we live in a world of uncertainty. If we do not achieve an awareness that the consciousness of uncertainty prevails in this dimension of existence, then we will never seek another realm. We may understand what the Zohar says in theory, yet not relate the theory with daily practice. Science states the physical world is uncertainty to the extent that whatever we determine in our consciousness as existing or not existing is created by our consciousness because there is nothing more than consciousness.

Yet if a person has cancer, they cannot declare to the cancer, "you do not exist," and because of this declaration, the disease does not exist. The problem is in the practice of the theory. This will remain a problem as long as the physical consciousness of our body has dominion over every decision we make. It is very difficult to leave the consciousness of the physical world by declaring to it, you do not exist.

Even if science, the Zohar, and the Bible tell us that this world is a world of illusion that does not exist, a moment later, after learning and even understanding this, we may feel hungry and then not hungry. How can it be that the situation of being hungry can disappear in a moment? Is it because we ate? Maybe. On the other hand, maybe the hunger could disappear without eating, by simply concentrating on how we are filling our body with food. Our hunger lies in the fact that we have already determined in our consciousness that if we do not eat, the body will remain hungry and it will have a gnawing effect upon us. With this consciousness, a person can even die if they do not eat. Yet there have been cases where people do not eat or drink and live. Moses did not eat or drink for 40 days.

Since we are subject to the physical rules, the theory does not always conform to the physical events. For example, we have an appointment. We have to fly there. The plane is delayed for six hours. We miss the appointment. As long as we are in this physical world, we have to deal with it. That is why we are here.

Nevertheless, as we deal with it, we have to have an awakened consciousness that what we are dealing with is an illusion. This is the ultimate objective and is required to achieve a stay of a plague, the stay of an earthquake—that will always exist in the world of Tree of Knowledge, the world of our existence.

Knowing that this realm is an illusion is so important because uncertainty is the root. If a person never has to think twice that something may go wrong, then they are in the realm of *Etz haChaim*, the Tree of Life Reality and *not* in the World of Good and Evil, which is a world of uncertainty where things will be good today and bad tomorrow.

Thus the first objective is to understand that this world is illusionary as is established by the Bible and by science. This is the most difficult task ahead of us. Uncertainty is being in the world of illusion.

Joseph and Pinchas

The Zohar makes a connection between Joseph and Pinchas. Superficially, it seems they have two things in common: they both deal with sexual energy and they both have a letter inserted into their name.

Joseph has the letter *Hei* (ה) inserted into his name to indicate that he left the world of uncertainty. And Pinchas has the *Yud* (י) added to his name, which removed him forever from the World of Illusion, a world from which it is so difficult to extricate ourselves.

In Joseph's case, the story only involved the wife of Potifar, who made an attempt to seduce him. In the case of Pinchas, it was the seduction of the entire people of Israel. Therefore, while they both deal with the same matter, nevertheless there is a difference. This is the reason for the difference in the letters.

Another similarity between Joseph and Pinchas is that the moment Joseph refused the wife of Potifar, he received the designation, *haTzadik* (the Righteous). He was not referred to as Yosef haTzadik (Joseph the Righteous) prior to his action of refusing to be seduced.

The Bible also tells us that when Pinchas performed the action of slaying the two people (*Lechen emor hineni noten lo et beriti shalom*) he earned and became in control of the High Priesthood forever, for all generations.

For both Joseph and Pinchas, their realm changed. Pinchas changed dimension to the extent that he reincarnated. His was the first account of a clinical death. According to the stipulation of the law, a Priest who murders, justifiable as it might have been becomes invalid to serve the Priesthood. Therefore, the Zohar asks how Pinchas could be permitted to perform the service of the Priesthood and be instilled with the consciousness of the High Priesthood forever because of this act.

The Zohar concludes that what we observe here is a clinical death. When the entire tribe of 147,000 people descended upon Pinchas to kill him, Pinchas literally died of fright. Moreover, at that very instant, he was reincarnated with the souls of the two sons of Aaron, Nadav and Avihu—his uncles. They had previously died and now incarnated into the physical body of Pinchas, which did not undergo any changes. It is supernatural for a body that dies not to undergo any change.

The reason we concentrate on the small Yud, inserted into the name Pinchas, when we read the Torah is that in doing so we exit the realm of the norm and enter into the realm of the supernatural. The letters of the Torah are all written the same size. Not only is there an injection of a Yud, which is not supposed to be there, it is a tiny Yud; a smaller, infinitesimal font size, different from the size of all the other letters. It is out of the norm. It is not just a Yud but also a tiny one.

Why is this here? To teach us that the norm is what we are confronted with in our everyday reality. The norm is every aspect of physical existence. As long as we live within the norm, we have no ability to move out of the physical reality and its consequences.

However the minute we go out of the norm or at least make an attempt to go out of the norm, there is another world, another nature waiting for us—the dimension of Pinchas and Joseph. Joseph became the Chariot for the Sefirah of Yesod, a Chariot of the World of the Tree of Life. The Sefirah of Yesod is in the realm of Zeir Anpin, which is the reality of *Etz haChaim*.

The instant Joseph resisted the wife of Potifar—and it was just an instant of restriction—he flipped into another dimension and became the controller of all the food supply of the world. His was what seemed to be an awful story of being separated from a father who loved him and whom he loved, then being sold into slavery by his brothers who perhaps wanted to kill him, to achieving the realm of the Tree of Life only to be locked up in a dungeon for two more years. This story defines the physical realm of existence, where one day is good the next day bad. Nonetheless, Joseph flipped it and went into another reality. The *Hei* that is inserted into Joseph's name flips him into another dimension in warp time. What does the *Hei* do? The *Hei* is the letter that was inserted in Abram's name. His name was first Abram and then it became Abraham. With the *Hei*, Abram was altered physically from a being who lived within the laws of nature and could never bear children to Avraham who flipped dimensions and fathered nations.

Pinchas too flipped existence, as he was not destined to be the High Priest. Yet he entered into another level and was incarnated with two of the highest souls that had ever inhabited this physical universe—Nadav and Avihu, whom the Zohar describes as souls who were beyond the physical reality, and he became the High Priest for eternity. In the name Pinchas, the *Yud*, the smallest letter in the Hebrew alphabet, is condensed even further to a smaller form.

In a matter of moments, one can go from one dimension into another dimension. We can all experience moving from one dimension into another.

The plague was stayed

Vate'atzar hamagefa means "and the plague was stayed." Why does it say it was stayed? Because while we can flip ourselves into another reality, the physical realm with a consciousness of uncertainty does not disappear, it does not come to an end. Only *Mashiach* (Messiah) means the end of uncertainty. It is not referring to a man arriving on a donkey, and all will be blissful. Uncertainty is one word that can open up such vistas. Therefore, the verse says *vate'atzar hamagefa*.

Although Pinchas underwent a clinical death, and with his newfound consciousness could remove everyone with him, nonetheless the realm of physical reality, where there are plagues of uncertainty, remained. The plague did not end. It was only stayed until the next plague of uncertainty. I like the word "stayed." We think the word "stayed" means that we have pushed it away. On the contrary. The idea that we face this physical reality stays—it remains. We, however with our consciousness can lift out of it.

Clinical Death

With regard to clinical death and reincarnation, I would like to mention what the Rav Isaac Luria (the Ari) tells us. Every time we move residences, we undergo an incarnation. It is like we undergo a clinical death. It is an opportunity to be new. Who wants to move or likes to move? No one likes to move. Everyone likes to stay in the same place, but if forced to move from one place to another, we actually undergo an incarnation or a clinical death.

Certainty

Uncertainty means we are unsure and is a belief in pure chance. What is chance? Is it really uncertainty? For example, in the case of a coin toss, the coin will land on heads or tails. Is this already known? Of course. It will land on either heads or tails. Do we think it will change? It will not change. Nonetheless, for us it is still chance because we have to guess. Is it really a head or tail? Or is it an illusion to us whether it is a head or tail? It is an illusion because it is not going to change by whatever we do; it is already established. Everything has already been established. Everything is certain but we inject a consciousness of uncertainty into whether it was a head or tail.

3 And Moses and Elazar, the priest, spoke with them in the plains of Moab by the Jordan at Jericho, saying: 4 "Take the sum of the people, from twenty years old and upward, as the Lord commanded Moses and the children of Israel, that came forth out of the land of Egypt." 5 Reuben, the first-born of Israel: the sons of Reuben: of Hanoch, the family of the Hanochites; of Pallu, the family of the Palluites; 6 of Hezron, the family of the Hezronites; of Carmi, the family of the Carmites. 7 These are the families of the Reubenites; and they that were numbered of them were forty-three thousand, seven hundred and thirty. 8 And the sons of Pallu: Eliab. 9 And the sons of Eliab: Nemuel, and Dathan, and Abiram. These are that Dathan and Abiram, the elect of the congregation, who contended against Moses and against Aaron in the company of Korach, when they contended against the Lord; 10 and the earth opened her mouth, and swallowed them up together with Korach, when that company died; what time the fire devoured two hundred and fifty men, and they became a sign. 11 Nevertheless the sons of Korach did not die. 12 The sons of Simeon after their families: of Nemuel, the family of the Nemuelites; of Jamin, the family of the Jaminites; of Jachin, the family of the Jachinites; 13 of Zerah, the family of the Zerahites; of Shaul, the family of the Shaulites. 14 These are the families of the Simeonites, twenty-two thousand, two hundred. 15 The sons of Gad

after their families: of Zephon, the family of the Zephonites; of Haggi, the family of the Haggites; of Shuni, the family of the Shunites; 16 of Ozni, the family of the Oznites; of Eri, the family of the Erites; 17 of Arod, the family of the Arodites; of Areli, the family of the Arelites. 18 These are the families of the sons of Gad according to those that were numbered of them, forty thousand, five hundred. 19 The sons of Judah: Er and Onan; and Er and Onan died in the land of Canaan. 20 And the sons of Judah after their families were: of Shelah, the family of the Shelanites; of Perez, the family of the Perezites; of Zerah, the family of the Zerahites. 21 And the sons of Perez were: of Hezron, the family of the Hezronites; of Hamul, the family of the Hamulites. 22 These are the families of Judah according to those that were numbered of them, seventy-six thousand, five hundred. 23 The sons of Issaschar after their families: of Tola, the family of the Tolaites; of Puvah, the family of the Punites; 24 of Jashub, the family of the Jashubites; of Shimron, the family of the Shimronites. 25 These are the families of Issaschar according to those that were numbered of them, sixty-four thousand, three hundred. 26 The sons of Zebulun after their families: of Sered, the family of the Seredites; of Elon, the family of the Elonites; of Jahleel, the family of the Jahleelites. 27 These are the families of the Zebulunites according to those that were numbered of them, sixty thousand, five hundred. 28 The sons of Joseph after their families: Manasseh and Ephraim. 29 The sons of Manasseh: of Machir, the family of the Machirites, and Machir begot Gilead; of Gilead, the family of the Gileadites. 30 These are the sons of Gilead: of Iezer, the family of the Iezerites; of Helek, the family of the Helekites; 31 and of Asriel, the family of the Asrielites; and of Shechem, the family of the Shechemites; 32 and of Shemida, the family of the Shemidaites; and of Hepher, the family of the Hepherites. 33 And Zelophehad the son of Hepher had no sons, but daughters; and the names of the daughters of Zelophehad were Mahlah, and Noah, Hoglah, Milcah, and Tirzah. 34 These are the families of Manasseh; and they that were numbered of them were fifty-two thousand, seven hundred. 35 These are the sons of Ephraim after their families: of Shuthelah, the family of the Shuthelahites; of Becher, the family of the Becherites; of Tahan, the family of the Tahanites. 36 And these are the sons of Shuthelah: of Eran, the family of the Eranites. 37 These are the families of the sons of Ephraim according to those that were numbered of them, thirty-two thousand, five hundred. These are the sons of Joseph after their families. 38 The sons of Benjamin after their families: of Bela, the family of the Belaites; of Ashbel, the family of the Ashbelites; of Ahiram, the family of the Ahiramites; 39 of Shefufam, the family of the Shufamites; of Hupham, the family of the Huphamites. 40 And the sons of Bela were Ard and Naaman; of Ard, the family of the Ardites; of Naaman, the family of the Naamites. 41 These are the sons of Benjamin after their families; and they that were numbered of them were forty-five thousand, six hundred. 42 These are the sons of Dan after their families: of Shuham, the family of the Shuhamites. These are the families of Dan after their families. 43 All the families of the Shuhamites, according to those that were numbered of them, were sixty-four thousand, four hundred. 44 The sons of Asher after their families: of Imnah, the family of the Imnites; of Ishvi, the family of the Ishvites; of Beriah, the family of the Beriites. 45 Of the sons of Beriah: of Heber, the family of the Heberites; of Malchiel, the family of the Malchielites. 46 And the name of the daughter of Asher was Serah. 47 These are the families of the sons of Asher according to those that were numbered of them, fifty-three thousand, four hundred. 48 The sons of Naphtali after their families: of Jahzeel, the family of the Jahzeelites; of Guni, the family of the Gunites; 49 of Jezer, the family of the Jezerites; of Shillem, the family of the Shillemites. 50 These are the families of Naphtali according to their families; and they that were numbered of them were forty-five thousand, four hundred. 51 These are they that were numbered of the children of Israel, six hundred and one thousand, seven hundred and thirty. 52 And the Lord spoke to Moses, saying: 53 "The land shall be

divided to you for an inheritance according to the number of names. 54 To those with more you shall give more inheritance, and to the fewer you shall give less inheritance; to each one according to those that were numbered of it shall its inheritance be given. 55 But the land shall be divided by lot; according to the names of the tribes of their fathers they shall inherit. 56 According to the lot shall their inheritance be divided between the more and the fewer."

Controlling the Zodiac

In this section, we have an opportunity to control the twelve signs of the zodiac. Each sign of the zodiac has beneficence in its influence and it also has chaos accompanied with a liability. For example, a Taurus is stubborn. Yet, in the Tree of Life Reality, this liability does not exist. We have the reading of the portion of Pinchas on Shabbat to remove the chaos that accompanies the signs of the zodiac, to remove their negative influences.

When we understand what the portion of Pinchas is really about, we understand God's compassion for us. This section provides us with the ability to control astrological influences. There are a few other places in the Bible where we are given this opportunity but there is something unique here because it embraces all the people— the counting of all the people in each tribe. For us, this means having the ability to control the next twelve months, as well as managing the negative energies also channeled through the months. How do we know this? It is in the name of the sign. Why cancer? It is to inform us that the disease of cancer is channeled into the world in this month represented by the zodiac sign of Cancer, and therefore we are told, be happy in this month. Happy people do not react and are therefore not vulnerable to cancer. This portion is always read in this month, always. While cancer is one of many illnesses that cause pain and suffering, nevertheless it is one of the most dreaded diseases. Therefore, with this portion, the twelve signs of the zodiac assist us in making life a little easier.

57 And these are they that were numbered of the Levites after their families: of Gershon, the family of the Gershonites; of Kohath, the family of the Kohathites; of Merari, the family of the Merarites. 58 These are the families of Levi: the family of the Libnites, the family of the Hebronites, the family of the Mahlites, the family of the Mushites, the family of the Korahites. And Kohath begot Amram. 59 And the name of Amram's wife was Jochebed, the daughter of Levi, who was born to Levi in Egypt; and she bore unto Amram, Aaron and Moses, and Miriam their sister. 60 And to Aaron were born Nadav and Avihu, Elazar and Ithamar. 61 And Nadav and Avihu died, when they offered strange fire before the Lord. 62 And they that were numbered of them were twenty-three thousand, every male from a month old and upward; for they were not numbered among the children of Israel, because there was no inheritance given them among the children of Israel. 63 These are they that were numbered by Moses and Elazar, the priest, who numbered the children of Israel in the plains of Moab by the Jordan at Jericho. 64 But among these there was not a man of them that were numbered by Moses and Aaron, the priest, who numbered the children of Israel in the wilderness of Sinai. 65 For the Lord had said of them: "They shall surely die in the wilderness." And there was not left a man of them, except Caleb, the son of Jephunneh, and Joshua, the son of Nun.

Bamidbar 27:1 Then drew near the daughters of Zelophehad, the son of Hepher, the son of Gilead, the son of Machir, the son of Manasseh, of the families of Manasseh, the son of Joseph; and these are the names of his daughters: Mahlah, Noah, and Hoglah, and Milcah, and Tirzah. 2 And they stood before Moses, and before Elazar the priest, and before the princes and all the congregation, at the door of the Tent of Meeting, saying: 3 "Our father died in the wilderness, and he was not among the company of them that gathered themselves together against the Lord in the company of Korach, but he died for his own sin; and he had no sons. 4 Why should the name of our father be done away from among his family, because he had no son? Give to us a possession among the brethren of our father." 5 And Moses brought their cause before the Lord.

Restoration

There are five final letters in the Hebrew alphabet—*Mem*, *Nun*, *Tzadi*, *Pei* and *Chaf* (מנצפ״ך). These five of the 22 letters take on another structure and characteristic when they appear as the last letter of a word. They are known as *MaNTzePaCh*, and comprise all the energy of the Resurrection of the Dead, the entire restoration, and the ability to retrieve all that has vanished from before our very eyes, which is an illusion. These letters have the power to restore life and all it requires is our absolute certainty.

Oversized letters in the Torah are a connection to Binah. In Bamidbar 27:5, there is a large final letter Nun (נ) in the word *mishpatan*, which means "judgment." *Mishpatan* also means "their court case." The Zohar says the enlarged Nun is to create for us a connection to the level of Binah, and all the power to restore health that has disappeared.

In the Ashrei, a Psalm of King David, there is no letter Nun—because Nun is the first letter of the word *nefila*, which means "falling"; the kind of falling a person experiences when one falls from health, or from security, and so on. With this reading, we have the opportunity to tap into the energy of Binah—the Tree of Life consciousness—and we can learn to channel the Light to protect us from falling into the illusions of uncertainty and chaos, and instead connect to an energy of restoration and rejuvenation.

6 And the Lord spoke to Moses, saying: 7 "The daughters of Zelophehad speak right: you shall surely give them a possession of an inheritance among their father's brethren; and you shall cause the inheritance of their father to pass to them. 8 And you shall speak to the children of Israel, saying: If a man dies, and has no son, then you shall cause his inheritance to pass to his daughter. 9 And if he have no daughter, then you shall give his inheritance to his brethren. 10 And if he have no brethren, then you shall give his inheritance to his father's brethren. 11 And if his father have no brethren, then you shall give his inheritance to his kinsman that is next to him of his family, and he shall possess it. And it shall be to the children of Israel a statute of judgment, as the Lord commanded Moses."

To Divide

There are 168 verses in this portion, which are equal to the sum of the numerical value of the letters in the word *lechalek*, which means both "to divide" and "to share." It is no coincidence the sages divided the portions in such a way that the verses of the portion of Pinchas would correspond to the word that means, "to divide." When an individual is with the Light, and shares it, *mechalek*, they are a conduit, therefore all that enters them from Above is emitted Below, and there is no dispute over what belongs to whom. Everything is shared because it is just passing through, and thus the conduit is always full. Where do we see the power of sharing, of *lechalek*? We see it with the daughters of Tzelophehad. As their father did not have a son, they had a question regarding their inheritance in the land of Israel.

What is an inheritance? A father works so that others will benefit and, as such, the father is a conduit or custodian. Everything accrues to him, not for himself, but for the generations that follow him. Why does an inheritance go specifically to the sons? Because a son, the male aspect, is the continuation of the revelation of the Light—while a daughter, the female aspect, is the manifestation of the Light. Therefore, the one who receives the inheritance is the one who is a conduit for continuing to draw the Light.

The word *chelek*, which means "a portion," is not the same as "sharing" because as soon as a person thinks about "their share," they are already consumed by the Desire to Receive for Oneself Alone. This is not how a conduit works. If an individual behaves in a giving way, then they are detached from their ego, from their own hardships, because they are now only a conduit for the Light.

Rav Isaac Luria explains that what the daughters of Tzelophehad wanted to say was that, although they were daughters, their inheritance is in the land of Israel, which is Malchut. Therefore the inheritance does not have to go to a male—Zeir Anpin, the one who inherits. Rather, in this case, because it will be revealed as an inheritance of Malchut, and the daughters reveal the energy of Malchut, there was no need for a continuation of Zeir Anpin. The dispute is about the land, which is Malchut, and they are Malchut. This is why Moses agreed that, in this case, they should receive a portion of the land.

12 And the Lord said to Moses: "Go up into this mountain of Abarim, and behold the land which I have given to the children of Israel. 13 And when you have seen it, you shall also be gathered to your people, as Aaron your brother was gathered; 14 because you rebelled against My Commandment in the wilderness of Zin, in the strife of the congregation, to sanctify Me at the waters before their eyes." These are the waters of Meribath-Kadesh in the wilderness of Zin. 15 And Moses spoke to the Lord, saying: 16 "Let the Lord, the God of the spirits of all flesh, set a man over the congregation, 17 who may go out before them, and who may come in before them, and who may lead them out, and who may bring them in; that the congregation of the Lord be not as sheep which have no shepherd." 18 And the Lord said to Moses: "Take Joshua, the son of Nun, a man in whom is spirit, and lay your hand upon him; 19 and set him before Elazar, the priest, and before all the congregation; and give him a charge in their sight. 20 And you shall put of your honor upon him, that all the congregation of the children of Israel may hearken. 21 And he shall stand before Elazar the priest, who shall inquire for him by the judgment of the Urim before the Lord; at his word shall they go out, and at his word they shall come in, both he, and all the children of Israel with him, even all the congregation." 22 And Moses did as the Lord commanded him; and he took Joshua, and set him before

Elazar the priest, and before all the congregation. 23 And he laid his hands upon him, and gave him a charge, as the Lord spoke by the hand of Moses.

Bamidbar 28:1 And the Lord spoke to Moses, saying: 2 "Command the children of Israel, and say to them: My food which is presented to Me for offerings made by fire, of a sweet savor to Me, shall you observe to offer to Me in its due season. 3 And you shall say to them: This is the offering made by fire which you shall bring to the Lord: he-lambs of the first year without blemish, two day-by-day, for a continual burnt-offering. 4 The one lamb you shall offer in the morning, and the other lamb you shall offer at dusk; 5 and one-tenth of an ephah of fine flour for a grain offering, mingled with one quarter of a hin of beaten oil. 6 It is a continual burnt offering, which was offered in Mount Sinai, for a sweet savor, an offering made by fire to the Lord. 7 And the drink offering shall be one-quarter of a hin for the one lamb; in the holy place you shall pour out a drink offering of strong drink to the Lord. 8 And the other lamb you shall present at dusk; as the grain offering of the morning, and as the drink offering thereof, you shall present it, an offering made by fire, of a sweet savor to the Lord. 9 And on the Sabbath day two he-lambs of the first year without blemish, and two-tenths of an ephah of fine flour for a grain offering, mingled with oil, and the drink offering thereof.

10 This is the burnt offering of every Sabbath, beside the continual burnt offering, and the drink offering thereof.

The Meaning and Nature of Shabbat

While the biblical portion of Pinchas primarily discusses the holidays, in particular, and some other issues, the Zohar regarding Pinchas deals with almost every aspect of life one can possibly conceive. It is strange how the Bible seems to be dealing with select subjects, while the Zohar delves into medicine, the cosmos, the holidays, zoology—everything.

In addition, there is the subject of Shabbat, which has become completely corrupted to an extent that it has, in effect, become solely viewed through the lens of religiosity. From a kabbalistic point of view, this aura of religiosity does not resonate with ideas possessed by most of humanity. The Sabbath, Shabbat, is unlike the other holidays that only come once a year. Shabbat, from a purely religious point of view, is something we have to observe once a week. In other words, it does not give us any breathing space, unlike the holidays, which only come once a year.

The phrase *shomer Shabbat* has been corrupted to mean, "observe or keep the Shabbat," when in fact the word *shomer* actually means "to watch." From a kabbalistic point of view, we always adhere to the word of the Bible, and in this regard, at the Kabbalah Centres we are fundamentalists. We will not change the meaning of a particular word because it suits the interpretation of a particular passage. I have always felt the discussion in reference to Shabbat a very difficult subject to approach but I believe the time has come for a meaningful interpretation.

To summarize in essence, for what Shabbat concerns, we turn to the Zohar, which will raise our level of consciousness so that what we are about to discuss can be comprehended on a higher level of consciousness. This is the immense power of the Zohar. It is instantaneous. As a society we seek instant relief, instant medication, instant everything, and the Zohar is one of the remedies of which I strongly urge everyone to partake. In fact, I think the Zohar is probably the only thing in this world that provides instant, temporary, and also permanent, relief from our many woes.

The Zohar says that those who have no idea what the Bible truly concerns will always claim that children, longevity, and the provision of sustenance do not depend on the merit of the individual, but are completely dependent upon *mazal*, the influence of the signs of the zodiac. They believe it is utterly out of our control, and completely depends on the position of the planets at the time of a person's birth.

The Zohar says Abraham the patriarch, who was probably the first known astrologer and is the author of the *Sefer Yetzirah* ("Book of Formation"), saw in his mazal, his astrological chart, that he would not have a son. And God took him outside to observe the stars. The Zohar explains that God told Abraham to remove himself, to leave behind the cosmic influences of his astrological chart, and raise himself *above* the stars. God said, "Look to the Heaven and count the stars. So shall be your children." (Beresheet 15:5)

We must delve more deeply into this idea, and seek a metaphysical explanation. Before the Revelation at Mount Sinai, every creature of the Four Kingdoms—Human, Animal, Vegetable, and Inanimate—depended completely upon the signs of the zodiac and the planets. At one time, the number of children one would have, how much money one would earn, how long an individual would live, all of it depended completely on the cosmos. Potentially, with the Revelation of the Bible on Mount Sinai, everyone was exempt from subjection to the rules and manipulations of the cosmos. We have learned from Abraham that humanity is no longer subject to these cosmic influences.

Rav Shimon has a very metaphysical and concealed way of explaining why the Revelation dealt with the changing of *mazal*. The Zohar uses the phrase "one who deals with the Bible" to describe people who have the ability to change their *mazal*. The Zohar does not say, "One who learns the Bible", but instead uses the word *esek*, meaning "deals" with the Torah. The word *esek* in this case means "deals" as in a business venture. The Zohar explains that those who do not treat the Bible in this way cannot achieve the level of consciousness by which they can become rulers over their own destiny—they will always be subject to what has been preordained.

The Zohar says that before the Revelation, the Israelites were not obligated to perform the Precepts because they could not touch and connect to the cosmos. "Obligated" is not a word we use in Kabbalah; nonetheless, this is the way it appears here. However, with the Revelation, they were then obligated to comply with the Precepts, and were then removed from the influence of the cosmos. What does Revelation have to do with the Precepts? The answer is this. When the Revelation took place, the energy the children of Israel received on Mount Sinai placed them at a higher level of consciousness. The Precepts are merely channels to bring the Israelites to the level of consciousness by which they would then be overseers of the planets and the stars. They would become the regulator of planets, rather than be regulated by them.

From this emerges the idea that there is both free will and predetermination or destiny. Both are possible, it depends on where we place ourselves. The Revelation on Mount Sinai gave the Israelites then, and it gives us now, the opportunity to raise ourselves above the astral influences. If we do not know how to raise ourselves above stars, then we shall be subjected to their influence in every respect—and our entire lives will be preordained. After the Revelation at Sinai, it was apparent that if one performed the Precepts of the Bible, one would have achieved a high level of consciousness.

According to the Zohar, the people of the world did not have free will prior to the Revelation—with the exception of those Chariots, Abraham, Isaac, Jacob, Moses and Aaron. Both the Midrash and the Talmud state that the Chariots, meaning all of the patriarchs, observed the Precepts of the Bible before it was given to the Israelites on Mount Sinai. They were not obligated to perform them, yet they were connected to the Bible because they were Chariots. They naturally had an elevated awareness.

During the time of Noah, there were seven Noahide Precepts, and people had the free will to perform or connect to these seven Precepts or not to connect. These seven Precepts were sufficient for them to achieve a higher level of consciousness; one that would permit them free will since their level of consciousness was already of a higher nature. However, there was the necessity of an additional 606 Precepts at the time of the Revelation of Mount Sinai because all the *klipot* from the fall of Adam came down and were revealed at the time of the Exodus. These souls existed at the time of the Deluge, and at the time of the Tower of Babel. However, they were not as powerfully evil as the *erev rav* of the exodus.

Therefore, to understand Shabbat, we shall discuss the section of the Ten Utterances in Shemot, Chapter 20, where it says, "Remember the Sabbath day, to keep it holy. You shall work six days of the week, and on the Seventh Day you shall rest, because on the Seventh Day the Lord rested. Six days He worked, but on the Seventh Day He rested. Therefore, He blessed this day and He made it holy. Because He rested, He made it holy."

The first discrepancy we find is the idea that God rested on the Seventh Day. In another section of the Bible, it says, "And on the Seventh Day, the Lord finished His work." (Beresheet 2:2) Here, the Bible does not say that on the Sixth Day He finished His work. It says, "He finished His work on the Seventh Day, and He rested on the Seventh Day." There seems to be a contradiction. God either finished His work on the Seventh Day, which means then He obviously did not rest that day, or else He finished His work on the Sixth Day, and on the Seventh Day He rested. Did God rest because He got tired? We can easily understand why God became fatigued creating universes; Heaven and Earth would require a great deal of effort.

There have been other poor explanations given of the Shabbat. To quote but one: "Everyone needs a rest because God rested on the Seventh Day." This was seemingly indicative that we cannot keep going—we cannot be workaholics. We must rest on at least one day of the week.

What does it mean to work? Is our work the same kind of work the Lord performed six days of the week? Why can we not rest on the third or fourth day of the week? I would claim I work one day of the week—and that is on Shabbat. I rest six days of the week. Shabbat is so exhausting that it permits me to take a vacation for the other six days of the week. Would this mean I am completely in conflict with what it says here—six days the Lord worked, and on the Seventh Day he rested?

Describing each day of Creation, the Bible says, there was night and then there was day—with the exception of the day of Shabbat. Instead, in the translation of Beresheet 2:3, it says, "And the Lord blessed the Seventh Day and made it holy." This is followed by the words, *Vayishbot bayom hashvi'i*, translated as "and He rested on the Seventh Day." However, if you know Hebrew, the word *vayishbot* comes from the word *shvita*, which means "strike." We might even be under the misconception that perhaps God went on strike on the Seventh Day. But concerning the Ten Utterances, the Bible says, "For in the six days the Lord made Heaven and Earth, the sea and all that is in them, and He rested on the Seventh Day." (Shemot 20:11) The word used here for "and He rested" is *vayanach* and not *vayishbot*. In Hebrew, the word for "rest" is *nach*. Why, in the Ten Utterances, does the Bible not repeat the same suggestion of resting as it does in the section on the creation of the Seventh Day—where it says, *vayishbot bayom hashvi'i*?

We might raise the question, if Shabbat is in essence a day when one should rest, what constitutes rest? I have not found any explanation of rest to mean literally a day of refraining from work. There is a Precept of Shabbat that, if one has the air conditioning running in the home with a temperature outside of 110 degrees and someone should accidentally flip the switch to the off position, no one is permitted to reset the operation of an air conditioner. However, if there are many guests in the home, and there is a lot of serving to be done, we may wash the dishes—there is nothing wrong with that. How do we reconcile the fact that even a waiter is permitted to perform his duties on Shabbat, yet we are not permitted to flip a simple switch?

The Bible says, "God blessed this day," but what does this mean? Why would He want to bless this day more than any other day? Why should this day be blessed and not the first or second day? Were all the days of Creation not of a phenomenal nature in producing something that never existed before? There were no Heavens, there was no Earth, there were no stars, no animals, no man or woman. These were days that God should have blessed, yet the day that God does not perform any task, or any form of work, is the day He decided to bless and make holy.

It is known that ninety percent of people who are actively working would rather be doing something else. Yet for financial reasons, they persist and remain where they are. They have to work because, without working, how else can they make a living. People work because it is what they know best—or because this toil is the means by which they can exact the greatest amount of remuneration.

The Zohar gives a definition of what work is and also provides us with an interpretation of what is meant by *vayehi erev vayehi boker*, "there was evening and there was morning." (Beresheet 1:5) The word *erev* (evening) according to the Zohar, refers to negativity, Left Column, and the word *boker* (morning) refers to positivity, Right Column. "And God called the light as day, and to the darkness as night. And therefore there was day and night." (Beresheet 1:5) Yet the sun and the moon were only created on the Fourth Day. How is that so? The answer is simple enough: we are to treat the words *erev* and *boker*, not as evening and morning, but rather as metaphysical energy-intelligences.

Genesis One does not deal with physical manifestations; it deals only with pure metaphysical energy-intelligences. God created negative energy-intelligences because there was not yet any light. We think the sun is what provides light for our world and yet, on the first day of Creation, the Bible says, "And the Lord said, 'Let there be light,' and there was light." (Beresheet 1:3) This appears as a contradiction. The Zohar tells us we are not discussing the sun and moon, or light as we understand it but rather everything in a purely refined thought energy-intelligence. When God said, "light," He meant, "let there be sharing," Right Column energy, and this is *yom* (day). When God said, *vayehi erev*, (there was evening), He was referring to the aspect of Desire to Receive. Thus, we are not discussing anything of a physical or corporeal nature in Genesis One.

Therefore, when it says *vayehi erev vayehi boker*, what the Bible is saying is that on the six days of the week, there are always two distinct opposing forces in conflict with each other—forces of negativity and forces of positivity, forces in total disharmony, forces that are not physical, in the corporeal sense but which exist in the cosmos. Each one always seeks to dominate the other.

What is the purpose of the sun, the moon, and all the signs of the zodiac? If there are only two energy-intelligences, negative and positive, what is the purpose of the astrological signs? They are to tell us that these positive and negative aspects were placed into this universe on a metaphysical basis and became manifest in different ways. This means the sun, for example, has both a positive and a negative aspect—and for this reason the Bible says, *vayehi erev vayehi boker*. Everything that confronts us during the six days of the week has these two opposing forces. They are not evil or good; one simply desires to rule over the other. Now, on the Third Day of Creation, God created what we refer to as the Central Column, which as we know, is restriction. The nature of these cosmic forces, which operate six days a week, is determined by the way we behave.

In Beresheet One, Shabbat was not included as the Seventh Day. Shabbat only came about with the Revelation at Mount Sinai, in the Book of Shemot. In Beresheet, we are dealing with Creation not Precepts. If the Seventh Day of Creation was the Precept of Shabbat, then there would have been eight Noahide Precepts instead of seven, and then not only the Israelites but also all the other nations would have been obliged to observe the Sabbath. Why, suddenly, in the Ten Utterances, the children of Israel are told that they now have an obligation to observe Shabbat?

The Zohar says the Seventh Day was not mentioned in Beresheet as a Precept, so why do the Ten Utterances concerning Shabbat refer back to Beresheet in saying that God rested during this day, which was before the creation of Shabbat? Why was it now considered a new precept? The answer is, just as the six days of Creation were cosmically established as Sefirot, so too, the Seventh Day was established as a cosmic event. What exactly was this cosmic event? To illustrate what took place, the Bible uses the word, *vayishbot*, from the word *shvita*, meaning "a strike."

Does strike mean you have a job to do yet, on a certain day you are going to refrain from performing those duties? Is this really what a strike refers to here? When the Bible says God finished His work on the Seventh Day, it means He worked on the Seventh Day—there is no way of twisting these words. God worked on the Seventh Day but not in terms of working, as we understand it. How could we have a Seventh Day if God did not create it for us? All seven days of Creation dealt with the creation of metaphysical energy-intelligences. When the Bible says God made the Seventh Day Holy, the Zohar explains that God created a full circuit.

The Zohar says that this is superficial; the inner meaning of Shabbat goes far beyond the notion of rest. On the Seventh Day, God took the two opposing forces, which were created on the other six days of the week, and He injected the natural force of restriction, which we call the Central Column. Whereas, during the first six days of Creation, there were positive and negative energies that were always to be in conflict, on the Seventh Day, God created a different phenomenon—the Central Column, which established, throughout the Universe, balance between the Right Column and the Left Column.

What did God create on the Third Day of Creation? From a kabbalistic point of view, the Third Day of Creation is referred to as the Sefira of Tiferet, which is a balancing thought-energy-intelligence. In fact, many people feel that the Third Day is a positive day because the Bible says, *ki tov*, "it was good," twice in reference to the creation of this day. Beresheet 1:11 says, "And He saw it was good" and in verse 12 it again says, "And the Lord saw that it was good." Therefore, from this emerged the idea that Tuesday, which is the Third Day, is a good day for moving into a new home, and also establishing a new business.

The Zohar says the Third Day of Creation is *tov* (good) because it is Tiferet, which has the power to balance. Therefore in the Shield of David's Upper Triad there is the Sefira of Tiferet, and from the Lower Triad there is Yesod as the balancing agent.

The Zohar asks why do we say *Shabbat vaykadesh oto*, "Shabbat, He made it Holy"? What about the Third Day and the Sixth Day? The Zohar explains it is different because the word Shabbat does not mean what it is commonly thought to mean. The word *vayishbot* is not from the word *shvita*, which means, "to strike."

The Zohar explains that on the Third Day of Creation, there was the manifestation of Chesed, Gevurah, and Tiferet—which created symmetry. Malchut, the Seventh Day of Creation, is Shabbat, the manifestation of everything that preceded it. It is like a finished building, where the thoughts of the architect are ultimately manifested as one complete structure in the Malchut, the physical realm. The Zohar says that Shabbat crowns all of the days of the week because Shabbat combines everything into one unified whole and we do not have to make the effort to forge a connection with it. It was created with an all-inclusive, harmonized energy-intelligence—without our effort, without our intervention.

God made the Seventh Day Holy because He infused the cosmos with an inbuilt filament. What about on Tuesday or Friday? God also injected the Lightforce into the universe on the other six days of Creation, but not the Lightforce that would combine and balance Right Column and Left Column. On the other six days, this would be only in a potential state, left to humankind to manifest. We have to work and restrict to bring about the symmetry of each of the six days.

The first letter of the word Shabbat is Shin, which kabbalistically is the letter of symmetry and balance. It represents the Three Columns. Shabbat does not mean a day of strike or not working. God finished the job and made the *Shin-bat* the "daughter of symmetry."

The seed represents the original, and Shabbat represents the seed all over again. This is Malchut, the final culmination beginning all over again. Without the revelation of the first six days, Shabbat cannot be revealed.

The Third Day and the Sixth Day, which are Tiferet and Yesod respectively, do not within themselves harmonize or create symmetry in the world. However, when we make our proper connections, we activate Tiferet and Yesod and by so doing we create balance and harmony between Right and Left, between *erev* and *boker*. The Bible does not say, *vayehi erev vayehi boker*, concerning Shabbat because Shabbat is not another Third Column energy force that was created. Shabbat is the culmination of everything—its merging into one unified whole.

When we plant the seed, a tree eventually emerges whose existence is inbuilt. The objective of the original planting of a seed is the fruit. No one would plant the seed of a fruit tree if they knew the result would not be a fruit. The objective is the fruit. In the seed, the fruit is inbuilt. However, with humankind, it requires work to achieve a complete unified whole.

From the last explanation of the Zohar, we see that the word *vayishbot* has nothing to do with working. We understand now that, on the Seventh Day God did work, He created Malchut, He brought together all of the Sefirot into a unified whole.

The Zohar states that in the Ten Utterances, it says, *vayanach ba'yom hashvi'i*. A new word comes into position—*vayanach* "and He rested". However, we have just seen that the Creator was very busy on the Seventh Day. God was working to create the crowning of all differentiated entities of thought energy-intelligence, bringing them into one unified whole. In fact, this is what the kabbalist does on Shabbat. *Vayanach* means that by crowning all of the separate, differentiated thought energy-intelligences, and bringing Right Column and Left Column together in harmony, God brought *them* to a rest. God brought not only positive and negative to a rest, even the Central Column was brought to a rest because Central Column is a thought energy-intelligence that has the potential, like the filament in a lightbulb, to bring positive and negative together. For the filament to produce a circuit of energy, it has to function. If the filament does not work, the bulb reverts to short-circuiting; the battle of Right and Left poles is lost. When functioning properly, it is put in a position where it constantly works through a process of restriction. On Shabbat, *vanach*, everything rested—all three components, Right, Left, and Central, both of the Upper Triad, which was potential, and the Lower Triad, which was actual. All six Sefirot or six days of Creation were laid to rest. There was no action.

The word *vayanach* means "to let go." The illusion of our physical world is the problem. Once we let it go, we connect with the level of King David—which is Malchut, where there are no problems. It is illusion that is our problem. There is unity in the physical world but it is our illusion that everything is fragmented, that everyone is separate. In reality, everything is in its unified state.

Restriction, achieving the level of balance, is what Kabbalah teaches us—but it requires activity, we have to work to restrict. On the Seventh Day of Creation, in cosmic terms, everything is put to rest. Everything is quiet. Therefore, "He blessed this day." What is *bracha* "blessing"? One man's curse is another man's blessing. The market goes up—for those who sold long it is a curse. The market goes down—for the one who sold short it is a blessing. What then is a blessing and what is a curse? Is there something that could be a blessing for everyone?

This was the principle of why the letter Bet (ב) was chosen to be the channel for Creation. The letter Bet has the power of providing blessing. Blessing, says the Zohar, is where there is no illusion; it is something that is good for everyone involved. If it is good for one and bad for another, it is an illusion. This is why even the entire Bible will ultimately disappear. Yet if it is eternal, how could it disappear? The answer is the Bible is not dealing with Zeir Anpin, the true reality, it is dealing with the illusory world—things of a very mundane element, things we have to deal with—which is why we are here in the first place.

However, God in His infinite wisdom realized we would never be able to succeed so, at the original Creation, the purpose in creating one day where there would be no effort was so at least for one day we would not struggle to keep our heads above water. There would be one day in the week where we would not have to fight this kind of battle. God created Shabbat for this purpose. The Precept of Shabbat is not a commandment to watch or observe a Holy Day. No, God is saying, *vayanach*, rest, make sure that whatever you do does not initiate this mad war that goes on throughout the rest of the week.

When we strike a match, we activate the electrons; we activate a negative force. Striking is binding. When we strike a match, we strike the incendiary head, we do not strike the match itself. We are igniting that which is in the match, and it comes into contact with Sulphur, then a flame erupts and light is created. It is beautiful but it requires effort to create. Before the match is struck, it is in a state of rest. The only requirement of Shabbat is to not upset rest.

If we participate in an action that takes something out of a potentially restful state and puts it into an active state, we are creating activity. The Precept of Shabbat says we should not work and neither should our animals labor. Everyone and everything around us has to be in the same state as it was at the time of Creation for us to be in the World of the True Reality, which is not to be in the World of Illusion.

Therefore, striking a match, and any other activity, is really an illusion. People seek one thing in life—peace of mind. Therefore, when we say Shabbat permits us to have this complete unified whole, just as when we strike a match, we have initiated dissension. There is activity, and activity is not peace of mind. An individual's mind could be active while they are not physically active. There are people who experience heart attacks while sitting quietly in a chair because there is so much thought-activity going on.

The Shabbat is a force that gives us this complete harmony. In fact, Shabbat is called a gift and I, for one, wonder what kind of a gift it is. Is it a wonderful thing, on a very hot day, not to be able to go to the beach because you have to seek proscribed transportation? There is a distinct lack of pleasure in being unable to go to the beach or, for that matter, to turn on the television. There is indisputable pleasure in being able to do such things, so why not enjoy them? What activity is really involved?

The flipping of a switch creates movement in the electrons, which in turn creates movement in the atoms. When we connect to activity, we have taken ourselves out of peace of mind. The Creator found it important enough to put it within the Ten Utterances because without the Shabbat we can never connect to the reality of quietude, of peace—to the ultimate, to that which is complete.

I am not denying there are people who can achieve a certain level of quietude. With this revelation from the Zohar, we should have no problem understanding what constitutes work, and what does not. There are 39 basic actions that constitute work on Shabbat.

When we go on a vacation to the mountains or to Florida to relax and have peace of mind, is it because we have gone there that we have achieved tranquility. The answer is no. According to the fourth Precept of the Bible, peace of mind is where there is no activity. Shabbat means that everything has been laid to rest, nothing labors. All that is required, if we want to maintain a connection with that elusive realm, which is not the physical dimension, is to achieve a space of no activity.

Does this mean you cannot be a waiter on Shabbat? The sages say, of course you can. Does it mean you cannot invite two hundred people to your home on Shabbat and thus work hard to provide them hospitality? Does it mean that you are not capturing the realm of peace of mind, of tranquility? The sages say of course not because it has nothing to do with physical activity. Physical activity, or the absence of physical activity, has nothing to do with Shabbat. You can work all Shabbat, if you wish.

As I have said, Shabbat for me is the most exhausting day of the entire week. When the power of Shabbat comes face-to-face with these six other days, or six other energy-intelligences that are always in activity, they come to an abrupt halt. Yet this does not mean there is no physical activity. However, the activation, the initiation of any aspect that would create the arousal of a proton, neutron or electron, results in activity—and now we have taken the world out of its tranquil cosmic state and, in essence, created fragmentation.

How does one desecrate a Shabbat? The words *mechalel Shabbat*, in fact, do not mean "desecrate." *Chalal* means "space; a vacuum." To help us understand what we mean by vacuum, consider this, if you throw a stone into water, there is activity from the impact, yet around the stone there is nothing. This is what activity generally results in, giving us the illusion of surrounding ripples. Activity results in emptiness.

According to the Bible, desecrating the Shabbat is punishable by death by stoning. Why stoning? What does stoning mean? Does this mean that a stone falls on top of someone's head and they die? The Zohar explains the Bible is telling us that Shabbat is laying everything to rest. Without the Zohar's interpretation, there is no explanation of the Shabbat—it has no logic and no place in human society. This precept has become so distorted that people today throw stones on those that they believe desecrate Shabbat. The real meaning of being stoned is the idea of complete fragmentation where nothing works. Mind and body are fragmented. The aspect of keeping Shabbat is that one receives a thought energy-intelligence that creates unity—a peace of mind. This is why it is called a gift.

11 And in your new moons you shall present a burnt offering to the Lord: two young bullocks, and one ram, seven he-lambs of the first year without blemish; 12 and three-tenths of an ephah of fine flour for a grain offering, mingled with oil, for each bullock; and two-tenths of fine flour for a grain offering, mingled with oil, for the one ram; 13 and a seven-tenth of fine flour mingled with oil for a grain offering to every lamb; for a burnt offering of a sweet savor, an offering made by fire to the Lord. 14 And their drink offerings shall be half a hin of wine for a bullock, and one-third of a hin for the ram, and one-fourth of a hin for a lamb. This is the burnt offering of every new moon throughout the months of the year. 15 And one he-goat for a sin offering to the Lord; it shall be offered beside the continual burnt offering, and the drink offering thereof. 16 And in the first month, on the fourteenth day of the month, is the Lord's Passover. 17 And on the fifteenth day of this month shall be a feast; seven days shall unleavened bread be eaten. 18 In the first day shall be a holy convocation; you shall do no manner of mundane work; 19 but you shall present an offering made by fire, a burnt offering to the Lord: two young bullocks, and one ram, and seven he-lambs of the first year; they shall be to you without blemish; 20 and their grain offering, fine flour mingled with oil; three-tenths shall you offer for a bullock, and two-tenths for the ram; 21 a seven-tenth shall you offer for every lamb

of the seven lambs; 22 and one he-goat for a sin offering, to make atonement for you. 23 You shall offer these beside the burnt offering of the morning, which is for a continual burnt offering. 24 After this manner you shall offer daily, for seven days, the food of the offering made by fire, of a sweet savor to the Lord; it shall be offered beside the continual burnt offering, and the drink offering thereof. 25 And on the seventh day you shall have a holy convocation; ye shall do no manner of mundane work. 26 Also in the day of the first-fruits, when ye bring a new grain offering to the Lord in your feast of weeks, you shall have a holy convocation: you shall do no manner of mundane work; 27 but you shall present a burnt offering for a sweet savor to the Lord: two young bullocks, one ram, seven he-lambs of the first year; 28 and their grain offering, fine flour mingled with oil, three-tenths for each bullock, two-tenths for the one ram, 29 a seven-tenth for every lamb of the seven lambs; 30 one he-goat, to make atonement for you. 31 Beside the continual burnt offering, and the grain offering and their drink offerings, you shall offer them; they shall be to you without blemish.

Bamidbar 29:1 And in the seventh month, on the first day of the month, you shall have a holy convocation: you shall do no manner of mundane work; it is a day of blowing the horn to you. 2 And you shall prepare a burnt offering for a sweet savor unto the Lord: one young bullock, one ram, seven he-lambs of the first year without blemish; 3 and their grain offering, fine flour mingled with oil, three-tenths for the bullock, two-tenths for the ram, 4 and one-tenth for every lamb of the seven lambs; 5 and one he-goat for a sin-offering, to make atonement for you; 6 beside the burnt offering of the new moon, and the grain offering thereof, and the continual burnt offering and the grain offering thereof, and their drink offerings, according to their ordinance, for a sweet savor, an offering made by fire to the Lord. 7 And on the tenth day of this seventh month you shall have a holy convocation; and you shall afflict your souls; you shall do no manner of work; 8 but you shall present a burnt offering to the Lord for a sweet savor: one young bullock, one ram, seven he-lambs of the first year; they shall be to you without blemish; 9 and their grain offering, fine flour mingled with oil, three-tenths for the bullock, two-tenths for the one ram, 10 a seven-tenth for every lamb of the seven lambs; 11 one he-goat for a sin-offering; beside the sin-offering of atonement, and the continual burnt offering, and the meal offering thereof, and their drink offerings. 12 And on the fifteenth day of the seventh month you shall have a holy convocation: you shall do no manner of mundane work, and you shall keep a feast to the Lord seven days; 13 and you shall present a burnt offering, an offering made by fire, of a sweet savor to the Lord: thirteen young bullocks, two rams, fourteen he-lambs of the

first year; they shall be without blemish; 14 and their grain offering, fine flour mingled with oil, three-tenths for every bullock of the thirteen bullocks, two-tenths for each ram of the two rams, 15 and a seven-tenth for every lamb of the fourteen lambs; 16 and one he-goat for a sin offering beside the continual burnt offering, the grain offering thereof, and the drink offering thereof.

Physicality and the Dot

We have a dot above the word *ve'esaron*, which means "one tenth." This is not usual because there are no vowels in the Torah scroll. A dot could be a vowel however, because it is on top of a letter not below it, this indicates for us something significant about the word that it crowns. And here the sages have chosen the word *esaron* on which to place a dot. The word *esaron* means a tenth. For those of us who have studied Kabbalah, and know about tithing, we understand we have Ten Sefirot, and that the tenth Sefira is Malchut, the place where chaos and the Satan have dominion.

When we come to this word in the Torah reading on Shabbat Pinchas, we meditate on this dot. The dot is the smallest aspect of physicality. Yet in the Tree of Life Reality a dot is an instrument, it is a beacon of Light—like a laser beam, but more powerful. While a laser beam cannot affect everything, this dot has no limitations and can pierce anything and everything within the physical realm.

As we remove physicality, we find in the metaphysical a more powerful instrument because it has almost been shorn of all of its physicality. When we see the dot above the word *esaron*, we are not looking at the physical dot, as it is only in the realm of physicality so that we can recognize the place this energy is located. It is a marking point in the Torah Scroll.

17 And on the second day you shall present twelve young bullocks, two rams, fourteen he-lambs of the first year without blemish; 18 and their grain offering and their drink offerings for the bullocks, for the rams, and for the lambs, according to their number, after the ordinance; 19 and one he-goat for a sin offering; beside the continual burnt offering, and the meal offering thereof, and their drink offerings. 20 And on the third day eleven bullocks, two rams, fourteen he-lambs of the first year without blemish; 21 and their meal offering and their drink offerings for the bullocks, for the rams, and for the lambs, according to their number, after the ordinance; 22 and one he-goat for a sin offering; beside the continual burnt offering, and the meal offering thereof, and the drink offering thereof. 23 And on the fourth day ten bullocks, two rams, fourteen he-lambs of the first year without blemish; 24 their grain offering and their drink offerings for the bullocks, for the rams, and for the lambs, according to their number, after the ordinance; 25 and one he-goat for a sin-offering; beside the continual burnt offering, the grain offering thereof, and the drink offering thereof. 26 And on the fifth day nine bullocks, two rams, fourteen he-lambs of the first year without blemish; 27 and their grain offering and their drink offerings for the bullocks, for the rams, and for the lambs, according to their number, after the ordinance; 28 and one he-goat for a sin offering; beside the continual burnt

offering, and the grain offering thereof, and the drink offering thereof. 29 And on the sixth day eight bullocks, two rams, fourteen he-lambs of the first year without blemish; 30 and their grain offering and their drink offerings for the bullocks, for the rams, and for the lambs, according to their number, after the ordinance; 31 and one he-goat for a sin offering; beside the continual burnt offering, the grain offering thereof, and the drink offerings thereof. 32 And on the seventh day seven bullocks, two rams, fourteen he-lambs of the first year without blemish; 33 and their meal offering and their drink offerings for the bullocks, for the rams, and for the lambs, according to their number, after the ordinance; 34 and one he-goat for a sin offering; beside the continual burnt offering, the grain offering thereof, and the drink offering thereof. 35 On the eighth day you shall have a solemn assembly: you shall do no manner of mundane work; 36 but you shall present a burnt offering, an offering made by fire, of a sweet savor to the Lord: one bullock, one ram, seven he-lambs of the first year without blemish; 37 their grain offering and their drink offerings for the bullock, for the ram, and for the lambs, shall be according to their number, after the ordinance; 38 and one he-goat for a sin offering; beside the continual burnt offering, and the grain offering thereof, and the drink offering thereof. 39 These you shall offer to the Lord in your appointed seasons, beside your vows, and your freewill

offerings, whether they are your burnt offerings, or your grain offerings, or your drink offerings, or your peace offerings.

Holidays as Cosmic Events

The instrument known as the Torah Scroll is the interface between the Lightforce of God and the individual. Without this interface, nothing can happen. Without it, union of the opposite aspects of the Light and the body is not possible.

The most unusual feature of the portion of Pinchas is that all the holidays or as we like to call them, cosmic events—Rosh Hashanah, Yom Kippur, Sukkot, Shemini Atzeret, Pesach and Shavuot—are mentioned. Each event is an opportunity to tap into a particular energy to provide us with the ability to manifest a life without chaos, a life that includes immortality.

In fact, all the Torah sections that are read at each cosmic event come from somewhere in the portion of Pinchas. There is a design to it. All the Hebrew letters and notes of the portion of Pinchas have the ability to transmit the Lightforce of God toward a particular holiday. From a kabbalistic point of view, holidays are not merely days of celebration; a holiday contains the ability to draw the Lightforce of God into our lives.

When we come to an event like Rosh Hashanah, Yom Kippur or Sukkot, each time we read the Torah, we are getting a unique infusion for that particular holiday. We call them whole days because there are certain times in the year when the Heavens are open and humankind can connect to the Tree of Life Reality. This is also true of Shabbat.

Bamidbar 30:1 And Moses told the children of Israel according to all that the Lord commanded Moses.

Pinchas and the Third Meal of Shabbat

When we recite the Kiddush, it means making the Lightforce of God manifest through this combination of words. We have become familiar with the Third Meal of Shabbat as the meal that can support us to achieve complete and ultimate healing. However, it is only recently that we began to understand just what the Third Meal means. Before Rav Isaac Luria, this was concealed. When it was revealed at the time of Rav Shimon bar Yochai and at the time of Pinchas, the Third Meal dealt with the Armageddon War. What does healing have to do with Armageddon? You may have heard it mentioned that we hope to bring healing, not only into our atmosphere and into our lives but also, at the same time, to prevent the Armageddon War with the Kiddush of the Third Meal. In the Gate of Meditations, Rav Isaac Luria says this is the information he received from Elijah the prophet with whom he studied, and that there is a connection between healing and preventing the Armageddon War. We accept it, but this does not necessarily mean we always understand it. This was one of the things not understood until recently because, until a condition arises on this physical level of reality, we cannot relate to these metaphysical teachings of Rav Isaac Luria and Rav Shimon.

We have all become accustomed to the idea that the Armageddon War means people are going to fight with one another, yet there are different versions of this prophecy for different religions. What could happen at the End of Days is mentioned twice in the Bible. Rav Isaac Luria provided us with this wisdom when he incorporated not only the prevention of the Armageddon War but also completely removed the whole idea of it, which is connected to healing. Our conception of Armageddon comes with healing. It comes with Pinchas. This is the origin.

In the previous portion, we read about an orgy that took place where 24,000 people perished in a resulting plague. Then Pinchas slew Cozbi and Zimri, the initiators of this act, and the plague was over. What is the relationship between this and the Armageddon War? Why would this plague occur? What kind of a plague was it? The Bible does not say.

Only today can we begin to understand what Armageddon concerns. According to Rav Isaac Luria., Armageddon is not a war between nations but rather it is about healing. Before the Kiddush of the Third Meal, we remind everyone that we are strengthening the immune system. Healing is about the immune system. Does this mean that if someone has problems with the heart, liver or lungs, they can simply listen to the Kiddush and tap into the healing power required for their particular ailment? The answer is no, because the cause of all illness is the inability of our immune system to fend off disease. The Lightforce created this pure and natural system within every single person.

According to what we learn at the Kabbalah Centre, and from the portion of Pinchas, a breakdown in our immune system is the reason diseases have been with us since the time of Creation. There is nothing new, no new strains of disease. It is only the inability of our immune system to confront these different situations. Today, airborne diseases that travel from place to place and infect, seemingly without contact, plague us. The solution to airborne disease seems to be beyond us, as we do not yet have any means of detecting them.

This is the Armageddon War, and it is because of Rav Isaac Luria that today we have incorporated the removal of the Armageddon War into our Third Meal connections, which primarily deal with the immune system. These days, we are in a state where our immune systems no longer function properly and this is true, not only among humans because trees, animals, and rocks are also affected. Everything exists in a state of inability to combat so many new diseases.

This Third Meal is designed to provide us, not only with the clues but also with the rejuvenation of our immune systems. Why the Third Meal, why not in the Second Meal of Shabbat? During the Mincha prayers of Shabbat, which we always complete before participating in the Third Meal, we can transform the energy of this negative time of day when the sun sets, rather than eliminate or obliterate this setting of the sun. The sun sets not only because the Earth is rotating, but also because there are various energies at work. The sun is constant; it will do the same thing the next day, and the day after that.

Furthermore, Rav Isaac Luria teaches us that we cannot cut out negativity; it will reappear because we have not eliminated its point of origin. The Third Meal, which is Central Column energy, has the ability to transform negative energy back into wholeness, and thereby restore circuitry. We cannot eliminate any energy that exists in this world, all we can do is take that energy and transform it. The End of Days is the breakdown of the immune system.

The letter Vav in the word *shalom* here is the immune system. It is split to indicate that Pinchas exists to restore our immune system. This is what we do in the Kiddush of the Third Meal. When we restore the immune system, health is restored, and there will be no more conflict. We have the opportunity to create an immune system within each of us that is so powerful and perfect anything outside of us will be transformed.

The Purpose of Creation

One might ask why things are the way they are. Why are they not better? Why are there so many wars, killings, robberies and illnesses in the world? For every illness, where a cure is discovered, five new diseases are revealed. As far as medicine is concerned, we are losing the race. God did not just plant us here so He could mete out his suffering or enjoy seeing the pain of humankind. This was never the intent of God, never the desire of God. We have all learned, in the Kabbalah courses, what it was that prompted God to do what he did. Was the Creation for God or for humankind? The answer is for both. Only humankind can make the Lightforce of God become manifest and revealed in this physical, terrestrial realm of creation.

The purpose of Pinchas is to provide us with this form of elevated consciousness. It is why there are so many tools presented in this portion. This is why Pinchas could feel strong enough to undertake the task of slaying Cozbi and Zimri. Upon achieving a particular level, our consciousness can direct the path of all physicality. The innate components of all physicality are atoms, and the human mind can manage and manipulate atoms—whether they are in a piece of wood, iron, or even in water.

Rav Shimon accomplished miraculous feats of controlling physical nature, to the extent that he refused to recognize the Angel of Death as an entity. He did not agree that humankind must necessarily be subject to forces that can still be considered as part of the physical realm. Rav Shimon decided for himself that he was capable of dealing with such a situation. Pinchas died the same way. He demonstrated clearly that he did not need to be governed by the laws of this physical realm, the Tree of Knowledge of Good and Evil. We know that thought is not physical, and yet for a thought to become manifested, if it is not infused into some form of physicality it becomes a force no one is aware even exists.

Conclusion

The portion of Pinchas includes all the great forces of energy whereby chaos may be removed in every respect, not just in realms of finance or health; there are many more aspects of life in which Satan is deeply involved. Pinchas is the solution to all those infinite forms of chaos.

The whole year's cosmic events are incorporated in the portion of Pinchas; all the events we usually have to wait months for. There is no other section of the Bible that contains this level of the Lightforce of God. Every Rosh Chodesh (New Moon) captures dominion for a month and all of the months and the connections to them too, are in the portion of Pinchas. We need to appreciate what is available, and have in our consciousness the idea that connecting with this reading on Shabbat can accomplish the removal of all chaos from our lives.

The Lightforce does not contain any form of uncertainty. The Lightforce is unlimited, and the Lightforce performs its work perfectly. The minute we wonder why it has not happened yet, we have injected uncertainty into our lives. Let us not get in our own way. We can capture the Lightforce; we simply need to let the Lightforce perform its work.

We now have the possibility of reading the Zohar in English, so we can appreciate the depths of understanding in what the Zohar reveals about the physical body. When the Zohar brings this to our attention, we are able to understand the healing power of Shabbat given to us in the portion of Pinchas. With the Zohar's explanations regarding the physical body's ability to affect its own healing, it becomes clear that we have lost the ability and knowledge that lie in the deepest recesses of consciousness. Every single individual can control every aspect of physical reality, regardless of time, space, and motion.

Edgar Cayce could heal from a distance in his sleep, meaning it was not the miracle of healing someone thousands of miles away but rather the idea that time, space, and motion did not apply to him. These limitations have weighed so heavily upon us, creating, in effect, a prison around us from which it is so difficult to break out because in the process, we are seeking something particular. We are not merely concerned with the obvious appearance of illness; we want to go back to the source, which might be hidden in the physical body. Pinchas defies today's understanding of medicine and healing, along with every rule with which humankind is familiar.

We have this great opportunity, but we must remember, when we are done connecting to the reading that, if the immediate appearance of our desired miracle or healing does not appear instantaneously (although sometimes it does happen right away), it is due to a correction process. The healing has to be remedied through a process, and this process should not create an opening for uncertainty. When we apply the tools provided us with discipline, there is no reason that we should not experience the miracle of what Pinchas really concerns.

If we take the statistics to heart, everyone is going to get cancer; this is, fundamentally, the current prediction. An opportunity to offset the likelihood of becoming a statistic comes only once a year in the physical world—on the Shabbat of Pinchas. Things in the physical world come and go but in the spiritual world, everything remains.

Rav Ashlag said that spiritual energy never disappears, so whatever you have accumulated in your spiritual energy account will remain there. There is no disappearance in the metaphysical realm.

The Zohar, in this particular section, deals with healing; it goes on to discuss every aspect of the physical body, while appearing to have no relationship with the portion of Pinchas. And more than just telling us the nature and function of a specific organ, it reveals the internal aspects of the significant driving-force behind every bone and every organ of our bodies. Why did Rav Shimon choose this particular section? He could have chosen a section more connected to healing, like the portion of Beshalach. In that portion, there are the four letter Yuds: *aylech ki ani adonai rofecha*, "for I am the Lord your healer." (Shemot 15:26) Alternatively, in the portion of Beha'alotcha, we have eleven coded letters that indicate healing: *El Na Refa Na La* "God, please heal please her." (Bamidbar 12:13)

Rav Shimon chose this section because it is so unusual. It has so many peculiarities about it, all of which provide us with the reason why it is so powerful. It begins with the second verse, where we have a letter *Yud* added to the name Pinchas. Aside from the fact that this is a small *Yud*, smaller than the usual size found throughout the Torah Scroll, the name Pinchas could have been written without the *Yud*—simply *Pei, Nun, Chet* and *Samech* (פנחס), but nonetheless, there was a *Yud* added to his name (פינחס). In addition to having this added letter, the *Yud* is reduced, meaning the physicality is further reduced to permit a greater outflow of the Lightforce of God and what is less is more, as we have learned from science. Consequently, in this portion, the Lightforce has greater opportunities to prevail.

Another element, so unusual and extraordinary that it even defies imagination, is what Pinchas accomplished in the previous portion. There was a plague, in which 24,000 perished, and Pinchas removed the forces of evil at that time; he put an end to the plague, and was rewarded with the Covenant of Peace. What does the Covenant of Peace mean? The Zohar explains that "peace" means "freedom," a reprieve from the Angel of Death. In other words, Pinchas never died and, to prove the point, Pinchas appeared as Elijah the prophet, the only known living person mentioned in scriptures who ascended in his physical form to the World to Come.

Elijah the prophet could travel freely from one world to another. We know that the World to Come does not mean the world hereafter with great rewards to be received after death, but rather it is when we enter into that dimension of the Pure Reality, the Tree of Life Reality where there is no chaos. Consequently, Pinchas achieved this level of consciousness, and he survived death because he had the courage to go against the wickedness that was going on, and he put an end to the plague.

A Kohen (Priest) who has murdered is ineligible to serve as Priest and yet, as a reward, Pinchas was provided with an everlasting service. The Zohar says this is a contradiction, and here we learn another lesson. As much as we tend to validate our negative activities, there is never a pure justification for them. The Zohar says that when the entire tribe of Shimon swept down upon him to kill him, Pinchas died. His body became separated from its present soul and in turn, he received a new soul. His own innate soul with which he came into this world, departed in order to provide an opportunity for his body to embrace the souls of Nadav and Avihu, the two dead sons of Aaron. So powerful were these two, who now became incarnated into Pinchas, that the souls of these two individuals were defined as embracing the consciousness of the entire nation of Israel and not only their own consciousness.

In this portion, Pinchas is provided with everlasting, eternal Priesthood and, with it, came the freedom, the knowledge that we can become free of mortality—to embrace immortality, which is a concept clearly stated here and nowhere else in the Bible.

We also find in the word *shalom*, meaning "freedom from death" that the letter Vav is intentionally split. Here, Moses was specifically instructed to create a hairline fracture in the letter of the word that gives us freedom from mortality, teaching us that it is only through paradox that we can connect to the Light. Splitting means the separating of soul and body denoting mortality. This is what happens at the time of death, and a body without a soul ultimately disintegrates. These two elements, the body and the soul, appear to have been eternally decreed as the principal rules of mortality. Yet while this is the way it appears, nevertheless each and every single individual can reinstate *shalom*, a completeness, a joining, an eternal connection between the body and the soul. When we connect with our reading on the Shabbat of Pinchas, this is no less than immortality itself.

BOOK OF BAMIDBAR:
PORTION OF MATOT

PORTION OF MATOT

Bamidbar 30:2 And Moses spoke to the heads of the tribes of the children of Israel, saying: This is the thing which the Lord has commanded. 3 When a man vows a vow to the Lord, or swears an oath to bind his soul with a bond, he shall not break his word; he shall do according to all that proceeds out of his mouth.

The Significance of Vows

The first verse begins with Moses speaking to the heads of the tribes (*rashei hamatot*), so that they in turn convey the message to the children of Israel. This is why the portion is called Matot (Tribes).

This verse is then followed by a discussion of the vows. The commentators attempt to explain why this verse does not begin as the Bible usually does. Whenever a particular precept is going to be mentioned, the Bible says, "And God says to Moses," and Moses tells the people. Why is there a change in the way the Bible is structured? Moreover, why was the section that speaks about vows chosen to distinguish the heads of the tribes, as opposed to any other section in the entire Bible? What is so significant about vows? There is something very unique here.

What is a vow? The commentators explain that it is human nature to make a vow when one is in distress. When Jacob encountered trouble, he vowed to God that if the Creator guided him through this difficulty, he would make a contribution. There are times that people make vows to God to donate, perhaps to a charity or similar institution.

Another kind of vow that people sometimes make is an *isar al nafsho* (to bind a bond on his soul), which means a prohibition on one's self—denying oneself of some pleasure in life, like vowing never again to eat cake. Placing a prohibition on a particular thing or action is also a form of a vow.

The Torah cautions, that if a person makes a vow they should not disobey the words that come out of their mouth, lo *yachel devaro* (what he utters from his mouth should not be desecrated). *Yachel*, comes from the root word *chilul*. This is one of the 613 precepts and one of the 365 prohibitions.

Here the statement is made in the negative, "one should not" lo *yachel devaro*. This verse could have used the positive: "one should observe his words;" meaning one who has made a promise, a vow, must keep his word. Nevertheless, the verse is not written this way. Why is this precept presented in the negative, as opposed to a positive precept? The last aspect concerning the vows is the following: If a parent, specifically a father hears the vow of his daughter, who lives at home and is not betrothed, he can nullify her vow. By the same token, if a husband hears the vow of his wife, he can also cancel her vow. If he hears it and he remains silent, then the vow becomes effective—a valid vow. This is what this entire section is dealing with.

There is only one page of actual Zohar text regarding the portion of Matot. However, there is a section in the portion of Pinchas that deals with the idea of vows as they relate to the most important cosmic event in the Kabbalistic calendar, Yom Kippur, and the connection known as the *Kol Nidrei*. On the eve of Yom Kippur, people attend a service to recite in Aramaic, the cancellation of all the vows we may have undertaken during the year. This is the way Yom Kippur begins. All of the rituals and fasting that make up the 24 hours of Yom Kippur, seem to center around the idea of *Kol Nidrei*, which translated means "All Vows."

Rav Isaac Luria (the Ari) says the origin of *Kol Nidrei* is found in the Zohar section of Pinchas. The Zohar explains that on Yom Kippur, the Tree of Life Reality is dominant, intermingled with no evil. Zohar, Pinchas B 120:809 says:

"Those over whom there is a verdict, A VERDICT NOT TO BE CHANGED under vow or oath, it was decreed for this reason that the following shall be recited: 'All vows (*Kol Nidrei*), bonds...' they shall all of them be released and annulled. They shall not be binding, nor shall they have any power. BUT THE VERDICT SHALL BE VOIDED FROM THEM. And this is why the vow is in the Name of *Yud, Hei, Vav,* and *Hei*, which is Tiferet, while the oath is in the name of *Alef, Dalet, Nun,* and *Yud*, which is Malchut, for they caused their own exile BY THEIR SINS. AND NOW, by means of Chochmah and Binah, 'they will be released and annulled; they shall not be binding, nor shall they have any power.' 'And all the congregation of the children of Israel shall be forgiven' (Numbers 15:26). Chesed is water, Gevurah is fire, and Tiferet is air, AND SINCE THE VOWS ARE IN TIFERET, WHICH IS AIR, the sages of the Mishnah therefore taught: release from vows hovers in the air, FOR THE RELEASE FROM CHOCHMAH AND BINAH HOVERS IN THE AIR, WHICH IS TIFERET, AND FROM THERE ANNULS THE VOW."

A verdict shall be voided for those who have won them over because they have not fulfilled a vow or transgressed upon a prohibition that they placed upon themselves.

Therefore, the prayer of *Kol Nidrei*, which annuls the decrees accompanying the violation of vows was chosen to be recited on Yom Kippur. There are many possible violations. Someone could have committed murder or another of the 365 prohibitions during the year and yet, when it comes to Yom Kippur, the day for attaining forgiveness, the *Kol Nidrei* has to do with vows and nothing else?

The Zohar explains that there is a difference between a vow and an oath—where someone is assuming an obligation. Vows are considered to be in the same framework as the Tetragrammaton—*Yud, Hei, Vav,* and *Hei,* which is Tiferet or Zeir Anpin. While an oath is in the framework of *Alef, Dalet, Nun,* and *Yud,* which is Malchut, since oath-breakers cause their own exile by the violation of their oath. The Zohar says that, since vows are in the framework of Tiferet, the sages taught that release from vows hovers in the air, and by means of Chochmah and Binah, the vows will be released and have no power. An oath comes from Malchut, which is below a vow, on the level of Tiferet. The sages taught that vows are higher than oaths, and that the *Kol Nidrei* refers to Zeir Anpin.

Vows are considered to be in the same framework as Zeir Anpin—the Tetragrammaton. There is a difference between a vow and swearing an oath. This is why the *Kol Nidrei* refers to the breaking of vows, as the violation of vows is where *Kol Nidrei* is found. Briefly stated, prohibitions in the Bible, such as "Thou shalt not steal," are either between oneself and God or between oneself and one's fellow man. Vows and oaths, on the other hand, deal with an obligation between man and himself. In other words, when a person has undertaken their own prohibition; it is not the Bible that has directed us to make a vow, we have personally made this vow, which must now be fulfilled. A vow is initiated by the individual. This is the only instance where man himself decides, and then of course, the precept is that one should not desecrate his own promise. Nonetheless, this precept refers to the vow that was initiated by the individual himself.

The Chieftain's Report

This, in essence, gives us an idea about why this relates to our question: "Why was this particular section concerning vows first transmitted by Moses to the heads of the tribes?" There was another incident with the heads of the tribes in the portion of Shlach Lecha, where the chieftains of the tribes request to make a reconnaissance of the land of Israel, and to return with a report for the Israelites regarding what they might expect when they entered into the land.

It is no coincidence that the biblical reading of Matot always occurs in the three negative weeks from the 17th day of Tammuz (Cancer)—when the enemy pierced and overtook the walls of Jerusalem during the time of the First and Second Temples—until the culmination on the 9th of Av (Leo), Tisha B'Av, when both Temples were destroyed. These Chieftains returned with a report that was very negative and, from that day on, there was a decree that those Israelites would not enter the land of Israel. God said they will always be crying, thus this will always be a period of mourning for them. And to this very day, we still refrain from certain aspects of pleasure from the 17th day of Tammuz until the 9th day of Av.

The Zohar, in Shlach Lecha, says the chieftains came back with a negative report because they were afraid that once the Israelites would enter the land of Israel, they would no longer need to be governed by chieftains—who would lose their political status in the community. The Zohar also says that these chieftains were *tzadikim* (righteous people). Nevertheless, it also raises the question, if they were *tzadikim*, why would they question God? If God had already told Moses this was a land of milk and honey, and there was no need to fear the people who inhabited the land of Israel at that time, why then did the chieftains come back with such a negative report? The report inevitably caused the Israelites to wail, asking, "God, why did You take us out of Egypt?"

The Zohar elucidates—and this is a great revelation—that, in sending these twelve chieftains, because they were *tzadikim* (righteous people), Moses and God were telling them that when they explore this land, their high level of consciousness would enable them to establish whether this was a land of milk and honey or just a land of want. When Moses asked the chieftains, meaning the heads of the tribes, to see if there were trees in that land, this question was not asked for itself, it was for these heads of the tribes to apply their consciousness to and establish the cosmic influences over Israel and thereby the entire world.

Though the world appears to be fragmented, there is no such thing as a fragmented universe. Unfortunately, most people experience each part of the world as separate, without adhering to the principles of modern physics, which says there is no such thing as separation or fragmentation. A butterfly flapping its wings in China will affect an action on the other side of the globe. The Zohar says even more so is Israel. What is consciously in the minds of the people in Israel is reflected to the consciousness of the entire world. What transpires in Israel goes on throughout the world. If there is hatred in Israel, there is hatred around the world. If there is murder in Israel, there is murder around the world. Violations of human dignity in Israel result in violation of human dignity around the world.

Therefore, these twelve heads of the tribes went to the land of Israel to establish the consciousness and influences that would govern not only the land of Israel but the entire world. These very same righteous people returned with a negative report—meaning that, by their very presence, they had established a negative consciousness in Israel. Yet they were chosen because of their high level of consciousness. They were not elected officials chosen by their tribes. These people were chosen because they were channels. If that was their purpose, why would they establish a negative consciousness? The Zohar says they established a negative consciousness because what they came back with was an exaggerated picture of the condition of the land of Israel—yet it was not a lie. The Zohar does not dwell on the fact that they were *tzadikim*—Rav Shimon bar Yochai simply mentions it. And he also mentions that they were responsible for the chaos that would, in the future, befall the world. Throughout history, the 9th of Av, the day they returned with their report, has played a significant role in world chaos and disorder because this was the consciousness established by these twelve chieftains in the land of Israel. What really happened?

From the Zohar, we will receive some insight regarding what the chieftains were about, and why this section is called Matot (Tribes). What do the tribes and the chieftains of the tribes have to do with vows? These twelve people of an elevated consciousness came to Israel and established there a consciousness of chaos and disorder. Had they come back with the true report—that this was indeed a land of milk and honey—they would have established the consciousness of the Tree of Life in Israel. The Zohar says that a land of milk and honey is a land where the presence of the Tree of Life and not the Tree of Knowledge of Good and Evil exists. In modern terms, this would be a reality where the second law of thermodynamics does not exist; where the world of chaos does not exist; where the world of death does not exist.

There is another world in our midst that we call the world of "occasional miracles," wherein, if we are faced with a certain situation and pray for a miracle, the miracle then occurs. What is a miracle? Is it an unnatural occurrence? Is an earthquake a miracle? Is a tidal wave a miracle? Naturally for most of us, a miracle is something out of the ordinary, supernatural; something above the normal course of events in our lives. A miracle is something that does not abide by physical laws.

If our definition of a miracle is a supernatural event, then earthquakes should also be termed miracles—but they are not. In our ill-informed definition of what a miracle is, we think of a miracle as something that only brings happiness; a miracle implies the end result is of a wonderful nature—yet such "miracles" are few and far between. From a kabbalistic point of view, experiencing miracles means being connected to the Tree of Life Reality; being connected to a supreme reality, a frame of reference where one is not governed by the world of chaos, meaning the world of the Tree of Knowledge of Good and Evil. When things of a non-chaotic nature happen, it is not a miracle; it is only that we have raised our consciousness to the level of the world where chaos does not exist. Only occasionally do we reach this level of consciousness—yet it should be the norm. Unfortunately, we find ourselves so seldom in the realm of the Tree of Life, the non-chaotic world, that we call it a "miracle."

A glance at the current condition of the Earth and its inhabitants finds mainly death, destruction, natural disasters, and so forth. This landscape of chaos seems to be much more a part of our personal lives than the world of miracles, yet the Zohar says it is of our own creation. It is of our own making because we have violated the realm of the Tree of Life Reality. The Zohar says this is what the chieftains established when they came to Israel because the land of Israel is the energy center of the world. It is the land from which the Tree of Life Reality emerges—the world of stability, the world of law and order. If people residing in Israel cannot live up to the standards of law and order, then their consciousness establishes the world of the Tree of Knowledge of Good and Evil. If they cannot raise themselves above the idea of chaos, if they cannot cooperate with one another, they create darkness. The fact is that if the consciousness of the people is connected to chaos for all the good and justifiable reasons—even if they believe they are 100 percent correct in the way they behave toward their neighbor—then what is being established is the world of Tree of Knowledge of Good and Evil by the inhabitant not by the neighbor. And because the inhabitant lives in that atmosphere, they bring the consciousness of the Tree of Knowledge of Good and Evil into the consciousness of Israel, and also the entire world. If there is chaos in any other part of the world, the source of that chaos is in Israel.

We now know that this is what these chieftains had established, so we can begin to understand the connection and why this particular portion is known as Matot.

A vow is a self-assumed prohibition, meaning it does not deal with me and someone else, but rather it deals with me and my own consciousness. I have chosen to make a vow. I have assumed an obligation. I have taken it upon myself to perform certain actions.

Lo yachel devaro (Do not desecrate your words)—this negative Precept is the connection to those chieftains. It is certainly true that there are influences that embed themselves in the lives of all Earth's inhabitants— yet who establishes whether there will be chaos or whether, instead, there will be a land of milk and honey? The individual establishes it. Where? It is done in Israel. One might thus ask whether one would need to observe Yom Kippur outside of Israel if the essential idea is that the consciousness established in Israel governs the rest of the world.

The Zohar explains that vows and oaths are not simply obligations we should not desecrate—it goes far beyond that. The Zohar states that a broken vow applies to both realms, and has nothing to do with any prohibition one assumes toward any physical element of this world. Rather it is dealing with the consciousness of both realms. It is worth reiterating that a vow deals solely with our own consciousness and its relationship to the realms of the Tree of Knowledge of Good and Evil and the Tree of Life. This is what the vows are about and the cancellation is through the *Kol Nidrei*. And what does cancellation mean? If we violate the atmosphere, the environment of this world, then we have caused chaos throughout the entire world. As an individual, we have contributed to the pollution, the hatred, with our consciousness. When fragmentation is a part of our consciousness then what results from that is a violation, meaning we are adhering to the Tree of Knowledge of Good and Evil. We are placing our consciousness into the Tree of knowledge of Good and Evil Reality. This is what the chieftains established because they could not handle the power that emanates in Israel. Even though they were righteous people, they were overcome by the energy and everything became magnified because it was of a quantum nature.

Moses asked, "Are there trees?" meaning are they going to establish the Tree of Life Reality or the Tree of Knowledge of Good and Evil Reality? Therefore, we can understand the verse in Shlach Lecha where God says, "What you have established, you will establish forever." (Bamidbar 14:28) Why forever? Why would the influence of a report of a negative nature remain throughout all of the centuries? It is because, being on an elevated level of consciousness, these people created the environment that we all endure—right up to this very day.

Lo Chalel Devaro

The phrase *lo chalel devaro* is translated to mean "do not desecrate your words." However, the Hebrew word *chalal* refers to "empty space." What physics says about empty space is so wonderful—more empty space is less revelation of the Light. This is the connection between the vow and the chieftains. It is not about what they said, the vow is not so important. What is vitally important is that the vow originated in their consciousness.

This brings us back to the question of Yom Kippur? Does the connection to Yom Kippur have to be in Israel? And the answer is yes because vows and oaths, which are removed from the universe by the *Kol Nidre*, deal with energy not words. Therefore, if we are outside of Israel, there is little influence we can have on the rest of the world. This is why in Kabbalah Centre War Rooms around the world we have pictures of the burial places of the great sages located in Israel. Righteous people are entombed where their interred presence makes a physical connection for us to a particular site of energy in Israel.

Therefore, when we say the *Kol Nidrei* on Yom Kippur outside of Israel, we can teleport ourselves to Israel in our prayers with the assistance of the images of these sites, so that we can influence not only our own environment but the world. This idea is supported by Rashi. Our prayers make changes in the world when we transport ourselves, as did the Heads of the tribes, who went into the land to establish the consciousness of the Tree of Life or the Tree of Knowledge of Good and Evil. Therefore, when we say the *Kol Nidrei* we, like the chieftains, are establishing the consciousness of both worlds, the physical world and the world of the Tree of Life. Both are metaphysical. Everything that happens on this level of reality is first established metaphysically before it makes its appearance. A human being does not just appear as a human being.

First there is a seed, an egg, a fetus and all are concealed. Everything in this physical world has already been placed into a position that will determine how it emerges in this physical realm. If we want to make changes here, we have to make changes there. Therefore, the *Kol Nidrei*, which is in Aramaic, as is the Zohar, transcends the level of Malchut to the levels of the Tree of Life where we can make the proper connections to change our own immediate environment and the environment of the entire world.

This is the connection between the vows and the heads of the tribes.

Burial Sites

There was a conflict between different cities in the area regarding where Rav Shimon should be buried. Each city wanted the honor of burying such a great *tzadik*—a man who could violate all of the Tree of Knowledge of Good and Evil reality, all of the chaos existing in our lives. These principles did not exist for him because he was totally connected to the Tree of Life Reality. Rav Shimon's body traveled to Meron by itself, on a device much like a ladder. It is buried at Meron to this day. No one chose the site where Rav Shimon lies, yet it is a powerful energy center.

Another example is Rabbi Yehoyada, the High Priest, who served for forty years in the Holy Temple and is buried in a valley on the side of a steep mountain, a site not readily accessible. It is as if he walked all the way from Jerusalem to be buried here. He was not buried in Jerusalem because sites where *tzadikim* are buried— like that of Joseph the Righteous in Shechem—make a physical connection for us to that particular energy-site. Rabbi Yehoyada knew that this particular location in Israel is a powerful energy-point—such as we find at Hebron, in the Cave of Machpela, where Abraham, Isaac, and Jacob are all buried.

4 Also when a woman vows a vow to the Lord, and binds herself by a bond, being in her father's house, in her youth, 5 and her father hears her vow, or her bond with which she has bound her soul, and her father holds his peace at her, then all her vows shall stand, and every bond with which she has bound her soul shall stand. 6 But if her father prohibits her in the day that he hears, none of her vows, or of her bonds with which she has bound her soul, shall stand; and the Lord will forgive her, because her father prohibits her. 7 And if she be married to a husband, while her vows are upon her, or the clear utterance of her lips, with which she has bound her soul; 8 and her husband hears it, whatever day that he hears it, and holds his peace at her; then her vows shall stand, and her bonds with which she has bound her soul shall stand. 9 But if her husband prohibits her in the day that he hears it, then he shall make void her vow which is upon her, and the clear utterance of her lips, with which she has bound her soul; and the Lord will forgive her. 10 But the vow of a widow, or of her that is divorced, everything with which she has bound her soul, shall stand against her. 11 And if a woman vowed in her husband's house, or bound her soul by a bond with an oath, 12 and her husband heard it, and held his peace at her, and prohibits her not, then all her vows shall stand, and every bond wherewith she bound her soul shall stand. 13 But if her husband make them null and

void in the day that he hears them, then whatever proceeded out of her lips, whether it were her vows, or the bond of her soul, shall not stand: her husband has made them void; and the Lord will forgive her. 14 Every vow, and every binding oath to afflict the soul, her husband may let it stand, or her husband may make it void. 15 But if her husband altogether holds his peace at her from day to day, then he causes all her vows to stand, or all her bonds, which are upon her; he has let them stand, because he held his peace at her in the day that he heard them. 16 But if he shall make them null and void after he has heard them, then he shall bear her iniquity. 17 These are the statutes, which the Lord commanded Moses, between a man and his wife, between a father and his daughter, being in her youth, in her father's house.

Male and Female; Cause and Effect

In this section, we read that if a husband hears the vow made by his wife he can cancel the vow. But what happens if the husband makes a vow—can the wife cancel his vow? No. From a superficial perspective, this seems chauvinistic. Nonetheless, thanks to the Zohar, we understand that when the Bible speaks about father, it is not referring to father in the physical sense. The Bible is only a combination of names, and has no reference to physical descriptions. This world is only a dim reflection of what exists on another level. And what it is reflecting in this case is that male refers to cause and female refers to effect.

Knowing a little about electricity we understand that a socket is termed "female" and the plug "male." In plumbing, when one pipe goes into another pipe, the outside pipe is called "female," and the pipe attached from within is called "male."

When the Zohar says the Bible only deals with labels, this means levels of consciousness—nothing more and nothing less. Therefore, the idea of sexism immediately falls away because this is not what is being discussed. Rather the subject is consciousness. What does male consciousness or female consciousness indicate? Like a sperm and an egg, or in the electrical and plumbing vernacular, we are referring to the expression of channeling, which is male and the expression of receiving, which is female. Each represents a particular aspect of consciousness.

When we are discussing vows, once again we are discussing consciousness. When the father or the husband hears a vow made by a female and can cancel it out, this has nothing to do with the standard notions of male or female physicality, it has to do with channeling and recipiency.

The Bible is telling us the male level is before the reaction, before the effect. The manifestation is the female level. Once something has been established as the effect there is little way to change it. Even if change is possible it requires a procedure. In this physical world, there is a reactive and a proactive consciousness. We can choose to belong to the reactive consciousness of the world or we can govern the consciousness of the physical world.

This section of the Bible is called Matot because, like the leaders, we have a choice of consciousness. And that which we choose becomes manifested on this level. When we plant an apple seed, is there any choice in what kind of fruit the eventual tree will bear? Can it be changed? Once it becomes a manifested corporeal entity, there is little if anything that can be done to change it. That which channels, governs. It is what provides the signals. The branches are the effect.

What the Bibles is teaching us with relation to the heads of the tribes is that, if we want to make changes or cancel things out, then our consciousness must be on the level of the seed, the head—that which channels, not the effect. The Bible refers to that as the father of the daughter, or the husband to the wife. Is the Bible saying that the male is of a higher nature? Not at all. It is saying to create change, be at the level of origin not the level of effect; to be proactive in our lives, not reactive. If someone slaps a person, there is an automatic reaction to respond. Instead, to be at a level of a higher consciousness in receiving a blow, one does not react, stopping for a moment to think.

This is what the whole portion of Matot is dealing with, providing us with the energy to establish proactive consciousness, because the physical environment can only be changed on the level of the male, at the origin level before the reaction, before the effect.

Once something is an effect, there is little or no way to change it. Even if there is a way of changing something, a procedure is required. In this case, it is *Hatarat Nedarim* (Annulment of the Vows) where three people are needed to form a *Bet Din* (Court of Judges), who try to undo the vows or oaths that have been made. There are ways vows or oaths can be undone, but it is preferable to undo them before the action becomes manifest because the extent to which it can be undone depends on the consciousness of the individual who made the vow.

Another example is with *Hatavat Chalom* (Annulment of a Dream), which means making a dream good. If an individual has a disturbing dream, they can come before three people, a

Bet Din, who use spiritual tools in the form of verses to change manifestations by transforming the origin. Even dreams, which are of a metaphysical nature, are still in a manifested state. These three people sit and create a *Hatavat Chalom*; they transform this negative dream, which is already in a manifested state, and can become a physical event in the life of a person having the dream. The dream makes contact with the future through consciousness. Science confirms what the Bible is saying that the future is here now. Tomorrow is a manifested state. Yesterday indicates origin, channeling, connecting with the source—male. The event, as it appears, is female. The dream can be changed at the origin level in the consciousness of the person who is partaking in the *Hatavat Chalom*. However, the person must understand what is happening, what is being created at this point. What is actually occurring is genetic engineering—changing the origin, changing the source, the root of what ultimately develops on the physical level we are familiar with.

Rav Isaac Luria (the Ari) says that when one makes a vow and does not fulfill it, this creates an empty space, a void in one's life that becomes filled with the forces of darkness—and these include all forms of chaos. Where there is no Light, the forces of darkness prevail. This dark matter represents the condition in which we all find ourselves. We live in a vacuum of chaos, and it is very difficult to extricate ourselves because there is so little Light.

The Torah scroll permits us to tap into the Lightforce of God, which is the only methodology available to humankind whereby we can create a protective security-shield around ourselves, our homes, the environment and, potentially, around the entire globe.

When the Bible speaks about the father, the daughter or the wife, these are all metaphors that give a name to different aspects of consciousness. Men and women represent a certain aspect of this reality but they are also a connection to the immaterial world. Woman is a vessel for the Lightforce of God, and a man represents the channeling of the Lightforce of God. Without a vessel, there can be no development of any sort, and so these combinations—a father and daughter, a husband and wife—permit access to the world of the Lightforce of God. This is the only method by which we can eliminate darkness. Darkness is a negative form of Satan, and it fills every empty space. Not keeping a vow is the simplest way to create dark matter. Yom Kippur is called the holiest of holy days because *Kol Nidrei* has the power to eliminate all the dark matter we have created.

Our Vows

There are rules in the game we play with Satan. Chaos comes when we make an appointment we do not keep. The power of the word cannot be forgotten. The moment we say we will meet someone; in the 99 Percent Reality the meeting has in fact already taken place.

The vows we make and do not keep create a condition of empty space, which is not filled—instead, an empty vessel with a negative charge is created. The recipient, which is negative, is female. This is not negative as in "bad." Negative, in this context, simply means a female recipient. The earth is female—it takes the seed and brings it to fruition. The egg absorbs the sperm—which is the negative drawing in the positive. When we do not fulfill a vow, we are creating a vessel that is not filled and this is an opportunity permitting Satan to enter. On Yom Kippur, we wash out all of our empty spaces. With the portion of Matot we can cancel out the vows we have made since the previous Yom Kippur.

This section regarding the husband and wife, father and daughter, is completely concealed. When, in our consciousness, we have made a decision, the effect of that decision is already extant on the 99 Percent level, even though on a 1 Percent level it has not yet manifested. When we establish an original consciousness, this action has already been completed in the metaphysical realm.

Tomorrow is here now. The idea of time, space, and motion is an illusory limitation. What the Bible is discussing here is not the issue of separate rights for a husband and a wife. Instead, we are being provided with the understanding that, when we think of anyone in a negative way, at that moment, on the 99 Percent level, the damage we thought to inflict has already become manifested.

When we experience chaos in our lives, it is important to understand that, invariably, we have said or done something to let in the chaos we experience. The words we speak reflect our mental states, yet often we are conflicted in our thoughts and actions. We are torn between two things because we have already established both—and this creates a problem.

Each of us possesses both female and male qualities. The right side of the face is not similar to the left, and our arms are not the same. Unfortunately, we comprise two opposite characteristics—the right and the left—but, by connecting to the reading we can experience a balance within. When we make decisions, it is as if one minute we think this, and the next minute we think something contrary to the first thought—and these are serious matters. We need to recognize the power of mind over matter, and realize there are fundamental rules of human existence; rules with which we cannot tamper.

Through the reading of the Bible, we connect to the positive energy of the week. Without listening to the reading of the Torah Scroll, we do not have any chance of overcoming negativity. We have to understand that the Bible is like Morse code; we need to know how to interpret it. The story about the man being able to nullify the woman's vow is a metaphor that explains how the universe functions.

We must keep in mind that there is nothing but consciousness and that the physical reality has no relevance, except to interfere with our ability to enact free will. We each get it in our own way because consciousness is all we are about.

The Bible is teaching us that a vow refers only to the physical reality. When we say we want to do this or that, we have already created a difficult situation. When we say we want a million dollars, why does it not appear instantaneously? The reason it does not just show up immediately is because our consciousness has to be developed to where it can attain a state of certainty. Only then will we be in control of the physical reality. We alone bring chaos to our own lives. We are the perpetrators, not the environment, not others. Only by looking within can we eliminate the source, the Keter of our chaos. If we understand the source of the chaos, we can remove it.

The story about the annulment of vows exists to tell us that male and female denote different modes of consciousness. The female refers to the effect, the male is the channel, the origin. We know that the woman is more important. If we read the Torah carefully, we notice it says that the vow can only be nullified on the day the father or husband hears it—not the next day, not a week later. This teaches us that we can only uproot chaos on the day it appears. The instant we recognize the chaos is when we can uproot it. Once it is manifested, it can no longer be nullified.

Bamidbar 31:1 And the Lord spoke to Moses, saying: 2 "Avenge the children of Israel of the Midianites; afterward you shall be gathered to your people." 3 And Moses spoke to the people, saying: "Arm men from among you for the war, that they may go against Midian, to execute the Lord's vengeance on Midian. 4 Of every tribe a thousand, throughout all the tribes of Israel, shall you send to the war." 5 So there were delivered, out of the thousands of Israel, a thousand of every tribe, twelve thousand armed for war. 6 And Moses sent them, a thousand of every tribe, to the war, them and Pinchas, the son of Elazar, the priest, to the war, with the holy vessels and the trumpets for the alarm in his hand. 7 And they warred against Midian, as the Lord commanded Moses; and they slew every male. 8 And they slew the kings of Midian with the rest of their slain: Evi, and Rekem, and Zur, and Hur, and Reba, the five kings of Midian; Balaam also the son of Beor they slew with the sword. 9 And the children of Israel took captive the women of Midian and their little ones; and all their cattle, and all their flocks, and all their goods, they took for a prey. 10 And all their cities in the places wherein they dwelt, and all their encampments, they burnt with fire. 11 And they took all the spoil, and all the prey, both of man and of beast. 12 And they brought the captives, and the prey, and the spoil, to Moses, and to Elazar the priest, and to the congregation of the children of Israel, to the camp, to the plains

of Moab, which are by the Jordan at Jericho. 13 And Moses, and Elazar the priest, and all the princes of the congregation, went forth to meet them outside the camp. 14 And Moses was angry with the officers of the host, the captains of thousands and the captains of hundreds, who came from the service of the war. 15 And Moses said to them: "Have you saved all the women alive? 16 Behold, these caused the children of Israel, through the counsel of Balaam, to revolt so as to break faith with the Lord in the matter of Peor, and so the plague was among the congregation of the Lord. 17 Now therefore kill every male among the little ones, and kill every woman that has known man by lying with him. 18 But all the women and children, that have not known man by lying with him, keep alive for yourselves. 19 And encamp outside the camp seven days; whoever has killed any person, and whoever has touched any slain, purify yourselves on the third day and on the seventh day, you and your captives. 20 And as to every garment, and all that is made of skin, and all work of goats' hair, and all things made of wood, you shall purify."

War with the Midianites

Most people would prefer to ignore and not discuss the above verses. But, incidentally, ignorance is not bliss. Most of us think that what we do not know, or what we have not heard, cannot hurt us—but this is not true. Just because we do not want to hear something does not change the fact that it has already manifested. There is no way we can escape the manifestation of what we do not wish to hear or see.

In this section, the Bible discusses war with the Midianites. The Israelites are told to wage war against the Midianites. We may recall that the Midianites were brought by Bilaam at the end of the portion of Pinchas. Their influence caused a catastrophe that killed 24,000 Israelites. The Bible states that the Israelites should annihilate all males—adults and children—and it then describes how to dispose of the women and girl captives.

There are no interpretations or explanations of these statements: The women of the Midianites and their children, their animals, their cattle, their possessions, all have to be dealt with. If women were married, or young girls had had sexual intercourse with a male, they were to be destroyed, and all of the physical possessions were to be burnt. The Bible does not describe the method of death.

Bamidbar 31:13 states that, when Moses and Elazar the High Priest and the heads of the tribes went out to meet the victorious army that was sent to destroy the Midianites, Moses was angry, because he saw that females were left alive. He had told them before battle that certain females were to be killed. He then repeats his initial order to kill all the male children, the captives, right now. Destroy all the male children and every woman that "knew" a man, meaning had sexual relations with a male. The Talmud says that sometimes a woman can lose her virginity, but not necessarily through sexual intercourse. They must have been very clever to know which women were virgins.

This is what the Bible actually says. I am not giving an interpretation—it is all there, in the translation of Bamidbar 31:14, and onwards. For millennia, we have avoided discussion of these troublesome verses.

Moses certainly received instruction from God. Moses would not have taught the people of Israel the laws without being instructed to do so by God. Yet, the Bible says, "Thou shalt not kill." I strongly urge all readers to review this portion in their spare time, although it may be sickening. In fact, it is designed to do this. Rav Shimon, in the Zohar, discusses these verses because he wants to arouse within us the curiosity to seek the truth.

We consider the Bible to be a roadmap, as Rav Shimon states it is. However, the Bible is absolutely baseless and useless if it is simply read on a literal level. Am I against translation? The answer is yes. We are accessing a living code here, and we cannot read the words of the Bible literally when we know there is so much more concealed in it—just as there is in this world. Why can we not accept the Bible as a work of total concealment? This way of thinking has to change if we hope to connect to that universe known as the Tree of Life.

Without understanding, the Bible can make no difference. We study Kabbalah to understand. The Bible says that, when someone kills, they should be put to death. However, the Talmud tells us that, of all the years of existence up to the era of the Second Temple, when a man was suspected of murder, two witnesses had to give an account of his violation for him to be convicted. Because two people could rarely agree on what they saw, the courts never decreed a death sentence. They would always find a basis for this accused to go free.

These sages are speaking about us. The Talmud is talking about *us* murdering *ourselves*. How many times are we self-destructive? With the exception of the mentally ill, of course. How many times do we make decisions and do certain things that we know are not good for us, thinking *Why shouldn't I?*

We are the agents of our own destruction. The Bible is teaching us about our own individual forces, which tell us to move in a direction that we should not go. However, when we leave it to God completely, the Tree of Life comes into play. What does this mean? I am not saying that leave it to the Lightforce means take a break, make no effort. On the contrary, I am saying we should take responsibility to make every conceivable connection to the Flawless Universe and bring it into our decisions. This is why we come to hear the Torah reading each Shabbat. This rather bizarre reading is the code. It brings us to the point where we can eliminate the chaos. We are here to destroy those internal dark forces that mislead us. This is not speaking about any men, women or children.

21 And Elazar, the priest said to the men of war that went to the battle: "This is the statute of the law which the Lord has commanded Moses: 22 Only the gold, and the silver, the brass, the iron, the tin, and the lead, 23 everything that can endure the fire, you shall make to go through the fire, and it shall be clean; nevertheless it shall be purified with the water of sprinkling; and all cannot endure the fire you shall make to go through the water. 24 And you shall wash your clothes on the seventh day, and you shall be clean, and afterward you may come into the camp." 25 And the Lord spoke to Moses, saying: 26 "Take the sum of the prey that was taken, both of man and of beast, you and Elazar, the priest, and the heads of the fathers' houses of the congregation; 27 and divide the prey into two parts: between the men skilled in war, that went out to battle, and all the congregation; 28 and levy a tribute to the Lord of the men of war that went out to battle: one soul of five hundred, both of the persons, and of the cattle, and of the donkeys, and of the flocks; 29 take it of their half, and give it to Elazar, the priest, as a portion set apart for the Lord. 30 And of the children of Israel's half, you shall take one drawn out of every fifty, of the persons, of the cattle, of the donkeys, and of the flocks, even of all the cattle, and give them to the Levites, that keep the charge of the Tabernacle of the Lord." 31 And Moses and Elazar, the priest, did as the Lord commanded Moses. 32 Now the prey, over and

above the booty which the men of war took, was six hundred and seventy-five thousand sheep, 33 and seventy-two thousand cattle, 34 and sixty-one thousand donkeys, 35 and thirty-two thousand persons in all, of the women that had not known man by lying with him. 36 And the half, which was the portion of them that went out to war, was three hundred and thirty-seven thousand, five hundred sheep. 37 And the Lord's tribute of the sheep was six hundred and seventy-five. 38 And the cattle were thirty-six thousand, of which the Lord's tribute was seventy-two. 39 And the donkeys were thirty thousand, five hundred, of which the Lord's tribute was sixty-one. 40 And the persons were sixteen thousand, of whom the Lord's tribute was thirty-two persons. 41 And Moses gave the tribute, which was set apart for the Lord, to Elazar, the priest, as the Lord commanded Moses. 42 And of the children of Israel's half, which Moses divided off from the men that warred, 43 now the congregation's half was three hundred and thirty-seven thousand, five hundred sheep, 44 and thirty-six thousand cattle, 45 and thirty thousand, five hundred donkeys, 46 and sixteen thousand persons, 47 even of the children of Israel's half, Moses took one drawn out of every fifty, both of man and of beast, and gave them to the Levites, that kept the charge of the Tabernacle of the Lord; as the Lord commanded Moses. 48 And the officers that were over the thousands of the host, the captains of thousands, and the

captains of hundreds, came near to Moses; 49 and they said to Moses: "Your servants have taken the sum of the men of war that are under our charge, and there lacks not one man of us. 50 And we have brought the Lord's offering, what every man has gotten, of jewels of gold, armlets, and bracelets, signet-rings, earrings, and girdles, to make atonement for our souls before the Lord." 51 And Moses and Elazar, the priest, took the gold of them, even all wrought jewels. 52 And all the gold of the gift that they set apart for the Lord, of the captains of thousands, and of the captains of hundreds, was sixteen thousand, seven hundred and fifty shekels. 53 For the men of war had taken booty, every man for himself. 54 And Moses and Elazar, the priest took the gold of the captains of thousands and of hundreds, and brought it into the Tent of Meeting, for a memorial for the children of Israel before the Lord.

Proactive and Reactive

This is one of those sections that is very difficult to understand. Aside from how to annihilate a nation, it also discusses what to do with the spoils of war. Imagine if we were to condemn a dictator—and there are so many of them around the world—could we possibly come to the conclusion that God contains this kind of negative consciousness, one whereby the Creator of the world could direct Moses to record such an incident? This portion is very lengthy and goes into great detail about how to divide the spoils of war, and the murder of men, women, and even children. How absurd can the Bible be?

Is it possible to read this section without puzzlement or even outrage? The reading of the Torah on Shabbat gives us strength, courage, and power for the entire week. Who among us would want to hear such a reading on Shabbat? This section gives us a wrong impression of the Israelites—to say the least.

One might think that perhaps this was the act of a rebellious nation, a people out for blood, out for spoils, yet the Bible very clearly states that Moses sent them. How do we justify murder, especially since the Midianites did not wage war against the Israelites? There is no mention of an act of aggression or of self-defense. Here the initiative was taken by Moses without an initial provocation from this alleged enemy known as Midian.

Within the paradox, and within the totally irrational, is where we find truth. Any normalcy of events in the Bible is just illusory or metaphorical. Those who have studied Kabbalah for a long time feel that, when things are normal, we should be concerned. When circumstances prove irrational, we know there is truth—no matter what the outcome of the event. This biblical section is so dramatic that we know there is a message because it is obvious Moses was not conquering any nation and dividing up the spoils. As I have often stated, if you want to write movies, the best source of inspiration is the Bible. The imagination can run wild in it. Some of the best scripts come from the Bible.

If someone opens the Bible and peruses only the section we are now discussing, it must raise the question, could this possibly be what God wants to teach us? Murder? Was Moses angry that women were kept alive? Is this about how to divide the spoils? This entire story is nonsensical—and this is why the Zohar is so essential to us. There is no logic as to why, with such an outpouring of wise interpretations in the Zohar, it has remained concealed for over two thousand years. As explained in the Zohar, there is something deeper here. It is impossible that Moses himself could utter those awful words: "Why did you not also kill the women?" This is far from the only section in which we find irrational, illogical or even inhuman occurrences. However, this is the one most glaringly obvious. The Zohar says that, if it was not presented for us in this manner, we would never raise the vital questions that the Zohar answers for us. War was the furthest thing from the minds of both Moses and God.

War is destruction. War is negative. War results in widows, orphans, and maimed people. The question then is, why is there war? Why does every civilization, every generation of humanity undergo war? There are many wars going on at any given time somewhere in the world. It seems endless. Why? Who instigates war? Presumably, people sitting down, having a meeting. Even with regard to the Iraq war, there was a meeting with many nations present, some who thought it was a good idea. No one goes to war for all the wrong reasons—there is always a justification.

That said, we cannot take this story literally; it is entirely irrational. There is no reasoning in any verse we read here. The only sense we can make of it is through what the Zohar reveals about this section. Matot is one of the longest sections in Bible and yet there are only twelve paragraphs of Zohar on this same portion. The fact that the shortest of all passages in the Zohar, which is, after all, a commentary on the Bible discussing one of the longest sections of the Bible seems almost illogical.

There are so many questions we could ask regarding this particular section, in addition to those already raised, and yet the Zohar does not find it necessary to elaborate. Rav Shimon could not take in all the information because it is not all there—it is concealed throughout the entire Bible. What Rav Shimon reveals for us here is that every aspect of this universe is governed by two causes or initiators—Positive and Negative. That is all the Zohar says on this matter.

This entire story is referring to the polarity that exists in physical nature. The binary system is a base-2 number system made up of only two numbers or digits: 0 (zero) and 1 (one). This numbering system is the basis for all binary code used to write digital data such as the computer processor instructions used every day. What the Zohar is saying is that there are only two forces in this world, and Rav Shimon says we activate either one or the other. When we behave in a positive way, we activate the positive force and when we are reactive, we activate the negative force. Either we are proactive or reactive—there is no other methodology in human behavior. In psychology, medicine, electrical or aeronautical engineering, everything will finally be reduced down to just two—positive and negative.

When we examine each and every single verse here, what emerges is only one word: Nanotechnology. Nothing else. There is nothing, either without or within, other than our consciousness. For 3,400 years, we have only been accustomed to what we can physically touch. All of us undergo chaos, and I am not discussing the chaos we do not know exists. How many times have we discovered something we did not know was going on? We know nothing.

The Zohar teaches us that, for the first twelve years, for a female, or thirteen years for a male, we have been embracing our chaos and our egos—which means acting from a reactive consciousness. Reactive consciousness is the cause of every single form of chaos, whether it is war, social strife or a family quarrel. In all of these disputes we act in a reactive state of consciousness—nothing more. The moment we act in a proactive state, all chaos disappears.

How can it be that things can be resolved without a lawyer, doctor or accountant? We are not accustomed to this kind of consciousness. We are dependent upon the physical supports we think are indispensable. Reality can be reduced to the simplicity of zero and one. This is the way the world works. We have not come to realize that the basis for human activity is reduced down to these two forces, and that there is only one area in which chaos can be reduced—and that is the nano-level of consciousness.

We can spend years pursuing liberty and happiness, yet somehow they constantly elude us. Freedom and joy are something we cannot hold onto because we are so involved with the physical manifestations of things. How can we expect a solution using only a fragment of our consciousness? At this level, we are duped. The Bible is teaching us there is nothing on the physical level— there is no rationale to the rational. There is no sense, no logic to the way we lead our lives. Today we are down, tomorrow we are up—just like the stock market, one day down, the next day up. There is no end to the rollercoaster ride. The solution is a positive consciousness, which is not easy to achieve. Nonetheless, we have to start somewhere.

Read superficially, this section is a discussion about how to divide the spoils of war. For nearly three and a half millennia we have read this literally and not thought anything was wrong with it. Today, nice people get pushed by the wayside. We constantly divide the spoils of life, even within our own families. Each person believes in the validity of their position and rights. We are hypocritical and dishonest with ourselves.

Bamidbar 32:1 Now the children of Reuben and the children of Gad had a very great multitude of cattle; and when they saw the land of Jazer, and the land of Gilead, that, behold, the place was a place for cattle, 2 the children of Gad and the children of Reuben came and spoke to Moses, and to Elazar the priest, and to the princes of the congregation, saying: 3 "Ataroth, and Dibon, and Jazer, and Nimrah, and Heshbon, and Elealeh, and Sebam, and Nebo, and Beon, 4 the land which the Lord defeated before the congregation of Israel, is a land for cattle, and your servants have cattle." 5 And they said: "If we have found favor in your sight, let this land be given to your servants for a possession; do not bring us over the Jordan." 6 And Moses said to the children of Gad and to the children of Reuben: "Shall your brethren go to the war, and shall you sit here? 7 And why will you turn away the heart of the children of Israel from going over into the land which the Lord has given them? 8 Thus did your fathers, when I sent them from Kadesh-Barnea to see the land. 9 For when they went up to the valley of Eshkol, and saw the land, they turned away the heart of the children of Israel, that they should not go into the land which the Lord had given them. 10 And the Lord's anger was kindled that day, and He swore, saying: 11 'Surely none of the men that came up out of Egypt, from twenty years old and upward, shall see the land which I swore to Abraham, to Isaac, and to Jacob; because they have not

wholly followed Me; 12 except Caleb, the son of Jephunneh, the Kenizzite, and Joshua, the son of Nun; because they have wholly followed the Lord.' 13 And the Lord's anger was kindled against Israel, and He made them wander to and fro in the wilderness forty years, until all the generation, that had done evil in the sight of the Lord was consumed. 14 And, behold, you have risen in your fathers' stead, a brood of sinful men, to augment yet the fierce anger of the Lord toward Israel. 15 For if you turn away from following Him, He will yet again leave them in the wilderness; and so you will destroy all this people." 16 And they came near to him, and said: "We will build sheepfolds here for our cattle, and cities for our little ones; 17 but we, ourselves, will be ready armed to go before the children of Israel, until we have brought them to their place; and our little ones shall dwell in the fortified cities because of the inhabitants of the land. 18 We will not return to our houses, until everyone of the children of Israel have inherited his inheritance. 19 For we will not inherit with them on the other side of the Jordan, and beyond, because our inheritance has fallen to us on this eastern side of the Jordan." 20 And Moses said to them: "If you will do this thing: if you will arm yourselves to go before the Lord to the war, 21 and every armed man of you will pass over the Jordan before the Lord, until He has driven out His enemies from before Him, 22 and the land be subdued before the Lord, and you return afterward; then you shall be clear before the Lord, and before Israel, and this land shall be your possession before the Lord. 23 But if you will not do so, behold, you have sinned against the Lord; and know your sin will find you. 24 Build you cities for your little ones and folds for your sheep; and do what has proceeded out of your mouth." 25 And the children of Gad and the children of Reuben spoke to Moses, saying: "Your servants will do as my lord commands. 26 Our little ones, our wives, our flocks, and all our cattle, shall be there in the cities of Gilead; 27 but your servants will pass over, every man that is armed for war, before the Lord to battle, as my lord said." 28 So Moses gave charge concerning them to Elazar, the priest, and to Joshua, the son of Nun, and to the heads of the fathers' houses of the tribes of the children of Israel. 29 And Moses said to them: "If the children of Gad and the children of Reuben will pass with you over the Jordan, every man that is armed to battle, before the Lord, and the land shall be subdued before you, then you shall give them the land of Gilead for a possession; 30 but if they will not pass over with you armed, they shall have possessions among you in the land of Canaan." 31 And the children of Gad and the children of Reuben answered, saying: "As the Lord has said to your servants, so will we do. 32 We will pass over, armed before the Lord, into the land of Canaan, and the possession of our inheritance shall remain with us beyond

the Jordan." 33 And Moses gave to them, even to the children of Gad, and to the children of Reuben, and to the half-tribe of Manasseh, the son of Joseph, the kingdom of Sihon, king of the Amorites, and the kingdom of Og, king of Bashan, the land, according to the cities within their borders, and the surrounding cities of the land. 34 And the children of Gad built Dibon, and Ataroth, and Aroer; 35 and Atroth-Shophan, and Jazer, and Jogbehah; 36 and Beth-Nimrah, and Beth-Haran; fortified cities and folds for sheep. 37 And the children of Reuben built Cheshbon, and Elealeh, and Kiriathaim; 38 and Nebo, and Baal-Meon— their names being changed—and Sibmah; and gave their names to the cities which they built. 39 And the children of Machir, the son of Manasseh, went to Gilead and took it and dispossessed the Amorites that were there. 40 And Moses gave Gilead to Machir, the son of Manasseh; and he dwelt there. 41 And Jair, the son of Manasseh, went and took its villages and called them Havvoth-Jair. 42 And Nobach went and took Kenath and its villages, and called it Nobach, after his own name.

The Land of Israel

Bamidbar 32 is a very little understood chapter with great significance, although it seems to have little relationship to our lives today. The tribes of Reuben, Gad, and the half-tribe of Menashe pleaded with Moses that they not enter the land of Israel. Because of their cattle, they preferred to remain on the opposite side of the

Jordan River, meaning the eastern side of the river, still known as the River Jordan today.

These people are part of the Twelve Tribes of Jacob, who Abraham promised would inherit the land of Israel. We are discussing the people of the Exodus, a people of the highest form of intelligence that ever existed. They were fully aware that the land of Israel was something special, and yet they begged Moses to permit them to settle outside the area known as Israel. Moses replies here that it is simply unfair that they remain on the opposite side of the Jordan, while the children of Israel go to war by themselves. Ultimately, Moses extracts a promise from the tribes of Reuben, Gad and the half-tribe of Menashe that they will assist their brethren in capturing the land of Israel, and then they will return to their land across the Jordan River.

We understand that the land of Israel is something special. It becomes the energy center of that time. Yet we see that some of the Israelites, reborn, after the Revelation on Mount Sinai, with a new Desire to Receive, did not want to inhabit the land of Israel—the land promised to Abraham.

Before the Israelites settled—when Abraham, Isaac and Jacob inherited the land—it was known as the land of Canaan. After the flood, Noah divided the land among his three sons. A portion of this land, which is Israel, was given to his son, Shem, because the nation of Israel descended from Shem. Through Divine Inspiration, Noah understood that ultimately this land would belong to the children of Israel, therefore he portioned out this particular section for Shem. With the arrival of the Canaanites, the land that rightfully belonged to the descendants of Shem was captured. This land was no longer known as the land of Shem, or the land of Israel, but was now called the land of Canaan.

243

When Abraham was promised that the land of Israel would belong to his descendants, he was also told the children of Israel would first have to go down to Egypt into exile, and only when they came out of Egypt would they inherit the land. What was the purpose of the long and arduous journey for the Israelites, back to the ancestral land? If God promised them the land, why not let the children of Israel inherit the land immediately? Why first send Jacob and his sons down to Egypt? In addition, a legend in the Talmud says that the reason Rav Chaim Vital, who produced the *Kitvei Ha'Ari* ("Writings of the Ari"), went to Damascus was because, when the Messiah finally arrives, the city called Jerusalem will extend up to Damascus, which is on the other side of the Jordan River. The Jordan River flows down what is presently the land of Israel, but Damascus is not part of Israel. Further up, we have Lebanon—but Damascus is just twenty-five miles away from the present borders of Israel.

Jacob and the Firstborn

When the Bible discusses what happened with the tribes of Reuben, Gad, and the half-tribe of Menashe, and their cattle, it is a code and not a story about people who did not want to go into the land of Israel. Rav Isaac Luria (the Ari), in *Sefer haLikutim* ("Book of Compilations"), provides us with an insight. He says the secret of the matter is as follows: When Jacob worked for seven years so he could marry Rachel, Laban tricked him, giving him Leah instead. In the moment Jacob was consummating his marriage, he was not aware that it was Leah and not Rachel that was his wife. Many customs have originated from this incident. Today, in traditional wedding ceremonies, the bridegroom meets the bride before the wedding to be certain she has not been exchanged. This is called *Badeken*.

Jacob was a chariot so how could he have been fooled? Jacob suspected Laban would try some kind of a trick, and he gave Rachel codes so that, on the night of the wedding he would ask her certain questions and if she knew the answers he could be certain she was Rachel. But Rachel gave away these secrets to Leah, and thus Jacob did not know it was not Rachel. On a very superficial level, this is what happens.

When Jacob married Leah, he was under the impression she was Rachel, and Reuben was born from the consummation of this marriage consciousness. There is a particular power in the firstborn, and because Reuben was conceived without Jacob's knowledge, Rueben could not enter the land of Israel. What does this mean? We know that the Bible is a cosmic code and when Reuben said he did not want to go into Israel, it was not a decision based on his cattle—it was because he *could* not enter the land of Israel.

There was a rebirth at the Revelation on Mount Sinai—and the land of Israel was already the supreme energy center at that time. The Ari said the reason Reuben did not enter the land of Israel was not because he decided against it but because of the energy-intelligence that came into Reuben as a result of Jacob thinking his wife was Rachel and not Leah. Why does the Bible give us the impression that it was purely an economic reason? The more we study the Bible, the more we learn how much it is concealed. Rather than just telling us Reuben was not fit to enter the land of Israel, the Bible says it was for an economic reason. There was a justification.

No one knew the land of Israel was the energy center of the world—which is why there was a Revelation on Mount Sinai. The Revelation meant that now the metaphysical world, which is generally concealed, was revealed. Things we cannot touch, see or feel are in the realm of metaphysics. On Mount Sinai, the world of metaphysics and the world of physics were one and the same.

Because of this transformation of the children of Israel, they realized that the place where they could directly draw energy was the land of Israel.

The children of Israel were promised this land and therefore the land of Israel belongs to them. The reason the tribes of Reuben, Gad and the half-tribe of Menashe could not enter the land promised to the children of Israel was not something purely physical—it was much deeper than that. The children of Gad could not enter the land because Gad was also conceived without Jacob's consciousness. The keyword here is Da'at (Consciousness). When Rachel could not bear children, she asked Jacob for permission to give him her handmaiden—it was with consciousness, and therefore everything was conducted appropriately.

Leah, however, did not ask for permission when she gave Jacob her handmaiden Zilpah. Jacob was unaware that she was not Leah, so there was no consciousness. The Bible calls Reuben the firstborn, and in Deuteronomy, it also calls Joseph the firstborn. Therefore, the Zohar and the Ari raise the question, how there could be two firstborns of Jacob? The answer is because Jacob's consciousness— his thought energy-intelligence—was so elevated that he was, in consciousness, connecting with Rachel, having intercourse with Rachel, and not Leah. Thus his internal energy force, manifested by his sperm, remained in suspended animation, and it became manifest when he physically had intercourse with Rachel, and she bore Joseph. Therefore, Joseph is the rightful firstborn son.

This teaches us the importance of the thought-consciousness of the parents, which becomes manifest at the time of conception, and how it affects the child conceived of that intercourse. In other words, the fact that Jacob's thought was for Rachel, enabled him to direct the internal energy-intelligence of that sperm.

We then ask how Reuben was born. The Ari explains that the physical aspect of this conception between Leah and Jacob did become manifest, however the internal energy-intelligence did not become manifest. The Ari says that Reuben had been created with a particular body, which could handle the power of the firstborn— but the power of the firstborn was lacking. The power of the firstborn remained in suspended animation, and was subsequently passed on to Joseph. The internal thought energy-intelligence of Jacob did not become manifest within Reuben. Therefore, the entire tribe of Reuben and Gad believed their future rested with the land in Jordan.

In many cases, there are people who do not have the best relationship with their father. We may even read in the newspaper that a son killed his father—which is this kind of discord taken to an extreme. There have been incidences where a parent passes away, and the son, who was not on the best terms with his parent, wants to know if he should say the prayer of Kaddish for this parent. This has nothing to do with whether or not he has the time for such an endeavor, nor is it because he does not want to assist his father's elevation—but rather it is because he internally feels it is a prayer that should be performed with a clear and honest consciousness, and not the old animosity.

The Ari, in *Sha'ar haGilgulim* ("The Gate of Reincarnations"), discusses how we can tell what the thoughts of the parents were at the time of intercourse and conception. Imagine looking at a person and knowing what this individual's parents thought about on the night their child was conceived. The Ari says there are times when it is obvious that the parent's intentions during intercourse were not pure. Then he discusses that if the child now reads The Gate of Reincarnations and understands fully what happened the night he or she was conceived, they still have to honor their father and mother, even though the spiritual aspect of the sperm—meaning all beneficial attributes also contained in it—were not transferred to the child.

The Ari explains that, even though this may have been the scenario, this child was born for the purpose of *tikkun* (spiritual correction). Thus, had this man and woman not conceived the physical body of this child, the soul of the child would not have the environment in which it could achieve its *tikkun*. Despite whatever qualities such a child was unable to derive from its parents, this child nevertheless has a place where the soul can rest—and this is what the particular child needs. Perhaps because, in a prior incarnation, he was not the most righteous person and, therefore he must return to such a situation. The body that would now incorporate that kind of soul was created by virtue of those two people and, therefore he would have to honor his mother and father forever all the same.

Jacob did not have Da'at consciousness, so he was unaware that it was Leah and not Rachel. This aspect of his consciousness did not become manifest—and thus Reuben is just dealing with his cattle. We shall come to understand why Reuben was in charge of the cattle. We know that sperm, which is in a potential physical state, is not activated until the point of Da'at—until that person becomes conscious he is having an ejaculation during intercourse. The Zohar says that Da'at is what initiates the internal thought energy-intelligence of the sperm.

When Joseph is sold as a slave, why does Jacob not know? We are dealing with a Chariot—someone who could see time, space, and motion, past, present and future all as one. Thus wherever Joseph was, there he was. Someone can only hide from us is because we are within the confines of time, space and motion. Given the limitations of time, space and motion, someone hiding in another room can be fully concealed from us. The question is why Jacob—a man freed from the restrictions of time, space, and motion—

could not have known? The answer to this is that his elevated consciousness was temporarily restricted. In accordance with the law of free will, his consciousness was taken away from him during that period of time.

Why would Rav Chaim Vital say, "I am poor and my eyes are failing, but I feel I must get the Writings of the Ari out?" What is the matter? With his visions, why could he not manipulate a couple of deals and make a small fortune in no time? All kabbalists could really do this—so why did he not get rich? Why did Chaim Vital, at the end, have to say, "I am poor," meaning he could not get rich—even though he once said being poor is one of the worst curses? The answer is because, under certain conditions, certain things must occur. If Chaim Vital and Shmuel Vital were not in that condition of being poor, the Writings of the Ari could never have appeared in the form it did.

This is much like when Rav Shimon was seen by his father-in-law, Rav Pinchas Ben Yair, in an emaciated and deteriorated condition because he had spent twelve years in a cave, buried in sand. Rav Shimon said, "Only because of the way you see me was I capable of acquiring the consciousness to receive the Zohar." There is no question that Rav Chaim Vital and Rav Shmuel Vital would answer in the same way. At certain times, a portion of our life must play itself out, and there must be no intervention.

While Jacob could have intervened and said that he knew Joseph was alive, and asked to have him brought back, there was a certain course of action that had to be enacted. The Israelites ultimately had to go down to Egypt, and Jacob understood this. Why did the Israelites have to go down to the land of Egypt and then, when they came out of Egypt, capture the land of Israel?

Certain things must take place where the kabbalist, or Jacob, or any of the other Chariots, are not permitted to interfere with the events that transpire. This does not mean the Chariot has a *tikkun* to fulfill in this situation; they are simply part of what has to take place. They had their function. However when their position could interfere with the rest of the cosmic events unfolding, they would be placed where they would not interfere—meaning they could not see the events from beginning to end as they normally could.

It was not a question of free will. Their advanced level of consciousness was not operable at such times. It was placed in a state of suspended animation, where they could not make use of it. They had no *tikkun* process here. This was part of a cosmic unfolding of events. Jacob, seeing that Joseph was alive, would interfere with the events that had to unfold.

It was the same with Gad. Leah did not ask Jacob for permission to give him Zilpah. When he had intercourse with Zilpah, Jacob thought it was Leah. The Ari says Jacob made the same mistake twice. He thought it was Leah, and Gad was conceived without Da'at consciousness. We now understand, from the Ari's explanation, why Gad also did not enter the land of Israel. It was not a question of a decision not to enter. Gad was not metaphysically or spiritually prepared as a vessel to adapt himself to the kind of centrality of energy that existed in the land of Israel.

With the story of the half-tribe of Menashe, the Ari shows us how the stories of the Bible suddenly take on another significance. And we hope one day, we will even come to the realization that there is no such thing as Judaism. The Bible is simply teaching us about life. When Joseph was in Egypt, he married Osnat, who was the daughter of Dina. Dina was the daughter of Jacob and Leah. In Genesis 34, we read that Dina was raped by the leader of the tribe of Nablus, Shechem. Osnat was conceived from this incident, and because these two souls were not of the same conscious level—Shechem was of the other nations and Osnat was an Israelite—consequently there was no totality of unification in their consciousness. Half of the consciousness came from Shechem and half from Dina—so there were two levels of consciousness now emerging in their daughter Osnat.

Joseph came from the level of total *kedusha*, which does not merely mean the word "holy" but also is a totality of the highest form of receptivity. In other words, the Desire to Receive was in a complete unified whole. When Joseph had intercourse with Osnat and she conceived, their firstborn was Menashe, who inherited the consciousness from his father and mother—meaning from his mother there was the consciousness of Dina and Shechem and from his father there was the consciousness of Jacob and Rachel. Therefore, within Menashe was instilled two different levels of consciousness. For this reason, the half of the tribe that manifested the consciousness of Osnat, the daughter of Dina—meaning Shechem of the other nations—did not enter the land of Israel for the same reason as Reuben and Gad. They could not handle the kind of energy that was subsequently to be revealed by the physical structure of the Holy Temple, and thus emanated from that land.

The Shechinah

We still have the question of why the Bible had to obscure the situation, saying the cattle were a reason—as if there was an economic reason these tribes wanted to remain in Jordan. To understand this, we turn to the Zohar, which says when someone is imbued with the Shechinah—the concentration of all knowledge, everything in this universe, past, present, and future; a single force of energy-intelligence above time, space, and motion—they know what is happening everywhere, with everyone. There are no secrets.

Most people are governed by the limitations of time, space, and motion but, for the one upon whom the Shechinah rests, there is no such thing as limitation. By forging this connection and tapping into this kind of consciousness, nothing is concealed.

The Zohar also explains that the Shechinah is not only revealed at the place in which She belongs—the Holy Temple in Israel. She is also found with the Israelites in exile all over the world. At the time of the destruction of the Holy Temple, the Shechinah went into *galut* (exile). What this means is that prior to the destruction of the Holy Temple the Shechinah was present, and all the Israelites could tap into Her influence and energy. Therefore, during the reign of King Solomon and the rule of the Holy Temple, peace prevailed in this universe as it had not done in any other period of history. Because, at that point in time, everyone could access the Shechinah, chaos simply did not exist.

Today, a major reason people keep busy trying to accumulate more wealth is because of the fear that tomorrow something bad might happen. Insecurity and uncertainty are what propel people. This is because the Temple does not exist, and the Shechinah is not revealed in its proper place. However, the Zohar says that today, the Shechinah reveals Herself only to an individual—who can be anywhere in the world, if they are a proper channel for this kind of revelation. They can tap into the Shechinah, no matter where they are. However, such a blessing is only for those who can adapt themselves, those who harmonize with the Shechinah.

Rav Ashlag says that what really happened with the tribes of Reuben, Gad, and half of Menashe, is the difference between the soul of an Israelite and souls of the other nations. There are two levels of consciousness. The Israelites have the kind of internal vessels where recipiency truly takes place. The example of a cup is useful. There is the exterior part of the cup and the interior part of the cup. With no exterior there is no interior with which the cup can receive anything. Yet, only the interior of the cup, which is empty space, is important to the general function of a cup. This is the real vessel. The external part of the cup is the support but it is not the actual part of the cup that holds within it that which it is receiving.

Rav Ashlag says that at the *Gemar ha Tikkun* (End of the Correction), everyone will be at this level of consciousness, tapping into all of this information and, consequently, this will bring peace on Earth and goodwill toward men—as it was during the time of the Holy Temple. Everyone will be happy because all people of the world will be accessing the Lightforce of God. Rav Shimon says the time of Messiah has not happened because all the souls from the exterior vessel have not yet entered this physical universe. Much as people who are separated, so is the physical structure of the universe separated into exterior and interior vessels. Before the *Gemar ha Tikkun*, (End of the Correction), only those who have this proper internal aspect can connect to the Shechinah. This is the revelation of the Zohar.

Rav Ashlag says that we can connect to the Shechinah by virtue of the land of Israel because there are two aspects. There are the people and there is the land, and only the land of Israel is our channel for connecting to the Shechinah. In order to connect with the Shechinah, we need physical channels. As the Zohar tells us, anyone praying outside the territorial borders of Israel should at least be informed that when we pray we must change our location. For example, if we are living in Queens and we are praying in a particular place, to connect to the Shechinah—an all-embracing unified whole—we need to transfer our consciousness to the land of Israel. If we have not transferred our consciousness to Israel, then we have only connected to the exterior of a vessel, which does not connect to the Shechinah.

How do we reconcile this with the fact that the Shechinah went into exile—went out of Israel, with the destruction of the Temple? It seems to be a contradiction because the Zohar says that the Shechinah can only rest in the place where it belongs. How then can it also rest on an individual, a person? A proper vessel can tap into the Shechinah. This means that an individual could be outside of Israel, and still be able to connect to the Shechinah, because they are a proper vessel. At the time of the destruction of the Temple, the Israelites were promised, with a guarantee that the Shechinah would go outside to assist them in exile. Yet the Zohar says the Shechinah can only rest where it belongs. The secret here is that the Shechinah is in Israel, and it is also not in Israel. If you are a proper vessel, an adaptable channel, and physically might dwell outside the territorial borders of Israel, then you can connect to the Shechinah despite the fact you are outside. If you are in Israel and you want to connect to the Shechinah, but you are not a proper channel, you will not make the connection. Therefore, the problems that exist in Israel are even more severe because they are closer to the world's great energy center.

How do we determine who is a Jew and who is a non-Jew? There are those who appear to be non-Jewish, and yet emerge as Rabbi Akiva did. This, again, depends on being able to observe the interior of the individual, which is the soul—rather than the exterior, which is the body. Both the Zohar and the Talmud say that, in Israel there shall never be one as great as Moses—but among the nations of the world there will be one as great as Moses. This was Bilaam. Both of these men were prophets who could see the past and the present, but the Shechinah could not rest on the level of Bilaam. Rav Shimon tells us that as great as Bilaam was, there was a level of consciousness in Moses that he did not attain. His was almost the same, but he did not have the consciousness of the Right Column. Moses came from the positive aspect of the Abel, and Bilaam came from the negative aspect. Negative consciousness is not the Shechinah. Bilaam could connect on a level of where time, space, and motion do not exist, but for the sake of negative purposes. The Shechinah only connects to the positive aspect.

In the case of Rav Chaim Vital, it was not that they could not get rich—they would not get rich because they knew this would have interfered with the way the *Kitvei Ha'Ari* ("Writings of the Ari") would have been revealed. It is the same with Rav Shimon. Had his body not deteriorated to the point it did, he could never have had the Zohar revealed through him. He would not have been a channel. Therefore, the *Kitvei Ha'Ari*, which emerged through Rav Shmuel Vital, was not despite, but because of, the fact that he was so poor. The Shechinah acts as our intermediary.

When there is an arousal of these exterior vessels—which are drawing down from Above to Below without restriction, as Balak and Bilaam were doing—they were able to make this kind of connection to the exterior. For example, there is a positive and negative aspect to the sun. Without the sun, there can be no life, and yet too much sunlight can cause fires or skin cancer. The negative aspect is called the exterior.

During the New Moon connections, we make specific meditations so we are connecting to the positive aspect of the month because everything contains an exterior and an interior. We too contain an interior and an exterior—our soul is the interior and the body is the exterior, because the energy-intelligence of the body is the Desire to Receive for the Self Alone.

We can now understand why they decided to remain outside the territorial borders of Israel. There had to be a physical reason compelling them to remain on the one side of the Jordan River, rather than enter Israel. But why did it have to be cattle?

Levels of Consciousness

We know there are four levels of consciousness. The kabbalists gave them names, which could be misleading but they had to choose some definition. The four levels of consciousness are referred to as Inanimate, Vegetable, Animal, and Human (known as Speaking).

Neo-Darwinism asserts that animals and all other apparent lifeforms have not evolved to the human level, where intercommunication exists. This could appear to be a completely egotistical statement because dogs can hear sounds that humans cannot—thus who is on a higher level, the dog or the human? The dog's capacity for detecting frequencies is much higher than that of any human being. It often seems that they communicate on a level that humans cannot understand. As humans, we tend to think that someone who cannot comprehend a conversation is at a lower level than our own. This may be a complete misconception. Dogs understand us on a fairly intimate level, and what they do is on an instinctive level of consciousness.

There is a precept in the Bible that, if a human being is in a field and goes to the bathroom, they must dig a hole and cover it up. Dogs do this instinctively, and thus the potential contamination becomes fertilizer.

In short, for us, "animal" means a lower level of intelligence. The Ari explains that the Bible says "cattle," and not some other reason, to indicate to us the level of consciousness of Reuben, Gad and the half-tribe of Menashe. We have just learned from the Ari that the children of these tribes were of a lower level of consciousness because there was no Da'at at the time of their conception. In other words, at the time of their conception, Jacob did not know at this level. Their free-will level of consciousness did not exist. However, the level of consciousness of cattle *did* exist. Meaning, they had a lower level of consciousness and they acted robotically without Da'at consciousness. This is why the Ari stresses the point of Da'at. With every level below the human, consciousness is absolutely robotic. The hearing of a dog, which is of a higher level of frequency than a human being, is nonetheless merely instinctive. When connected to the *Shechinah* and the level of Da'at, a human being hears everything resounding throughout the universe.

Yet Reuben, Gad, and the half-tribe of Menashe, as the Ari described, were not of that level. They were at the level of consciousness of cattle, meaning the level that is one-step down from Human. There was no consciousness free will, no ability to rise above a destiny. All the instinctive consciousness that is in the Inanimate, Vegetable, and Animal can be achieved by a human being who connects to the Shechinah. These people were not on that level of consciousness, though, and they were not born with Da'at. They were born without the consciousness of Jacob. Without the internal energy-intelligence of Jacob, the rest was instinctive. In essence, they did not decide they would prefer to live outside of Israel—it was inevitable. These things happened because they were destined.

As a final note, the Zohar, in the portion of Vayera, says that during the time of the Coming of the Messiah, the tribe of Reuben will return to Israel and make a claim on his firstborn birthright. Preceding the incident of the golden calf, all the firstborn males were destined to be the High Priests, which is why the firstborn sons fast on the eve of Passover. The tribe of Reuben will return at the time of the Messiah to reclaim his birthright, which is not rightfully his, and they will go to war against their fellow Israelites—because, on another level of consciousness, Reuben feels he is the firstborn. The Zohar says that only the proper vessel can connect with the Shechinah. These two and a half tribes that never entered into Israel are now dispersed, and we do not know who they are. However, at the time of the Coming of Messiah, they will emerge as they really are.

Conclusion

There are only two short pages of Zohar on this section, and yet we know that, where the Zohar either omits or has very little to say on a subject, it is thus left for us to delve into the secret that must be revealed here—because that which is less is always more.

There are 112 verses in the portion of Matot. According to Kabbalah, the number 112 represents the interface between the World of the Tetragrammaton—*Yud, Hei, Vav,* and *Hei,* the numerical value of which is 26, the world of the metaphysical, the Flawless Universe, beyond the limitations of time, space, and motion—and Elohim, represented by the number 86, another Name of God that represents our world of chaos. God is not a renegade or a criminal who needs at least 72 different Names or aliases because he is running from city to city. The different Names of God refer to different dimensions. The Zohar says there are only two aspects in this world. Similarly, computers operate entirely on zero and one. Here we have 112 verses to tell us that these two almost opposite realms, the Flawless Universe and the chaotic universe, can be combined into one. This is the secret of Matot.

The Bible, in the opening verse, says that Moses spoke first to the chieftains and then to the other Israelites about vows. Why did Moses first speak to the chieftains? Why did Moses choose this time to discuss vows with the chieftains, and then move on? The Zohar says simply that a chieftain represents control. You control if you rule, and vows are only about control. Here, the Bible is teaching us that we can eliminate the black holes in our lives. This is what this portion concerns. The chieftain in this section is only to indicate that if we want to be in control, we must interface with the world of consciousness, which is connected to the Flawless Universe, and bring this to bear on our physical world, known as Elohim, and there is no other choice—which is beautiful.

We need to remove the limitations of space, time, and motion, but how is it to be done? We say what is missing is the interface that will bring these two worlds together. The Torah scroll is what brings this interface. We have been given the system by which we can exercise control over two different elements. The mind over the body, over physicality, and over chaos—wherever it might exist. This is Matot.

BOOK OF BAMIDBAR:
PORTION OF MASEI

PORTION OF MASEI

Bamidbar 33:1 These are the journeys of the children of Israel, by which they went forth out of the land of Egypt with their armies under the hand of Moses and Aaron. 2 And Moses wrote their goings forth, stage by stage, by the commandment of the Lord; and these are the stages of their journeys. 3 And they journeyed from Rameses in the first month, on the fifteenth day of the first month; on the day after the Passover, the children of Israel went out with a high hand in the sight of all the Egyptians, 4 while the Egyptians were burying those that the Lord had smitten among them, all their first-born; upon their gods, also the Lord executed judgments. 5 And the children of Israel journeyed from Rameses, and pitched in Succoth. 6 And they journeyed from Succoth, and pitched in Etham, which is in the edge of the wilderness. 7 And they journeyed from Etham, and turned back unto Pihahiroth, which is before Baal-Zephon; and they pitched before Migdol. 8 And they journeyed from Penehahiroth, and passed through the midst of the sea into the wilderness; and they went three days' journey in the wilderness of Etham, and pitched in Marah. 9 And they journeyed from Marah, and came unto Elim; and in Elim were twelve springs of water, and seventy palm trees; and they pitched there. 10 And they journeyed from Elim, and pitched by the Red Sea. 11 And they journeyed from the Red Sea, and pitched in the wilderness of Sin. 12 And they journeyed from the wilderness of Sin, and pitched in Dophkah. 13 And they journeyed from Dophkah, and pitched in Alush. 14 And they journeyed from Alush, and pitched in Rephidim, where was no water for the people to drink. 15 And they journeyed from Rephidim, and pitched in the wilderness of Sinai. 16 And they journeyed from the wilderness of Sinai, and pitched in Kibroth-Hattaavah. 17 And they journeyed from Kibroth-Hattaavah, and pitched in Hazeroth. 18 And they journeyed from Hazeroth, and pitched in Rithmah. 19 And they journeyed from Rithmah, and pitched in Rimmon-Parez. 20 And they journeyed from Rimmon-Parez, and pitched in Libnah. 21 And they journeyed from Libnah, and pitched in Rissah. 22 And they journeyed from Rissah, and pitched in Kehelathah. 23 And they journeyed from Kehelathah, and pitched in mount Shepher. 24 And they journeyed from mount Shepher, and pitched in Haradah. 25 And they journeyed from Haradah, and pitched in Makheloth. 26 And they journeyed from Makheloth, and pitched in Tahath. 27 And they journeyed from Tahath, and pitched in Tarach. 28 And they journeyed from Tarach, and pitched in Mithkah. 29 And they journeyed from Mithkah, and pitched in Hashmonah. 30 And they journeyed from Hashmonah, and pitched in Moseroth. 31 And they journeyed from Moseroth, and pitched

in Bene-Jaakan. 32 And they journeyed from
Bene-Jaakan, and pitched in Hor-Haggidgad.
33 And they journeyed from Hor-Haggidgad,
and pitched in Yotvata. 34 And they journeyed
from Yotvata, and pitched in Abronah. 35 And
they journeyed from Abronah, and pitched
in Ezion-Gaber. 36 And they journeyed from
Ezion-Gaber, and pitched in the wilderness
of Zin—the same is Kadesh. 37 And they
journeyed from Kadesh, and pitched in
Mount Hor, in the edge of the land of Edom.
38 And Aaron, the priest went up into Mount
Hor at the commandment of the Lord, and
died there, in the fortieth year after the
children of Israel were come out of the land
of Egypt, in the fifth month, on the first day
of the month. 39 And Aaron was a hundred
and twenty-three years old when he died in
Mount Hor. 40 And the Canaanite, the king
of Arad, who dwelt in the South in the land of
Canaan, heard of the coming of the children
of Israel. 41 And they journeyed from Mount
Hor, and pitched in Zalmonah. 42 And they
journeyed from Zalmonah, and pitched in
Punon. 43 And they journeyed from Punon,
and pitched in Oboth. 44 And they journeyed
from Oboth, and pitched in Iyei-Ha'abarim,
in the border of Moab. 45 And they journeyed
from Ijim, and pitched in Dibon-Gad. 46 And
they journeyed from Dibon-Gad, and pitched
in Almon-Diblathaim. 47 And they journeyed
from Almon-Diblathaim, and pitched in the
mountains of Abarim, in front of Nebo. 48
And they journeyed from the mountains of

Abarim, and pitched in the plains of Moab by the Jordan at Jericho. 49 And they pitched by the Jordan, from Beth-Jeshimoth even unto Abel-Shittim in the plains of Moab.

The Journeying of the Israelites

Why would the Bible use 132 verses to tell us where in the wilderness the Israelites traveled? What we hope to achieve with this reading about the 42 different encampments, is to reach the point where we can be present in the moment before confusion set in. Cancer always becomes manifest in the month of Cancer, and the portion of Masei always occurs at the end of the month of Tammuz (Cancer), when both the disease and the confusion occur. This reading connects us to the power of the Ana Beko'ach. The Ana Beko'ach is so powerful because it embraces the entire physical reality. Time, space, and motion are an illusion. The universe has already decided that what we connect to now is the very root of Creation itself.

Among the many things the portion of Masei discusses are the travels of the Israelites from place to place. And while this may be historically interesting, it seems ridiculous that, for 3400 years, people come to listen to a reading about places that do not exist What the Bible wants to teach us here is a concept revealed in the Zohar, which science recognizes but has buried. As long as it remains suppressed, chaos will never come to an end. Only through the process of quantum—when yesterday, today, and tomorrow are one—can chaos be removed. It is somewhat innately understood that if we could see tomorrow, chaos cannot rule our life. Once we can see tomorrow, we can avoid catastrophic events. They can no longer inflict chaos upon us. Quantum physics states that everything is one. This is true even within ourselves. Being the prime cause, the mind should affect every effect. If there is some form of physical chaos, such as illness, there is no reason why we cannot control that chaos with our minds.

The Ana Beko'ach

For those who study Kabbalah, the number 42 always refers to the Ana Beko'ach, the instrument by which this entire physical world was created.

There are some who do not take the Ana Beko'ach as seriously as it was intended to be taken, which is not to say they do not use it, only that they do not use it to its full potential. The Ana Beko'ach is an interface between the Lightforce of God and that which was created—meaning this entire universe. Therefore, when the Bible refers to 42 journeys, it is merely a code for the opportunity to tap into this force, this great power.

Using the spiritual technology of the Ana Beko'ach we interface two worlds. With our minds alone we can bring the Flawless Universe into this world. If we have not removed chaos from our lives, then we need to understand we are either involved in the process, or ensnared by uncertainty. There is no question that we can bring an end to chaos in our personal lives by connecting with this reading on the Shabbat of Masei.

The 42 letters that make up seven verses of the Ana Beko'ach are the method by which God created every aspect of this universe, and what we can capture with the reading is a reconnection to that Flawless Universe—the state before the confusion and chaos we generally experience.

Masei is the final portion of the Book of Bamidbar—which has in it every conceivable form of chaos that humankind can suffer. We listen to the reading of this Torah portion on Shabbat, not to prolong the reading because there are so many verses, but to power up a system that can literally remove all forms of chaos without repeating what we have gained in each reading of Bamidbar. This is a more extensive spiritual, immaterial device that permits us to remove every form of chaos, at the very moment we read or listen to the Torah reading—whether it be plague, bankruptcy, death, or any other disaster conceivable. The reason there are so many verses here is because this is the way God devised the system whereby we can have some chance of survival without the usual snares that have lain in wait for us ever since the beginning—before the sin of Adam, before the world of corruption.

The only dimension that was affected by Adam and Eve's eating from the Tree of Knowledge is the physical reality. The Bible appeared in order to give us a physical system—the letters of the Hebrew alphabet, which are the channels we can use to connect to that incorporeal world, the Flawless Universe.

Why do we need to know which places the Israelites went to, or that there were in fact 42 locations? Kabbalah teaches that the number 42 always refers to the Ana Beko'ach. We need to instill within our consciousness that there is only one objective—to connect to the Flawless Universe. The world was created with 42 letters, 42 Names. With the Ana Beko'ach we can go back to the time before the Creation, before the world was polluted by humankind. The only reason we are affected in this reality is because we are weak and without antidotes.

The Bible gives us a unique opportunity here. With the Hebrew letters *Yud, Chaf, Shin* (ש.כ.י) of the Ana Beko'ach, we access the full energy of the 42 Names. Whether we are aware of it or not, when we read or listen to this Torah portion on Shabbat, we are in fact doing the Ana Beko'ach. It makes sense if we feel life has improved because, as Rav Shimon bar Yochai says, the proof of the pudding is in the eating. If your life has not improved, why waste your time?

For the most part the world is ignorant to these tools. This is why the Kabbalah Centres exist. If we can restore our environment, our society, and ourselves to the state of the Flawless Universe, we will be rid of pollution, and the world can return to its natural state. Let us take advantage of this opportunity and use all of our consciousness. Whatever is in our minds is what we are—nothing more, nothing less. We are connecting to the greatest, most awesome physical channel—which is the Lightforce of God.

In this section, we are learning about the Ana Beko'ach, and, with it, we are establishing certain security shields around us—shields which will protect us in the future, so that disease and chaos do not get through.

50 And the Lord spoke to Moses in the plains of Moab by the Jordan at Jericho, saying: 51 "Speak to the children of Israel, and say to them: When you pass over the Jordan into the land of Canaan, 52 then you shall drive out all the inhabitants of the land from before you, and destroy all their figured stones, and destroy all their molten images, and demolish all their high places. 53 And you shall drive out the inhabitants of the land, and dwell there; for to you I have given the land to possess. 54 And you shall inherit the land by lot according to your families—to those with more you shall give more inheritance, and to the fewer you shall give the less inheritance; where the lot falls for each man that shall be his; according to the tribes of your fathers shall you inherit. 55 But if you will not drive out the inhabitants of the land from before you, then shall those that you let remain be as thorns in your eyes, and as pricks in your sides, and they shall harass you in the land wherein you dwell. 56 And it shall come to pass, that as I thought to do to them, so will I do to you."

Bamidbar 34:1 And the Lord spoke to Moses, saying: 2 "Command the children of Israel, and say to them: 'When you come into the land of Canaan, this shall be the land that shall fall to you for an inheritance, the land of Canaan according to its borders. 3 Thus, your south side shall be from the wilderness of Zin, close by the side of Edom, and your southern border shall begin at the end of the Salt Sea eastward; 4 and your border shall turn around the southern side of the ascent of Akrabbim, and continue to Zin; and be on the south of Kadesh-Barnea; and it shall go on to Hazar-Addar, and continue to Azmon; 5 and the border shall turn around from Azmon to the Brook of Egypt, and it shall end at the Sea. 6 And for the western border, you shall have the Great Sea for a border; this shall be your west border. 7 And this shall be your north border: from the Great Sea you shall mark out your line to Mount Hor; 8 from Mount Hor you shall mark out a line to the entrance to Hamath; and the direction of the border shall be at Zedad; 9 and the border continue to Ziphron, and it shall end at Hazar-Enan; this shall be your northern border. 10 And you shall mark out your line for the eastern border from Hazar-Enan to Shepham; 11 and the border shall go down from Shepham to Riblah, on the eastern side of Ain; and the border shall go down, and shall reach the eastern slope of the sea of Kinnereth; 12 and the border shall go down to the Jordan, and shall end at the Salt Sea; this shall be your land according to its surrounding borders." 13 And Moses commanded the children of Israel, saying: "This is the land where you shall receive inheritance by lot, which the Lord has commanded to give to the nine tribes, and to the half-tribe; 14 for the tribe of the children of Reuben, according to their fathers' houses, and the tribe of the children of Gad, according to their fathers' houses, have received, and the half-tribe of Manasseh have received, their inheritance; 15 the two tribes and the half-tribe have received their inheritance beyond the Jordan at east of Jericho, toward the sun rise." 16 And the Lord spoke to Moses, saying: 17 "These are the names of the men that shall take possession of the land for you: Elazar, the priest, and Joshua, the son of Nun. 18 And you shall take one prince of every tribe, to take possession of the land. 19 And these are the names of the men: of the tribe of Judah, Caleb, the son of Jephunneh. 20 And of the tribe of the children of Simeon, Shemuel, the son of Ammihud. 21 Of the tribe of Benjamin, Elidad, the son of Kislon. 22 And of the tribe of the children of Dan, a prince, Bukki, the son of Jogli. 23 Of the children of Joseph: of the tribe of the children of Manasseh, a prince, Hanniel, the son of Ephod; 24 and of the tribe of the children of Ephraim, a prince, Kemuel, the son of Shiphtan. 25 And of the tribe of the children of Zebulun, a prince, Elitzahpan, the son of Parnach. 26 And of the tribe of the children of Issaschar, a prince, Paltiel the son of Azzan. 27 And of the tribe of the children of Asher, a prince, Ahihud, the son of Shelomi. 28 And of the tribe of the children of Naphtali, a prince, Pedahel, the son of Ammihud. 29 These are they whom the Lord commanded to divide the inheritance to the children of Israel in the land of Canaan."

Bamidbar 35:1 And the Lord spoke to Moses, in the plains of Moab by the Jordan at Jericho, saying: 2 "Command the children of Israel that they give to the Levites of the inheritance of their possession cities to dwell in; and open land around the cities you shall give to the Levites. 3 And the cities they shall have to dwell in; and their open land shall be for their cattle, and for their substance, and for all their beasts. 4 And the open land around the cities, which you shall give to the Levites, shall be from the wall of the city and outward a thousand cubits around. 5 And you shall measure outside the city on the east side two thousand cubits, and on the south side two thousand cubits, and on the west side two thousand cubits, and on the north side two thousand cubits, the city being in the middle. This shall be to them the open land around the cities. 6 And the cities which you shall give to the Levites, shall be the six cities of refuge, which you shall give to the manslayer to flee to; and to these you shall add forty-two cities. 7 All the cities which you shall give to the Levites shall be forty-eight cities: you shall give them with the open land around them. 8 And concerning the cities which you shall give as the possession of the children of Israel, from the many you shall take many, and from the few you shall take few; each tribe according to its inheritance which it inherits shall give of its cities to the Levites." 9 And the Lord spoke to Moses, saying: 10 "Speak to the children of Israel, and say to them: When you pass over the Jordan into the land of Canaan, 11 then you shall appoint cities to be cities of refuge for you, that the manslayer that kills any person through error may flee to. 12 And the cities shall be to you for refuge from the avenger, so that the manslayer does not die, until he stands before the congregation for judgment. 13 And as to the cities which you shall give, there shall be for you six cities of refuge. 14 You shall give three cities beyond the Jordan, and three cities shall you give in the land of Canaan; they shall be cities of refuge. 15 For the children of Israel, and for the stranger and for the settler among them, shall these six cities be for refuge, that every one that kills any person through error may flee to. 16 But if he smote him with an instrument of iron, so that he died, he is a murderer; the murderer shall surely be put to death. 17 And if he smote him with a stone in the hand, whereby a man may die, and he died, he is a murderer; the murderer shall surely be put to death. 18 Or if he smote him with a weapon of wood in the hand, whereby a man may die, and he died, he is a murderer; the murderer shall surely be put to death. 19 The avenger of blood shall himself put the murderer to death; when he meets him, he shall put him to death. 20 And if he thrust him with hatred, or hurled at him anything, lying in wait, so that he died; 21 or in enmity smote him with his hand, that he died; he that smote him shall surely be put to death: he is a murderer; the avenger of blood shall put the murderer to death when he meets him. 22 But if he thrust him suddenly without enmity, or hurled upon him anything without lying in wait, 23 or with any stone, whereby a man may die, seeing him not, and cast it upon him, so that he died, and he was not his enemy, nor sought his harm; 24 then the congregation shall judge between the smiter and the avenger of blood according to these ordinances; 25 and the congregation shall deliver the manslayer out of the hand of the avenger of blood, and the congregation shall restore him to his city of refuge, where he fled; and he shall dwell there until the death of the High Priest, who was anointed with the holy oil. 26 But if the manslayer shall at any time go beyond the border of his city of refuge, where he fled; 27 and the avenger of blood find him without the border of his city of refuge, and the avenger of blood slay the manslayer; there shall be no blood-guiltiness for him; 28 because he must remain in his city of refuge until the death of the High Priest; but after the death of the High Priest, the manslayer may return to the land of his possession. 29 And these things shall be for a statute of judgment to you throughout your generations in all your dwellings. 30 Who ever kills any person, the murderer shall be slain at the mouth of witnesses; but one witness shall not testify against any person, that he dies. 31 Moreover you shall take no ransom for the life of a murderer that is guilty of

death; but he shall surely be put to death. 32 And you shall take no ransom for him who is fled to his city of refuge, that he should come again to dwell in the land, until the death of the priest. 33 So you shall not pollute the land where you are; for blood pollutes the land; and no expiation can be made for the land for the blood that is shed there, but by the blood of him that shed it. 34 And you shall not defile the land which you inhabit, in the midst of which I dwell; for I the Lord dwell in the midst of the children of Israel."

The 42 Trials of the Israelites

Why is it so important that we read the portion of Masei before Tisha B'Av? It is because this entire section deals with destruction. Masei recounts the journeys of the Israelites after the Revelation on Mount Sinai. They set up camp at 42 places. How are we meant to interpret this part of the Bible? Why does the Bible enumerate all 42 locations? For some, the historical information has relevance—but the real purpose of this section has been lost.

Before Kabbalah, I had no understanding of what these journeys meant. The reason the Bible mentions all these journeys is not generally known. The 42 stops are trials. The number 42 is the number of letters that make up the Ana Beko'ach, connecting us to the power of the Alef-Bet. Almost every acronym of the Ana Beko'ach is without meaning. We are not simply talking about 14 acronyms (seven sentences constructed of two acronyms each) made up of 42 letters. The Zohar says 42 was responsible for the Creation of the world. When read, the 42 letters are in fact Names of God that take us back to that moment in time when Creation was established. Using the 42 names, we are our own creators—we are a part of God. If God is able to create, and we are part of God, then we are able to create—we can govern our lives. Yet, if everyone is a part of God, why can we not perform miracles?

We do not know how God does this. We think miracles are when God answers our prayers. God is the producer of the entire universe. The Talmud and the Zohar say that we are only a part of God. Yet we are the creators of our personal experience of our environment—and ignorance is no excuse. Today, we know the *kavanot* (meditations) for the 42 Names of God, and thus we can recite them. With the Ana Beko'ach we can use the same instrument that the Creator used to make this world.

Why are these travels mentioned, and why must they be read before Tisha B'Av?

Has warfare ever accomplished anything? We never seem to learn from the lessons of history. There is a dual purpose here, and one is to tell the generations what occurred—yet the Bible is not a mere history book. Could the Holy Temple's destruction in Jerusalem, which occurred two thousand years ago, have been avoided? Nothing in the physical reality is ever the cause—it is only the outcome. Thought is the metaphysical energy behind the cause.

Jerusalem is not a holy city because of any physical Holy Temple. Jerusalem is the holy city because it is the metaphysical energy-center of the world.

The Zohar is a result of desire. Think about how we move our hands. Even when we talk, we constantly move our hands. But the motivation for movement lies deeper, and we do not even see it—so we think our hands move automatically. There is so much we are unaware of going on in the concealed world. Our unfamiliarity with these deeper forces makes us rely on the physical reality that has already been established. No matter how intelligent we may be, the moment we surrender to Murphy's Law, Satan finds his way in. In general, humanity does not believe we can affect things on the physical level by our own consciousness alone—Kabbalah says we can.

In the portion of Masei, we also hear how the land of Israel was divided, how the boundaries between the tribes were set up— which, as the Bible documents, was by allotment. Israel was divided amongst the tribes by a lottery, a number. Is the Bible attempting to lead us off course? No, the Zohar says that this division concerned the power of the land—that each tribe is a channel for a particular heavenly constellation. But what value did each of these parcels of land have? It was not about the physical monetary value. The land was divided by determining which tribes could be the channels for which pieces of land.

Cities of Refuge

There is also a section about the six cities of refuge—three beyond the River Jordan, and three in the land of Canaan. If someone committed unpremeditated murder, they had to flee to one of these cities in order to remain alive. The Bible says that when an individual commits unpremeditated murder, a member of the victim's family has the right to kill the perpetrator before they escape to the city of refuge. However, once the killer reaches the city, nothing can happen to them while the current High Priest is alive. However, if a murderer flees the city while the High Priest is still alive, and is then killed in revenge by someone, the avenger is not guilty of murder because the killer was meant to remain in the city until the death of the High Priest. Only when the High Priest dies can the killer leave the city of refuge and return to his city.

This is one of the most difficult sections of the Bible to understand. The High Priest is the Sefira of Chesed, and thus responsible for channeling the unified whole of the Lightforce of God to humanity.

During the time of the destruction of the Temple, the election of the High Priest was invalid—because bribes were offered to secure the office. This was one of the causes of the destruction of the Holy Temple. The Sefira of Chesed cannot be fooled. Chesed is represented by the first verse of the Ana Beko'ach—which is the most powerful. It contains all there is to know.

The reason this portion is read before Tisha B'Av is to teach us that it is our actions that create either misfortune or fortune—no matter the reason or justification for it. When the Kohen (Priest) chose one animal to be sacrificed for Yom Kippur, and the other one to be thrown off the mountain to atone for the sins of all the people, this decision was made by a lottery.

The Bible wants to teach us here that everything in the physical world is predetermined. Quantum states that tomorrow is known today. A murderer could go to trial and argue that he or she was affected by the influence of their victim, and thus did not have free will at the time. According to our current laws, if a person kills another in an automobile accident, it is not considered murder— but, on the metaphysical level, accidents are not really accidental. Consciousness is our bridge to the metaphysical realm. If we imagine a person falling off a ladder, we are to a certain extent responsible if they fall and injure themselves or if the ladder kills someone. Another way a person climbing the ladder could fall is if they were thinking negative thoughts. The metaphysical profoundly affects the physical.

The idea of quantum is that everything in the universe was known long before this moment. What exists as thought in our minds is already happening. If we think positively, positive things will happen. If we think negatively, negative things will happen. Everything originates in our consciousness. The purpose of the Ana Beko'ach is to help us get rid of the negative thoughts we have.

Bamidbar 36:1 And the heads of the fathers' houses of the family of the children of Gilead, the son of Machir, the son of Manasseh, of the families of the sons of Joseph, came near, and spoke before Moses, and before the princes, the heads of the fathers' houses of the children of Israel; 2 and they said: "The Lord commanded my lord to give the land for inheritance by lot to the children of Israel; and my lord was commanded by the Lord to give the inheritance of Zelophehad, our brother, to his daughters. 3 And if they are married to any of the sons of the other tribes of the children of Israel, then their inheritance will be taken away from the inheritance of our fathers, and will it be added to the inheritance of the tribe to which they shall belong; so it will be taken away from the lot of our inheritance. 4 And when the jubilee of the children of Israel shall be, then their inheritance will be added to the inheritance of the tribe to which they shall belong; so their inheritance will be taken away from the inheritance of the tribe of our fathers." 5 And Moses commanded the children of Israel according to the word of the Lord, saying: "The tribe of the sons of Joseph speak right. 6 This is the thing which the Lord has commanded concerning the daughters of Zelophehad, saying: 'Let them be married to whom they think best; only into the family of the tribe of their father shall they be married. 7 So shall no inheritance of the children of Israel be removed from tribe to tribe; for the children of Israel shall cleave every one to the inheritance of his fathers' tribe. 8 And every daughter who possesses an inheritance in any tribe of the children of Israel, shall be wife to one of the family of the tribe of her father, that the children of Israel may possess the inheritance of his father. 9 So shall no inheritance be removed from one tribe to another tribe; because the tribes of the children of Israel shall cleave each one to its own inheritance." 10 Even as the Lord commanded Moses, so did the daughters of Zelophehad. 11 ForMahlah, Tirzah, and Hoglah, and Milcah, and Noah, the daughters of Zelophehad, were married to their father's brothers' sons. 12 They were married into the families of the sons of Manasseh, the son of Joseph, and their inheritance remained in the tribe of the family of their father. 13 These are the commandments and the ordinances, which the Lord commanded by the hand of Moses to the children of Israel in the plains of Moab by the Jordan at Jericho.

Conclusion

With this portion, we bring to a close the Book of Bamidbar, the Book of Numbers. At the conclusion of the reading we say the word *chazak* three times. The word *chazak* has a numerical value of 345— the same value as the word *Mashiach* (Messiah), as well as the letters *Mem, Hei, Shin* (72; מ.ה.ש Name for healing). When we complete one of the books of the Bible, we draw together all the energy we gained from every portion that was read in previous Shabbat connections. The word *bamidbar* means "in the wilderness," and here we bring together all the previous sections, and all that the Israelites experienced in the wilderness, using the energy of those readings to remove the chaos that has been with humankind for the past four thousand years.

We do not call this wisdom "new age," since there is nothing new here. It has simply been neglected. For some reason, humanity has not availed ourselves of this wisdom until recently. We now have this energy available to us to keep chaos at bay, to create a security shield against the destruction that is all around us. How else can we avoid chaos in our lives? Where else can we acquire this kind of energy? Who knows what the future will bring? We want to manage the future now, and control destiny through the use of the unique Torah readings each Shabbat.

This has been going on for four thousand years, and this claim has had a life of its own—it has not been lost. Nor has the Zohar been lost, and it too has a Light of its own. It is all-inclusive, available to Jew and non-Jew alike. We cannot deny this opportunity to our non-Jewish brethren. According to Rav Shimon bar Yochai, denying people this technology, not sharing it with the world, is what brings about anti-Semitism. This is also a very significant insight revealed by the portion. We have regular readings so we can enlarge our vessel to contain the vast energy awaiting us. If we are not aware of it, we do receive it. We have another opportunity with this complete book to capture the different energies of each of these portions, and thereby keep chaos away. We need it for the hostile environment in which we live—for the pollution, for the financial and social chaos. We need it in order to heal.

About the Centres

Kabbalah is the deepest and most hidden meaning of the Torah or Bible. Through the ultimate knowledge and mystical practices of Kabbalah, one can reach the highest spiritual levels attainable. Although many people rely on belief, faith, and dogmas in pursuing the meaning of life, kabbalists seek a spiritual connection with the Creator and the forces of the Creator, so that the strange becomes familiar, and faith becomes knowledge.

Throughout history, those who knew and practiced the Kabbalah were extremely careful in their dissemination of the knowledge because they knew the masses of mankind had not yet prepared for the ultimate truth of existence. Today, kabbalists know that it is not only proper but necessary to make the Kabbalah available to all who seek it.

The Research Centre of Kabbalah is an independent, non-profit institute founded in Israel in 1922. The Centre provides research, information, and assistance to those who seek the insights of Kabbalah. The Centre offers public lectures, classes, seminars, and excursions to mystical sites at branches in Israel and in the United States. Branches have been opened in Mexico, Montreal, Toronto, Paris, Hong Kong, and Taiwan.

Our courses and materials deal with the Zoharic understanding of each weekly portion of the Torah. Every facet of life is covered and other dimensions, hithertofore unknown, provide a deeper connection to a superior reality. Three important beginner courses cover such aspects as: Time, Space and Motion; Reincarnation, Marriage, Divorce; Kabbalistic Meditation; Limitation of the Five Senses; Illusion-Reality; Four Phases; Male and Female, Death, Sleep, Dreams; Food; and Shabbat.

Thousands of people have benefited from the Centre's activities, and the Centre's publishing of kabbalistic material continues to be the most comprehensive of its kind in the world, including translations in English, Hebrew, Russian, German, Portuguese, French, Spanish, Farsi (Persian).

Kabbalah can provide one with the true meaning of their being and the knowledge necessary for their ultimate benefit. It can show one spirituality that is beyond belief. The Research Centre of Kabbalah will continue to make available the Kabbalah to all those who seek it.

—Rav Berg, 1984

About The Zohar

The Zohar, the basic source of the Kabbalah, was authored two thousand years ago by Rabbi Shimon bar Yochai while hiding from the Romans in a cave in Peki'in for 13 years. It was later brought to light by Rabbi Moses de Leon in Spain, and further revealed through the Safed Kabbalists and the Lurianic system of Kabbalah.

The programs of the Research Centre of Kabbalah have been established to provide opportunities for learning, teaching, research, and demonstration of specialized knowledge drawn from the ageless wisdom of the Zohar and the Jewish sages. Long kept from the masses, today this knowledge of the Zohar and Kabbalah should be shared by all who seek to understand the deeper meaning of this spiritual heritage, and a deeper and more profound meaning of life. Modern science is only beginning to discover what our sages veiled in symbolism. This knowledge is of a very practical nature and can be applied daily for the betterment of our lives and of humankind.

Darkness cannot prevail in the presence of Light. Even a darkened room must respond to the lighting of a candle. As we share this moment together we are beginning to witness, and indeed some of us are already participating in, a people's revolution of enlightenment. The darkened clouds of strife and conflict will make their presence felt only as long as the Eternal Light remains concealed.

The Zohar now remains an ultimate, if not the only, solution to infusing the cosmos with the revealed Lightforce of the Creator. The Zohar is not a book about religion. Rather, the Zohar is concerned with the relationship between the unseen forces of the cosmos, the Lightforce, and the impact on humanity.

The Zohar promises that with the ushering in of the Age of Aquarius, the cosmos will become readily accessible to human understanding. It states that in the days of the Messiah "there will no longer be the necessity for one to request of his neighbor, teach me wisdom." (Zohar, Naso 9:65) "One day, they will no longer teach every man his neighbor and every man his brother, saying know the Lord. For they shall all know Me, from the youngest to the oldest of them." (Jeremiah 31:34)

We can, and must, regain dominion of our lives and environment. To achieve this objective, the Zohar provides us with an opportunity to transcend the crushing weight of universal negativity.

The daily perusing of the Zohar, without any attempt at translation or understanding will fill our consciousness with the Light, improving our well-being, and influencing all in our environment toward positive attitudes. Even the scanning of the Zohar by those unfamiliar with the Hebrew *Alef Bet* will accomplish the same result.

The connection that we establish through scanning the Zohar is one of unity with the Light of the Creator. The letters, even if we do not consciously know Hebrew or Aramaic, are the channels through which the connection is made and can be likened to dialing the right telephone number or typing in the right codes to run a computer program. The connection is established at the metaphysical level of our being and radiates into our physical plane of existence. But first there is the prerequisite of metaphysical "fixing." We have to consciously, through positive thought and actions, permit the immense power of the Zohar to radiate love, harmony, and peace into our lives for us to share with all humanity and the universe.

As we enter the years ahead, the Zohar will continue to be a people's book, striking a sympathetic chord in the hearts and minds of those who long for peace, truth, and relief from suffering. In the face of crises and catastrophe, the Zohar has the ability to resolve agonizing human afflictions by restoring each individual's relationship with the Lightforce of the Creator.

—Rav Berg, 1984

Kabbalah Centre Books

72 Names of God, The: Technology for the Soul
72 Names of God for Kids, The: A Treasury of Timeless Wisdom
72 Names of God Meditation Book, The
And You Shall Choose Life: An Essay on Kabbalah, the Purpose of Life, and Our True Spiritual Work
AstrologiK: Kabbalistic Astrology Guide for Children
Becoming Like God: Kabbalah and Our Ultimate Destiny
Beloved of My Soul: Letters of Our Master and Teacher Rav Yehuda Tzvi Brandwein to His Beloved Student Kabbalist Rav Berg
Consciousness and the Cosmos (previously Star Connection)
Days of Connection: A Guide to Kabbalah's Holidays and New Moons
Days of Power Part 1
Days of Power Part 2
Dialing God: Daily Connection Book
Education of a Kabbalist
Energy of the Hebrew Letters, The (previously Power of the Aleph Beth Vols. 1 and 2)
Fear is Not an Option
Finding the Light Through the Darkness: Inspirational Lessons Rooted in the Bible and the Zohar
God Wears Lipstick: Kabbalah for Women
Gift of Being Different, The: (Spiritually Hungry Publishing, an imprint of Kabbalah Centre Publishing)
Holy Grail, The: A Manifesto on the Zohar
If You Don't Like Your Life, Change It!: Using Kabbalah to Rewrite the Movie of Your Life
Immortality: The Inevitability of Eternal Life
Kabbalah Connection, The: Preparing the Soul For Pesach
Kabbalah for the Layman
Kabbalah Method, The: The Bridge Between Science and the Soul, Physics and Fulfillment, Quantum and the Creator
Kabbalah on the Sabbath: Elevating Our Soul to the Light
Kabbalah: The Power To Change Everything
Kabbalistic Astrology: And the Meaning of Our Lives
Kabbalistic Bible: Genesis
Kabbalistic Bible: Exodus
Kabbalistic Bible: Leviticus
Kabbalistic Bible: Numbers
Kabbalistic Bible: Deuteronomy
Light of Wisdom: On Wisdom, Life, and Eternity
Miracles, Mysteries, and Prayer Volume 1
Miracles, Mysteries, and Prayer Volume 2
Nano: Technology of Mind over Matter

Navigating The Universe: A Roadmap for Understanding the Cosmic Influences that Shape Our Lives (previously Time Zones)

On World Peace: Two Essays by the Holy Kabbalist Rav Yehuda Ashlag

Origins of Consciousness, The: A Study of the Ten Luminous Emanations Volume 1

Path to the Light: Decoding the Bible with Kabbalah: Book of Beresheet Volume 1

Path to the Light: Decoding the Bible with Kabbalah: Book of Beresheet Volume 2

Path to the Light: Decoding the Bible with Kabbalah: Book of Beresheet Volume 3

Path to the Light: Decoding the Bible with Kabbalah: Book of Beresheet Volume 4

Path to the Light: Decoding the Bible with Kabbalah: Book of Shemot Volume 5

Path to the Light: Decoding the Bible with Kabbalah: Book of Shemot Volume 6

Path to the Light: Decoding the Bible with Kabbalah: Book of Vayikra Volume 7

Path to the Light: Decoding the Bible with Kabbalah: Book of Bamdibar Volume 8

Prayer of the Kabbalist, The: The 42-Letter Name of God

Power of Kabbalah, The: 13 Principles to Overcome Challenges and Achieve Fulfillment

Rebooting: Defeating Depression with the Power of Kabbalah

Rethink Love: 3 Steps to Being the One, Attracting the One, and Becoming One

Satan: An Autobiography

Secret, The: Unlocking the Source of Joy & Fulfillment

Secrets of the Bible: Teachings from Kabbalistic Masters

Secrets of the Zohar: Stories and Meditations to Awaken the Heart

Simple Light: Wisdom from a Woman's Heart

Shabbat Connections

Tale of the Other Glove, The: (Spiritually Hungry Publishing, an imprint of Kabbalah Centre Publishing)

Taming Chaos: Harnessing the Secret Codes of the Universe to Make Sense of Our Lives

Thought of Creation, The: On the Individual, Humanity, and Their Ultimate Perfection

Tikunei HaZohar: Volumes 1-3

Times of Elevation: Volumes 1

To Be Continued: Reincarnation & the Purpose of Our Lives

To the Power of One

True Prosperity: How to Have Everything

Two Unlikely People to Change the World: A Memoir by Karen Berg

Vokabbalahry: Words of Wisdom for Kids to Live By

Way Of The Kabbalist, The: A User's Guide to Technology for the Soul

Well of Life: Kabbalistic Wisdom from a Depth of Knowledge

Wheels of a Soul: Kabbalah and Reincarnation

Wisdom of Truth, The: 12 Essays by the Holy Kabbalist Rav Yehuda Ashlag

Zohar, The

www.ingramcontent.com/pod-product-compliance
Lightning Source LLC
Chambersburg PA
CBHW020537100426
42813CB00038B/3472/J